The Daily Telegraph Murder File

Also by Jonathan Goodman

Crime History

The Killing of Julia Wallace
The Burning of Evelyn Foster
The Stabbing of George Harry Storrs
The Slaying of Joseph Bowne Elwell
The Passing of Starr Faithfull
Bloody Versicles: The Rhymes of Crime
Posts-Mortem: The Correspondence of Murder
The Trial of Ian Brady and Myra Hindley (*re-issued as* The Moors Murders)
The Trial of Ruth Ellis (*with Patrick Pringle*)
The Crippen File
The Oscar Wilde File
Acts of Murder
Underworld (*with Ian Will*)
The Black Museum (*with Bill Waddell*)
Murder in High Places
Murder in Low Places
Anthologies: The Pleasures of Murder, The Railway Murders, The Seaside Murders, The Country House Murders, The Christmas Murders, The Vintage Car Murders, The Lady Killers, The Art of Murder, The Medical Murders, The Supernatural Murders, Masterpieces of Murder

Novels

Instead of Murder
Criminal Tendencies
Hello Cruel World Goodbye
The Last Sentence

Verse

Matinee Idylls

Others

Who He?: Goodman's Dictionary of the Unknown Famous
The Master Eccentric: The Journals of Rayner Heppenstall, 1969–81 (*editor*)

The Daily Telegraph
Murder File

Edited by
JONATHAN GOODMAN

Mandarin

A Mandarin Paperback

THE DAILY TELEGRAPH MURDER FILE

First published in Great Britain 1993
by Mandarin Paperbacks
an imprint of Reed Consumer Books Ltd
Michelin House, 81 Fulham Road, London SW3 6RB
and Auckland, Melbourne, Singapore and Toronto

Reprinted 1993

A CIP catalogue record for this title
is available from the British Library
ISBN 0 7493 1126 6

Typeset by CentraCet, Cambridge

The Random House Group Limited supports The Forest Stewardship Council® (FSC®), the leading international forest-certification organisation. Our books carrying the FSC label are printed on FSC®-certified paper. FSC is the only forest-certification scheme supported by the leading environmental organisations, including Greenpeace. Our paper procurement policy can be found at
www.randomhouse.co.uk/environment

Printed and bound in Great Britain by Clays Ltd, St Ives PLC

Contents

Foreword

by Neil Darbyshire,
Chief Crime Correspondent of the *Daily Telegraph*

On 1 October 1992, the Home Secretary, Kenneth Clarke, refused to grant a posthumous pardon to Derek Bentley, effectively scotching a forty-year campaign to prove the simple-minded teenager's innocence of murdering a London policeman.

The intensity and duration of that campaign, joined by many prominent figures and followed assiduously by the press and media over the decades, illustrate the continuing public fascination with crime and punishment.

To win a full pardon for any convicted person, campaigners must convince the authorities, and to a large extent the public, that there was either a judicial error or some crucial piece of evidence which was not put before the jury at the original trial.

In the case of Bentley, they failed to do so. The vociferous claims of his supporters that, given the benefit of hindsight, the jury would have returned an acquittal, were rejected.

One of the great strengths of this book is that it allows the reader to judge for himself whether such campaigners had a valid case for appeal. Through contemporaneous *Daily Telegraph* reports of the trial, the reader is able to establish what was and what was not put before the jury.

Interestingly, it does not seem illogical from the Bentley reports to conclude that they tend to support Kenneth Clarke's argument. Whatever the morality of the original verdict, it was certainly correct in law.

The Bentley case is just one of an intriguing selection of notorious murders described in this book. All were committed before the abolition of capital punishment in Great Britain, and almost all the perpetrators paid the ultimate penalty.

The 'Brides in the Bath' murders, the Lefroy 'railway murder', the last public execution, the first private one, and the short story of the last two men to hang – all are contained here.

It is of particular interest to note how much newspaper reports have changed in style over the past 136 years. The closely detailed coverage of some of these cases is in marked contrast with the general press treatment of comparable murder cases now.

Instead of the current tendency to provide banner headlines at the beginning and end of each major trial and very little of the evidence and legal argument in between, the journalistic hacks of days gone by supplied mountains of copy from each day's court evidence in order to quench the public thirst for minutiae.

This is owing to three main factors.

Firstly, before the rise of the electronic media in the last three or four decades, newspapers were the only real means of mass communication, and the public was not yet conditioned to expect its news to be neatly contained in easily digestible sound-bites.

Secondly, the prospect of a murder defendant being hanged if found guilty increased the tension of the trial and led to a more sharply-focused desire to know the full circumstances of the allegations.

Thirdly, and most crucially, there are simply more recorded murders now than in the past. If every one were to be covered in detail, there would be little room in today's truncated and picture-dominated newspapers for anything else.

The advantage of taking a selection of murders from a period of more than a century, however, is that some of the most intriguing are chosen – and any of the cases chosen for this book would certainly make front-page news today.

The story of George Joseph Smith, for example, is tailor-made for the Sunday tabloids. Rogue, bigamist and harmonium player, Smith murdered three 'wives' (he had married them in false names) in quick succession and almost escaped justice entirely.

His *modus operandi* was simple. He married his woman, albeit illegally, persuaded her to sign her possessions over to him, contacted the local GP to tell him his beloved wife was prey to epilepsy, then drowned her in the bath.

With the unwitting support of the respective GPs, who assumed epileptic fits had caused the drownings, he was able three times to convince coroners to return verdicts of death by misadventure.

He came unstuck some days after the third inquest – but only because the father of a previous victim had read press reports which rang a familiar note. He contacted the police, and the game was up.

Perhaps the most chilling aspect of the trial was the evidence of the landlady at one of the lodging-houses used by the killer. She testified that, shortly after hearing noises and splashing from the bathroom, she heard Smith singing 'Nearer My God to Thee' to his own accompaniment on the harmonium.

It is the period flavour of testimony like this which helps to make *The Daily Telegraph Murder File* a pleasure to read.

Introduction

The first issue of the *Daily Telegraph & Courier* (tuppence for the four pages, the front one entirely of advertisements) appeared on Friday, June 29, 1855.

It was a slack day for news. As the telegraph line from near Sebastopol to Paris was out of action, there were only some 'IMPORTANT RUMOURS' about the Siege. But still – 'Yesterday being the [eighteenth] anniversary of Her Majesty's coronation, the usual display of flags, ringing of bells, and other loyal demonstrations took place throughout the metropolis.'

Most of the mast-head page, the third, was devoted to comment: a tirade against 'the illicit traffic in Militia Commissions'; the suggestion that the worthy cause of administrative reform had attracted unworthy advocates – including Mr Dickens: 'Whatever use he may righteously suffer himself to be put in furtherance of Administrative change, he is not, and never can be, a practical politician'; and 'the raising of a voice in reprehension of the mild system of chivalry, better expressed as weakness, which British commanders appear to have adopted in combating the perfidious Russians in the Crimea'. Pride of place went to the new paper's manifesto 'as a candidate for popular favour', in which credit was given to established papers for helping towards 'the gradual improvement in the moral and intellectual condition of the great masses of the people of this country, within the last half-century':

> The Parliament and the Press re-echoed the sentiments of the classes, and the Crown assented to the wishes of the subject. The Whipping-post, the Pillory, and the Stocks – those instruments of a degraded people – were levelled to the ground when a free Press taught man, moulded in the image of his Maker, that cruelty and vengeance deterred not from

crime, and that more was to be achieved by reforming the refractory than by indelibly branding shame and ignominy upon the body and brutalising the mind so as to render it unfit for a saving thought of the soul hereafter.

Within a year (during which *& Clarion* was dropped), the *Telegraph*'s circulation was higher than that of *The Times*, which was far and away the best-selling paper among the other ten published in London. The main reason for the *Telegraph*'s early and spectacular success was its lavish, many-editioned coverage of an event that everyone, but everyone, wanted to know about: the murder trial of Doctor William Palmer of Rugeley.

And so, when I came to choose according-to-the-*Telegraph* accounts of matters to do with murder for this book, the Palmer case was already chosen. Deciding what else to include was made hardly less daunting by my having decided to stay within the 113 years till the abolition of capital punishment in Great Britain: during those years, there were some 40,000 known murders in England and Wales alone – not all of them attributed, of course, and no more than a few each year with ingredients making them memorable; but even so – and never minding cases in Scotland, all of Ireland for most of the time, and Ulster for the rest – a too-considerable total.

Rather than adopting the scientific, eeny-meeny-miney-mo approach to the problem, I have simply ignored the problem – and, in so doing, have finished up with three long accounts and several that are much shorter. They are spread fairly evenly over the chosen period. Of the long accounts, the Palmer case is one, the Bentley-Craig case another. As for the third, the Lefroy case, my intention was to include merely a snippet, just to take notice of a police-assisting innovation by the *Telegraph*, but I was so fascinated by bits of the story that are left out of retrospective essays on the case, and so entranced by the several daily reports of the committal proceedings in a usually sleepy village (I wish I knew who the special correspondent was), that I felt that it would be criminally selfish to keep the pleasures to myself.

Just as the contents of this book are only a comparatively

tiny sampling of the *Telegraph*'s 'murder file', each part – and I am speaking even of each of the long ones – is made up of only a little of what the paper had to say on the particular murderous subject. I have made few textual alterations; no more than once or twice have I thought it really necessary to signify an elision, by inserting triple points; occasionally I have transposed paragraphs. I have kept explanatory footnotes to the minimum.

I am grateful to my researchers, Toby Mitchell and David Ward; and, for specific information, to David Allen of the Bank of England; Ivan and Hilda Butler; Detective Constable Rod Elwood, Curator of the Kent County Constabulary's Museum (who also provided the illustrations on pages 79 and 114); T. J. Leech; Cyril Pike, Chairman of the Board of Trustees of the Cuckfield Museum, West Sussex (who also provided the illustrations on pages 104, 105 and 115); Beth Richardson of the Royal Pharmaceutical Society of Great Britain; and Richard Whittington-Egan.

Jonathan Goodman

1856

First leading article on Wednesday, May 14:

THIS day, one of the most remarkable trials in the annals of crime will commence at the Central Criminal Court, Old Bailey, and in referring to the case of Dr WILLIAM PALMER and the poisonings at Rugeley, in Staffordshire, we shall abstain from criticisms which could by any possibility prejudice the accused before a jury of his countrymen.

The subject of poison and poisoning has always been attended with a peculiar interest. The operation of the poison, the tragical character of the event in many cases, the part which poisons have played in history, all combine to invest cases of poisoning with a kind of dramatic interest. What can be more wonderful than that a drop of clear fluid like prussic acid, a compound of carbon, nitrogen and hydrogen, ingredients existing simple in the first instance, and pure in the diamond, when given to an animal – nay, if only applied to its eye – should still all that subtle machinery of life in a moment! One convulsive shudder, and the brain, were it that of NEWTON, will cease to think, the senses to feel, the heart to beat, and the limbs to move. And what machine of man's construction is comparable to that which this single drop has deprived of motion for ever? It has separated the animating force from the matter, and dismissed the soul.

Or when we take other instances, and reflect on the tortures which a few grains of a tasteless white powder like arsenic can inflict – the burning, consuming pain, the paralysed limb, the shrunk countenance, and the sinking pulse – can we fail to marvel at the mysterious influence by which this is accomplished? Or again, in the case of strychnia, the singular convulsions which throw every muscle into violent spasmodic action when the least disturbing force is applied to a body bent backwards by a power of inscrutable origin. Nothing in natural history is more wonderful than the action of poisons.

How are we to define a poison? Various definitions have been given, of which the one generally received is that of ORFILA. A poison, he says, is a substance which is deleterious or fatal to the animal frame when administered in small quantities. But this definition appears to us exceedingly vague and unsatisfactory. For what is a small quantity? Some substances, too, are beneficial in small quantities and deleterious in large. Thus alcohol in small quantity is an article of nutriment, in larger quantities a stimulant, and in very large quantities, to all intents and purposes, a poison. We will venture to propose a new definition, by way of contrasting poison with food. Food is amenable to the laws of the organisation, is assimilated by it, and becomes part of the system. Poison, on the other hand, forces the animal frame to obey its laws. Thus poison and drug are synonymous terms, for when other modes of cure fail in medicine, such as alteration in diet, regimen, or hygiene, recourse is had to drugs to compel the system to certain modes of action which otherwise could not be accomplished.

Poisons are variously classed. The most common division is into irritant, narcotic, and narcoctico-acrid. The first class act chiefly by producing inflammation in the stomach or parts to which they are applied; the second, by stupefying the brain, or some part of the nervous system; and the last combine the properties of the other two. But, in point of fact, it is exceedingly difficult to draw any such distinction, because hardly any poison has a pure action, so to speak, upon one organ, or one set of organs, or one mode of operation. Most poisons, however, act more upon particular organs; thus arsenic, however introduced, either given internally or inserted in a wound, will produce inflammation of the stomach; prussic acid will produce convulsions like those of epilepsy, arising from some peculiar action of the nervous system not yet understood; and strychnia will produce symptoms resembling those of tetanus, or lock-jaw, from its effect upon the spinal cord.

The effect of this last-named poison is well shown on a frog: the animal becomes quite rigid, the legs thrown out; but on striking the table on which it is placed, or irritating it with a needle, the whole body is thrown into violent convulsions. The effects are nearly the same in all animals. In human subjects the intellect is quite clear; it is the spinal cord that is affected.

Perhaps the most curious recorded instance of the peculiar actions of some poisons is that of picrotoxin, the active principle of cocculus indicus (or grains of paradise used by some brewers), according to the experiments of Dr GLOVER. It causes animals to walk or run backwards. The same results, or similar results, are produced by the mutilation of certain parts of the brain. The inference is, therefore, that this poison acts upon those parts of the brain.

Very strange notions of the effects of poison have been entertained, and are so yet. When our knowledge of poisons was much more limited than it is now, it was supposed that poisons could be conveyed in gloves, and a conspirator against QUEEN ELIZABETH was accused of plotting to poison the saddle of her horse. Perhaps, indeed, a glove might be poisoned by means of pure prussic acid, but the glove should be immediately put on, and could not be sent so as to act. In the same way, it was supposed that poisoners could produce death at any determinate period, a week after the administration of the dose, six weeks, or a year. No such power exists. It is possible, no doubt, to kill instantly and directly, as by the administration of a sufficient quantity of prussic acid, or conia, the active principle of hemlock, and a few more such poisons, and *rather* more slowly but as certainly by strychnia and other poisons. But beyond that there is no certainty as to time, the result depending upon the relations between the nature of the poison and the strength of the patient's constitution, and many adventitious circumstances; thus, when Pope ALEXANDER and his still more atrocious son poisoned themselves by mistake, the Pope died after nine days' illness, and after having undergone fearful torments, but his son survived and partially recovered, although he seems never to have recovered his former vigour of body and mind.

The comparative impunity enjoyed by poisoners in former times depended far more on the imperfection of the means employed to detect poison than on the popularly supposed mysterious skill of the poison. The aqua tofanas, so much used in Italy at the end of the 17th and beginning of the 18th century, was undoubtedly a solution of arsenic. The poisons used by St CROIX and Madame BRINVILLIERS were chiefly arsenic and corrosive sublimate. Now, no poisons are more *certain* of detection in the present day than these, however *difficult* the process may sometimes be.

The fact of poisoning is revealed in several ways, but chiefly by the symptoms, the appearance after death, and the detection of the poison in the system by chemical tests. With regard to the symptoms, it is important to observe whether they have come on after meals, and at what period after a meal or meals, or the taking of any drink, and also whether they occur during a state of health. Two examples may serve to illustrate the meaning of this. Thus, a Crown Prince of Sweden fell from horseback while reviewing his troops, with symptoms closely resembling those of apoplexy, but which were ascribed to poison. He had not, however, partaken of anything for several hours, and the only poison likely to produce such symptoms was opium, and the symptoms of poisoning by opium do not come on in this sudden manner after a period of hours intervening from the taking of the drug. Again, in the celebrated case of Sir THEODOSIUS BOUGHTON, who was poisoned by his brother-in-law DONELLAN, the symptoms came on in two minutes after the fluid in which the poison was contained was administered. This was justly deemed a suspicious circumstance.

Generally speaking, it may be regarded as a remarkable fact that those poisons which are most difficult of detection by chemical means in the body are easiest of recognition by their symptoms; thus arsenic and corrosive sublimate, and, on the whole, metallic poisons, the mineral acids and such like, are very similar in their symptoms, but the chemical means for detecting their presence are almost infallible. Such poisons as prussic acid and strychnia, again, are difficult of detection by analysis, but their symptoms are well characterised.

With regard to post-mortem appearances, it was formerly supposed that various external appearances might indicate poisoning; thus, swelling of the body, sudden putrefaction, lividity of the countenance, and such like, were often reckoned as proofs of poison having been given. It is now known that there are hardly any external appearances of much value. In prussic acid poisoning, the eye has a peculiar glistening appearance for some time after death. In poisoning by strychnia, we should expect to find the joints excessively rigid, the limbs stretched out, and the jaws clenched. The *internal* appearances are in some cases very characteristic. This is particularly so with the mineral acids and metallic poisons, exhibiting all the stages of corrosion and irritation, from ordinary inflammation to ulceration and corrosion of the stomach and intestines. With the organic poisons – as opium, prussic acid, and strychnia – the appearances are more likely to be those of congestion of the brain and spinal cord, the last especially in the case of strychnia.

The union of certain symptoms with certain *post-mortem* appearances may be sufficient evidence of the fact of poisoning, without the detection of the poison by chemical means in the body; but when human life is at stake, it is much to be desired that they should be thus confirmed.

Chemical analysis has of late made vast strides in regard to the detection of poisons. Formerly it was usual to examine, at most, the contents of the stomach. Since 1842, especially when ORFILA published his researches on the absorption of acids and salts, it has become customary to seek for poisons in the internal organs, especially in the lungs, liver, and spleen.

As a general rule, poisons are detected in three ways in the dead body, either by their mechanical separation: for instance, arsenic can sometimes be detected by merely washing the contents of the stomach and pouring off the washings, when the white powder will remain at the bottom, and can be tested easily; or the contents of the stomach may be so clear of food and other organic matter as to allow of the various tests being applied, but if there be much organic matter present, tests usually will not act, and the poison must be separated from the organic matter or from the tissue of the stomach, liver, and so forth, in which it is contained. This constitutes the great difficulty in testing for poisons. Metallic poisons little destructible by heat are generally tested for by destroying the animal or organic matter by means of acids and heat, dissolving the tissue first, and then burning off the organic matter and the acid, leaving the metal in the ash, when it can be re-dissolved in an acid and tested. When acids are sought for, an alkali is generally added, and this fixes the acid, and allows the animal matter to be burnt off, and leaves a salt which can be tested. With the vegetable and animal poisons easily detructible by heat, different methods must be employed: sometimes the poison is distilled off and collected in a receiver, as in the case of prussic acid; at other times it is removed by dissolving it out by alcohol or ether, which would be the case with strychnia. When the poison is thus obtained, in a form which admits of the application of tests, the task is much simplified. It is a mistake to suppose, then, that there is so much difficulty in detecting organic poisons. The difficulty consists in two things: first, in the fact that many organic poisons soon undergo decomposition, and all are destructible by heat, at comparatively low temperatures; second, which is a corollary of the first, that the direct destruction of organic matter to get at them is thus precluded.

There is one observation with which we shall at present conclude. Tests may give results with a poison, every one of which is fallacious in itself; but which, *taken together*, are infallible. For instance, arsenic in solution gives a green colour with ammoniacal salts of copper, a yellow with ammonia, and a yellow with sulphuretted hydrogen. Now, objections in certain cases may be taken to every one of these tests singly; and lawyers generally require the reduction of the arsenic to the metallic form, as a *sine quà non*. But this is a mistake, for no known substance will give these results, with these *three* tests, but arsenic. This may have to be borne in mind in the trial of PALMER; and in the above observations, which we have considered it appropriate to make, we desire to prepare the public mind for the professional evidence, upon which chiefly will rest the acquittal or conviction of the accused.

In fact, the trial is one of chemical science, and the crucible, more than the eloquence of counsel, will 'well and truly try and true deliverance make between our Sovereign Lady the Queen and the prisoner at the bar'.

Thursday, May 15.

Yesterday having been appointed for the long-pending trial of William Palmer, for the murder of John Parsons Cooke, at Rugeley, in Staffordshire, in November last, by administering to him various quantities of strychnia, all the portals of the building in the Old Bailey devoted to the administration of justice, and which, in that character, remains as a relic of the past ages and a scandal to the present one, were stormed at an early hour in the morning by persons of various conditions and both sexes, desirous of being present at the important inquiry; but no inducement whatever, either by the exhibition of blue, pink, or yellow tickets, could gain the slightest relaxation of the inflexible order which had been laid down, that no person whatever should be admitted until 9 o'clock, although several ladies complained grievously of the inconvenience to which they were subjected by having to stand in the rain, which was falling tolerably heavy at the time.

However, at nine o'clock the doors were opened, and one of the most fearful rushes for admission took place that we ever remember to have seen on a similar occasion, but fortunately no accident occurred, and in a few minutes every part of the court was crowded, but not to such an extent as might have been anticipated. On the bench we observed the Earl of Denbigh, the Marquis of Anglesea, Lord W. Lennox, Lord Gordon Lennox, Earl Grey, Prince Edward of Saxe Weimar, the Duke of Wellington, the Earl of Derby and the Dean of Ripon.

The seats appropriated to the members of the bar were by no means sufficient for their accommodation, and many of them were compelled to take their chance amongst the strangers in the body of the court.

Shortly before ten o'clock, the Attorney-General, Sir Alexander Cockburn, entered the Court, accompanied by Mr Edwin James, Mr Welsby, Mr Bodkin, and Mr Huddlestone; and in a few minutes the counsel for the defence appeared, and took their places – viz. Mr Serjeant Shee, Mr Grove, QC, Mr Grey, and Mr Kenealy.

We think it as well to refresh the memory of our readers by a few antecedent particulars.

William Palmer is a member of a very wealthy family. He was educated for the medical profession, was a pupil of St Bartholomew's Hospital, London, received the diploma of the Royal College of Surgeons in 1846, and shortly afterwards settled at Rugeley, his native place. He seems, however, to have paid more attention to the 'turf', and what are commonly called sporting pursuits, than to his own profession, and to have confined his practice to his own family and friends.

He married, in 1847, Anne, the natural daughter of Colonel William Brookes and Mary Thornton, the Colonel's housekeeper. Colonel Brookes, who, after quitting the East Indian service, took up his residence at Stafford, died in 1834, leaving considerable property, and more than one natural child. To Anne Thornton he bequeathed nine houses at Stafford, besides land, and the interest of 20,000 sicca rupees,* for herself and her children. To Mary Thornton, the mother of Anne, the Colonel bequeathed certain property, which was to pass to the daughter at the decease of the mother. Mary Thornton departed this life, it is said, while a guest at Mr Palmer's house, in 1848 or 1849.

Now, although the will of Colonel Brookes would seem clear enough to anyone who was ignorant of law, and although in the present state of the law, as we are informed, it would be sufficient, yet it was discovered by the legal fraternity, some years since, that the language conveying the bequest to Anne Thornton was not sufficiently forcible to convey it to her absolutely, but only to give her a life interest in it, inasmuch as, at her decease, it was liable to be claimed by the heir-at-law to Colonel Brookes. Under these circumstances, there was nothing unusual or unnatural in the idea that Palmer should insure his wife's life, in order to protect himself from the inevitable loss which would ensue in case of her decease; and since her property consisted of 17 acres of land, valued at between £300 and £400 per acre, besides nine houses, and the interest of the sicca rupees – probably altogether worth at least £400 per annum, upon which he had borrowed largely from his mother – there could be no doubt of his having such an interest in his wife's life as would justify insurance. Accordingly, in January 1854 he insured her life for £3,000 in the Norwich Union and in March in the Sun for £5,000; there was also an insurance in the Scottish Equitable for £5,000.*

Mrs Palmer died on Sept. 29, 1854, leaving only one surviving child, a boy of seven years; and, as if to justify the husband in effecting an insurance, an action was brought within a month by Colonel Brookes's heir-at-law, to obtain possession of Mrs Palmer's property. Palmer brought up the life policies on the Sun and Norwich Union on the 16th of October, 1854, and employed Mr Thomas Pratt, a solicitor, to obtain the money from the offices. Mr Pratt, who seems to have acted with the caution usual among lawyers, required to be furnished with evidence of the husband's pecuniary interest in his wife's life, took counsel's opinion on every step, and obtained the £8,000 from the offices on the 6th of February, 1855; strangely enough, the £5,000 from the Scottish Equitable was paid through a banker, unknown to Pratt.

If proofs were wanted that circumstances of peculiar interest invest this case, they might be found in the fact that so great was the local excitement created by the

* Coined under the government of Bengal, they remained legally current till 1836, when each was worth about half a crown in English money. Since the 1993 purchasing power of the 1836 half-crown is reckoned to be about £4.10, 20,000 sicca rupees then would be worth about £82,000 in 1993.

* The 1993 purchasing power of the 1854 £ is reckoned to be about £33 – therefore, £13,000 in 1854 was roughly equivalent to £430,000 in 1993.

circumstances connected with its earlier stages that the prisoner's counsel found it necessary to apply for the removal of the trial to another county, and that to carry out their (under the circumstances)

Thomas Pratt

reasonable proposition, it was found necessary that the Legislature itself should interfere and pass a special Act of Parliament authorising the change of venue.* By such imposing and unusual machinery, the case was removed to the Metropolitan court, whither the public interest has followed it in as strong a current as at Rugeley and Stafford – so much so that the court-house has had to be completely metamorphosed to meet, in some degree, the extraordinary influx of applicants for admission. The whole of the large central table has been removed, and the vacant space filled with seats and desks, as in the courts at Westminster, to accommodate the bar; while in the other parts of the court every possible device has been resorted to, to increase the amount of accommodation.

The Lord Chief Justice of England, assisted by two of our most eminent criminal judges, tries the case, and the certainty of an impartial jury is obtained by the character of the panel. Some of the ablest names at the bar are ranged on either side, and the most eminent of our scientific men have been summoned as witnesses to give their opinions as to the causes of the symptoms by which the death of Cooke are alleged to have been attended.

We have good authority for believing that 'in the multitude of counsellors there is wisdom', but, if report speaks truth, there is reason for fearing, in the present case, that in the multitude of scientific men there will be nothing but confusion. It is understood that a violent schism has been raging in the regions of toxicological experiment, as to the symptoms following the administration of strychnine and antimony, and a relentless crusade has been waged against the domestic animals to disprove or verify, as the case might be, the different theories of the discordant professors.

At five minutes to ten o'clock, Lord Chief Justice Campbell, Justice Cresswell, and Baron Alderson, accompanied by the Lord Mayor and the Recorder, entered the Court and took their seats on the bench.

The Crier of the Court, Mr Harker, having delivered the usual

* *19 Vic cap 16*, afterwards known as 'Palmer's Act'. The local prejudice against Palmer arose mainly from strong suspicion that, prior to the death of John Parsons Cooke, Palmer had killed, among others, his mother-in-law, his wife, a brother, an uncle (who died after a 'brandy-drinking match'), sundry creditors, and several of his legitimate and illegitimate children.

proclamation, Mr Straight, the Deputy Clerk of Arraigns, ordered the prisoner William Palmer to be placed at the bar. He entered the dock with a firm step, and bowed somewhat stiffly to the bench. He looked extremely well, and was dressed in black.

The prisoner stands described thus: – William Palmer, 31, surgeon, superior education, committed by the Court of Queen's Bench, received in custody May 4, standing indicted for the wilful murder of John Parsons Cooke. The prisoner has the appearance of a man about 40 years of age, and we think there must be a mistake in the comparatively brief term of past existence assigned to him in the calendar. He was dressed with genteel plainness – black frock-coat, cravat, vest, trowsers, and gloves. He appeared, as he might have said himself when describing a horse, 'sleek, fat, and in good condition'.

Throughout the whole day's proceedings he presented a calm, composed and tranquil front, indicating the most perfect self-possession and a mind quite at ease as to the result of the inquiry; and if anxiety, alarm and kindred emotions had a place at all under the placid exterior, William Palmer must be pronounced one of the most consummate actors that ever trod the real or mimic stage of life. Severe physiognomists, in contemplating the features of the prisoner, while they would be perhaps unable to distinguish the 'outward and visible signs' that proclaim cunning and ferocious criminals, would, in all probability, be apt to discern strong evidences of sensuality in the broad face, thick neck, and intellectual forehead, and in a certain firmness about the mouth (the lips of which were frequently compressed) – a determination not to allow conventional obstacles or 'compunctious visitings' to stand in the way of its owner's designs, whatever they might be.

Palmer, during the first few minutes after he was placed in the dock, occupied himself in scanning the Court, the bar, and the assembly generally, and enquiring of the gaoler the names of the different persons who more particularly arrested his attention. He was furnished with pen, ink, and paper – a privilege of which he made ample use during the trial.

Next to the prisoner, the persons whom the public were most anxious to see were his brother Joseph from Rugeley, with a strong family resemblance, but darker, and Mr Smith, his very active solicitor. It was mentioned in court that this gentleman had endeavoured to secure the services of Sir Fitzroy Kelly,* but that the latter had demanded one thousand guineas with his brief, and consequently, and in the absence of Serjeant Wilkins, the leadership was entrusted to Serjeant Shee.

The jurors were, it appears, all taken from the panels of the counties of Surrey, Essex, and Middlesex. After the gentlemen were sworn in, the prisoner was formally indicted for having, at Rugeley, in the county of Stafford, on the 21st November last, feloniously, wilfully, and with malice aforethought, committed murder on the person of John Parsons Cooke.

* Known as 'Apple-pip Kelly' since 1845, when, unsuccessfully defending John Tawell at his trial at Aylesbury for the murder of his girlfriend Sarah Hart, he suggested that Sarah, who had eaten pounds of pippins shortly before her death, may have been the victim of apple-pip poisoning.

Mr Huddleston, Q.C. Mr Bodkin Mr Welsby
The Attorney-General Mr Edwin James, Q.C.

THE COUNSEL FOR THE CROWN

Mr Gray Mr Kenealey
Mr Serjeant Shee Mr Grove, Q.C.

THE COUNSEL FOR THE PRISONER

The Attorney-General stated the case.* He said: Gentlemen of the jury, the duty you are called upon to discharge is the most solemn which a man can by possibility have to perform – it is to sit in judgement and to decide an issue on which depends the life of a fellow human being who stands charged with the highest crime for which a man can be arraigned before a worldly tribunal.

I am sure that I need not ask your most anxious and earnest attention to such a case; but there is one thing I feel it incumbent on me to urge upon you. The peculiar circumstances of this case have given it a profound and painful interest throughout the whole country. Standing here as a minister of justice, with no interest and no desire save that justice shall be done impartially, I feel it incumbent on me to warn you not to allow any preconceived opinion to operate on your judgment this day. Your duty – your bounden duty – is to try this case according to the evidence which shall be brought before you, and according to that alone. You must discard from your minds anything that you may have read or heard, or any opinion that you may have formed.

The prisoner at the bar, William Palmer, was by profession a medical practitioner. In later years, however, he became addicted to turf pursuits, which gradually drew off his attention and weaned him from his profession. Within the last two or three years, he made over his business to a person named Thirlby, formerly his assistant, who now carries it on. In the course of his pursuits connected with the turf, Palmer became intimate with the man whose death forms the subject of this inquiry – Mr John Parsons Cooke.

Thirlby's Shop

Now, Mr Cooke was a young man of decent family, who originally had been intended for the profession of the law. He was articled to a solicitor; but after a time, inheriting some property, to the extent of some £12,000 or £15,000, he abandoned the laborious profession of the law, and betook himself also to the turf. He kept racehorses, and betted considerably; and in the course of his operations he became much connected and familiarly intimate with the prisoner William Palmer. The case which, on the part of the prosecution, I have to urge against Palmer is this – that, being in desperate circumstances, with ruin, disgrace, and punishment staring him in the face, which could only be averted by means of money, he took advantage of his intimacy with Cooke, when Cooke had become the winner of a considerable sum, to destroy him, in order to obtain possession of his money.

* EDITOR: The *Telegraph*'s report of the speech (indeed, of the entire trial) was virtually verbatim. I have omitted a considerable amount of the speech.

It appears that as early as the year 1853 Palmer had got into difficulties, and that he began to raise money upon bills. In 1854 his circumstances became worse, and he was at that time heavily indebted to different persons.

Among the bills on which Palmer raised money in 1853 was one for £2,000, which he had discounted by a person named Padwick. That bill bore the acceptance of Sarah Palmer, the mother of the prisoner. She was, and is, a woman of considerable property, and, her acceptance being believed to be genuine, was a security upon which money could be readily raised. The prisoner forged that acceptance, and that was, if not the first, at all events one of the earliest transactions of that nature by means of which for a long period of time money was obtained by him upon bills, with his mother's acceptance forged by him.

He owed in 1854 a very large sum of money. On the 29th of September in that year his wife died. He had effected an insurance upon her life for £13,000, and he discharged some of his most pressing liabilities. But that still left Palmer with considerable liabilities, and among other things, the bill of £2,000, which was discounted by Padwick, remained unpaid. In the course of the same year he effected an insurance for £13,000 on his brother Walter's life, and upon the strength of that policy Palmer proceeded to issue fresh bills, which were discounted by a solicitor, Pratt, at the rate of 60 per cent; Pratt kept the policy as collateral security. The bills which were discounted in the course of that year amounted in the whole to £12,500. £1,000 of this sum, however, he contrived to pay off, so that there was due in November, 1855, no less than £11,500 upon bills, every one of which bore the forged acceptance of the prisoner's mother.

Under these circumstances, a pressure naturally arose – the pressure of £11,500 of liabilities, with not a shilling in the world to meet them, and the still greater pressure resulting from a consciousness that the moment when he could no longer go on and his mother was resorted to for payment, the fact of those forgeries would at once become manifest, and would bring upon him the peril of the law for the crime of forgery.

The prisoner's brother died in August 1855. The prisoner, of course, expected that the proceeds of the insurance would pay off his liabilities; but the office in which the insurance was effected declined to pay, and consequently there was no assistance to be derived from that source.

Now, in these transactions to which I have referred, the deceased John Parsons Cooke had been to a certain extent concerned. It seems that in May 1855, Palmer was pressed to pay £500 to a person named Serjeant, and he wanted Pratt to advance him £190. Pratt declined to do that except upon security; upon which Palmer offered him the acceptance of Cooke, representing him to be a man of substance. Accordingly the acceptance of Cooke for £200 was sent up, and upon that Pratt advanced the money. When that bill for £200 became due, Palmer failed to provide for it, and Cooke had to meet it himself.

In August of the same year, an occurrence took place to which I must call your particular attention. Palmer wrote to Pratt, to say that he must have £1,000 by a day named. Pratt declined to advance it without security; upon which Palmer offered the security of

Cooke's acceptance for £500. Pratt still declined to advance the money without some more tangible security. Now, Palmer represented this as a transaction in which Cooke required the money, and it may be that such was the fact. I have no means of ascertaining how that was; but I will give him the credit of supposing it to be true. Pratt still declining to advance the money, Palmer proposed an assignment by Cooke of two racehorses, one called Polestar, which won at the Shrewsbury races, and another called Sirius. That assignment was afterwards executed by Cooke in favour of Pratt, and Cooke, therefore, was clearly entitled to the money which was raised upon that security, which realised £375 in cash and a wine warrant for £65. Palmer contrived, however, that the money and wine warrant should be sent to him and not to Cooke. Mr Pratt sent his cheque to Palmer, on a stamp as the Act of Parliament required, and he availed himself of the opportunity now offered by law by striking out the word 'bearer', and writing 'order', the effect of which was to necessitate the endorsement of Cooke on the back of the cheque.

It was not intended by Palmer that those proceeds should fall into Cooke's hands, and accordingly he forged the name of John Parsons Cooke on the back of that cheque. Cooke never received the money, and you will see that within ten days from the period when he came to his end, the bill in respect to that transaction, which was at three months, would have fallen due, when it must have become apparent that Palmer received the money, and that, in order to obtain it, he had forged the endorsement of Cooke.

I wish these were the only transactions in which Cooke had been at all mixed up with the prisoner Palmer; but there is another to which it is necessary to refer. In September, 1855, Palmer's brother having died, and the proceeds of the insurance not having been realised, Palmer induced a person named Bates to propose his life for insurance. Palmer had succeeded in raising money upon previous policies,

George Bates

and I have no doubt that he persuaded Cooke to assist him in that transaction, so that, by representing Bates as a man of wealth and substance, they might get a policy on his life, by which policy, deposited as a collateral security, they might obtain advances of money. Bates had been somewhat better off in the world, but he had fallen into decay, and he had accepted employment from Palmer as a sort of hanger-on in his stables. He was a healthy young man; and, being in the company of Palmer and Cooke at Rugeley, on the 5th of September, Palmer asked him to insure his life, and produced the form of proposal to the office. Bates declined, but Palmer pressed him, and Cooke interposed and said, 'You had better do it; it will be for your benefit, and you'll be quite safe with Palmer.' At length they succeeded in persuading him to sign the proposal for no less a sum than £25,000, Cooke attesting the proposal, which Palmer filled in, Palmer being referred to as medical attendant, and his former assistant, Thirlby, as general referee. That proposal was sent up to the Solicitors and General Insurance Office, and in the ensuing month – that office not being disposed to effect the insurance – they sent up another for £10,000 to the Midland Office. That proposal also failed, and no money, therefore, could be obtained from that source. All these circumstances are important, because they show the desperate straits in which the prisoner at that time found himself.

On the 6th of November, two writs were issued by Pratt for £4,000, one against Palmer, and the other against his mother; and Pratt wrote on the same day to Palmer to say that the writs were not to be served until he sent further instructions, and he strongly urged Palmer to make immediate arrangements for meeting them, and also to arrange for the bills for £1,500 due on the 9th of November. Between the 10th and 13th of November, Palmer succeeded in paying £600; but on that day Pratt again wrote to him, urging him to raise £1,000, at all events, to meet the bills due on the 9th.

That being the state of things at that time, we now come to the events connected with Shrewsbury races. Cooke was the owner of a mare called Polestar, which was entered for the Shrewsbury Handicap. She had been advantageously weighted, and Cooke, believing that the mare would win, betted largely upon the event. The race was run upon the 13th of November – the very day on which that last letter was written by Pratt, which would reach Palmer on the 14th. The result of the race was that Polestar won, and that Cooke was entitled, in the first place, to the stakes, which amounted to £424, minus certain deductions, which left a net sum of £381 19s. His bets had also been successful, and he won, upon the whole, a total sum of £2,050. He had won also in the previous week, at Worcester, and I shall show that at Shrewsbury he had in his pocket, besides the stakes and the money which he would be entitled to receive at Tattersall's, between £700 and £800. The stakes he would receive through Mr Weatherby, a great racing agent in London, with whom he kept an account, and upon whom he would draw; and, the race being run on Tuesday, he would be entitled on the ensuing Monday to receive his bets at Tattersall's, which amounted to £1,020.

Within a week from that time Mr Cooke died, and the important inquiry which we have now to make is how he came by his death – whether by natural causes or by the hand of man? and if the latter, by whose hand?

It is important, in the first place, that I should show you what was his state of health when he went down to Shrewsbury. He was a young man, but twenty-eight when he died. He was slightly disposed to a pulmonary complaint, and, although delicate in that respect, he was in all other respects a hale and hearty young man. For four years he had occasionally consulted a physician in London, Dr Savage, being at that time a little anxious about the state of his throat, in which there happened to be one or two slight eruptions. He had been taking mercury for these eruptions, having mistaken the character of the complaint. Dr Savage at once saw that he had made a mistake, and desired him to discontinue the use of mercury, substituting for it a course of tonics. Mr Cooke's health immediately began to improve; but, inasmuch as the new course of treatment might have involved serious consequences in case Dr Savage had been mistaken in the diagnosis of the disease, he asked Cooke to look in upon him from time to time, and Cooke had, as recently as within a fortnight of his death, gone to call upon Dr Savage. Dr Savage then examined his throat and whole system carefully, and found that at that time he had nothing on earth the matter with him, except a certain degree of thickening of the tonsils, or some of the glands of the throat, to which anyone is liable, and there was no symptom whatever of ulcerated sore throat, or anything of the sort.

Having then seen Dr Savage, he went down to Shrewsbury races, and his horse won. After that he was somewhat excited, as a man might naturally be under the circumstances of having won a considerable sum of money, and he asked several friends to dine with him to celebrate the event. They dined together at the Raven, the hotel where he was staying, and had two or three bottles of wine; but there was no excess of any sort, and there is no foundation for saying that Cooke was the worse for liquor. Indeed, he was not addicted to excesses, but was, on the contrary, an abstemious man on all occasions. He went to bed that night, and there was nothing the matter with

Shrewsbury Races

him. He got up the next day, and went again on the course, as usual.

That night, Wednesday, the 14th November, a remarkable incident happened. A friend of his, a Mr Fisher, and a Mr Herring, were at Shrewsbury races, and Fisher, who, besides being a sporting man, was an agent for receiving winnings, and who received Cooke's bets at the settling day at Tattersall's, occupied the room next to that occupied by Cooke. Late in the evening, Fisher went into a room in which he found Palmer and Cooke drinking brandy and water. Cooke gave him something to drink, and said to Palmer, 'You'll have some more, won't you?' Palmer replied, 'Not unless you finish your glass.' Cooke said, 'I'll soon do that'; and he finished it at a gulp, leaving only about a teaspoonful at the bottom of the glass. He had hardly swallowed it, when he exclaimed, 'Good God! there's something in it, it burns my throat.' Palmer immediately took up the glass, and drinking what remained, said, 'Nonsense, there's nothing in it': and then, pushing the glass to Fisher and another person who had come in, said, 'Cooke fancies there is something in the brandy-and-water – there's nothing in it – taste it.' On which one of them replied, 'How can we taste it? you've drank it all.'

Cooke suddenly rose and left the room, and called Fisher out, saying that he was taken seriously ill. He was seized with most violent vomiting, and became so bad that after a while it was necessary to take him to bed. He vomited there again and again in the most violent way, and as the sickness continued after the lapse of a couple of hours, a medical man was sent for. He came and proposed an emetic and other means for making the sick man eject what he had taken. After that, medicine was given him – at first some stimulant of a comforting nature, and then a pill as a purgative dose. After two or three hours he became more tranquil, and about two o'clock he fell asleep and slept till next morning. Such was the state of the man's feelings all that time that I cannot tell what passed; but he gave Fisher the money which he had about him, desiring him to take care of it, and Mr Fisher will tell you that that money amounted to between £800 and £900 in notes.

The next morning, feeling better, he went out on the course; and he saw Fisher, who gave him back his notes. That was the Thursday. He still looked very ill, and felt very ill; but the vomiting had ceased. On that day Palmer's horse, the Chicken, ran at Shrewsbury. He had backed his mare heavily, but she lost. When Palmer went to Shrewsbury, he had no money, and was obliged to borrow £25 to take him there. He and Cooke then returned to Rugeley, Cooke going to the Talbot Arms Hotel, directly opposite the prisoner's house.

There is an incident, however, connected with the occurrence at Shrewsbury, which I must mention. About eleven o'clock that night, a Mrs Brooks, who betted on commission, and had an establishment of jockeys, went to speak to the deceased upon some racing business, and in the lobby she saw Palmer holding up a tumbler to the light; and, having looked at it through the gas, he withdrew to an outer room, and presently returned with the glass in his hand, and went into the room where Cooke was, and in which room he drank the brandy and water from which I suppose you will infer that the sickness came on. I do not charge that by anything which caused that sickness Cooke's death was occasioned; but I shall

The Chicken

show you that throughout the ensuing days at Rugeley he constantly received things from the prisoner, and that during those days that sickness was continued. I shall show you that, after he died, antimony was found in the tissues of his body and in his blood – antimony administered in the form of tartar emetic, which, if continued to be applied, will maintain sickness.

It was not that, however, of which this man died. The charge is that, having been prepared by antimony, he was killed by strychnine.

Palmer was a medical man, and it is clear that the effect of strychnine had not escaped his attention. I have a book before me which was found in his house after his arrest, called 'Manual for Students Preparing for Examination at Apothecaries' Hall,' and on the first page, in his handwriting, I observe this remark; 'Strychnine kills by causing tetanic fixing of the respiratory muscles.' I don't wish to attach more importance to that circumstance than it deserves, because nothing is more natural than that, in a book of this kind belonging to a professional man, such notes should be made; but I refer to it to show that the effect of poison on human life had come within his notice.

I now revert to what took place after the arrival of these people at Rugeley. They arrived on the night of Thursday, the 15th of November, between ten and eleven o'clock, when Mr Cooke took some refreshment and went to bed.

He rose next morning and went out, and dined that day with Palmer. He returned to the inn about ten o'clock that evening, perfectly well and sober, and went to bed. The next morning, at an early hour, Palmer was with him, and from that time, throughout the whole of Saturday and Sunday, he was constantly in attendance on him. He ordered him coffee on Saturday morning. It was brought in by the chambermaid, Elizabeth Mills, and given to the prisoner, who had an opportunity of tampering with it before giving it to Cooke. Immediately after taking it, the same symptoms set in which had occurred at Shrewsbury. Throughout the whole of that day and the next, the prisoner constantly administered various things to Cooke, who continued to be tormented with that incessant and troublesome sickness. Again, toast and water was brought over from the prisoner's house, instead of being made at the inn, as it might have been, and again the sickness ensued.

It seems also that Palmer desired a woman named Roney to procure some broth for Cooke from the Albion. She obtained it, and gave it to Palmer to warm, and when Palmer had done so he told her to take it to the Talbot for Mr Cooke, and to say that Mr Smith had sent it – there being a Mr Jeremiah Smith, an intimate friend of Cooke. Cooke tried to swallow a spoonful of the broth, but it immediately made him sick, and he brought it off his stomach. The broth was then taken downstairs, and after a little while the prisoner came across and asked if Mr Cooke had had his broth. He was told, 'No; that he had tried to take it but that it had made him sick, and that he could not retain it on his stomach.' Palmer said that he must take it, and desired that the broth should be brought upstairs. Cooke tried to take it again, but again he began to vomit and throw the whole off his

The Talbot Arms

stomach. It was then taken downstairs, and a woman at the inn, thinking that it looked nice, took a couple of tablespoonfuls of it. Within half an hour she also was taken severely ill. Vomiting came on, and continued almost incessantly for five or six hours. She was obliged to go to bed, and she had exactly the same symptoms which manifested themselves in Cooke's person after he drank the brandy and water at Shrewsbury.

On that Saturday, about three o'clock, Dr Bamford, a medical man at Rugeley, was called in, and Palmer told him that Cooke had had a bilious attack – that he had dined with him on the day before, and had drunk too freely of champagne, which had disordered his stomach. Now, I shall show to you, by the evidence of medical men, both at Shrewsbury and Rugeley, that although Palmer had on one or two occasions represented Cooke as suffering under bilious diarrhoea, there was not, during the continuance of the violent vomiting which I have mentioned, a single bilious symptom of any sort whatever. Dr Bamford visited him at half-past 3, and when he found Mr Cooke suffering from violent vomiting, and the stomach in so irritable a state that it would not retain a tablespoonful of anything, he naturally tried to see what the symptoms were which could lead him to form a notion as to the cause of that state of things. He found to his surprise that the pulse of the patient was perfectly natural – that his tongue was quite clean, his skin quite moist, and that there was not the slightest trace of fever, or, in short, of any of those symptoms which might be expected in the case of a bilious man. Having heard from Palmer that he ascribed his illness to an excess of wine on the previous day, he informed Cooke of it, and Cooke then said, 'Well, I suppose I might have taken too much, but it's very odd, for I only took three glasses.' The representation, therefore, made by Palmer, that Cooke had taken an excess of champagne, was not correct.

Dr. William Bamford

Coffee was brought up to Cooke at 4 o'clock when Palmer was there, and he vomited immediately. At 6 some barley-water was taken to him when Palmer was not there, and the barley-water did not produce vomiting. At 8 some arrowroot was given him, Palmer was present, and vomiting took place again. These may, no doubt, be mere coincidences, but they are facts which, of whatever interpretation they may be susceptible, are well deserving of attention – that during the whole of that Saturday Palmer was continually in and out of the house in which Cooke was sojourning; that he gave him a variety of things, and that whenever he gave him anything, sickness invariably ensued. That evening Dr Bamford called again, and finding that the sickness still continued, he prepared for the patient two pills containing half a grain of calomel, half a grain of morphia, and four grains of rhubarb.

On the following day, Sunday, between 7 and 8 o'clock in the morning, Dr Bamford is again summoned to Cooke's bedside, and finds the sickness still recurring, but fails to detect any symptoms of bile. He visited him repeatedly in the course of that day, and on leaving him in the evening found that, though the sickness continued, the tongue was clean, and there was not the slightest indication of bile or fever. And so Sunday ended. On Monday, the 19th, Palmer left Rugeley for London – on what business I shall presently explain. Before starting, however, he called in the morning to see Cooke, and ordered him a cup of coffee. He took it up himself, and after drinking it, Cooke, as usual, vomited. After that, Palmer took his departure.

Presently Dr Bamford called, and finding Cooke still suffering from sickness of the stomach, gave him some medicine. From that time a great improvement was observed in Cooke. Palmer was not present, and during the whole of the day Cooke was better. Between 12 and 1 o'clock he is visited by Dr Bamford, who, perceiving the improvement, advises him to get up. He does so, washes, dresses, recovers his spirits, and sits up for several hours. Two of his jockies and his trainer call to see him, are admitted to his room, enter into conversation with him, and perceive that he is in a state of comparative ease and comfort, and so he continued till a late hour.

I will now interrupt for a moment the consecutive narration of what passed afterwards at Rugeley, to follow Palmer through the events in which he was concerned in London. He had written to a person named Herring to meet him at Beaufort Buildings, where a boarding-house was kept by a lady named Hawks. Herring was a man on the turf, and had been to Shrewsbury races. Immediately on seeing Palmer, he inquired after Cooke's health. 'Oh,' said Palmer, 'he is all right; his medical man has given him a dose of calomel and recommended him not to come out, and what I want to see you about is the settling of his accounts.' Monday, it appears, was settling-day at Tattersall's, and it was necessary that all accounts should be squared. Cooke's usual agent for effecting that arrangement was the person named Fisher, and it seems not a little singular that Cooke should not have told Palmer why Fisher should not have been employed on this as on all similar occasions.

On this point, however, Palmer offered no explanation. He was himself a defaulter, and could not show at Tattersall's. He produced a piece of paper which he said contained a list of the sums which Cooke was entitled to receive, and he mentioned the names of the different persons who were indebted to Cooke, and the amounts for which they were respectively liable. Herring held out his hand to take the paper, but Palmer said, 'No, I will keep this document; here is another piece of paper, write down what I read to you, and what I have here I will retain, as it will be a check against you.' He then dictated the names of the various persons, with the sums for which they were liable. Herring observed that it amounted to £1,020. 'Very well,' said Palmer, 'pay yourself £6, Shelly £30, and if you see Bull, tell him Cooke will pay him on Thursday or Friday. And now,' he added, 'how much do you make that balance?' Herring replied that he made it £984, Palmer replied that the tot was right, and then went on to say, 'I will give you £16, which will make it £1,000. Pay yourself the £200 that I owe you for my bill; pay Padwick £350, and Pratt £450.'

So we have it here established, beyond all controversy, that Palmer did not hesitate to apply Cooke's money to the payment of his own debts.

Palmer desired Herring to send cheques to Pratt and Padwick at once, and without waiting to draw the money from Tattersall's. To this Herring objected, observing that it would be most injudicious to send the cheques before he was sure of getting the money. 'Ah, well,' said Palmer, 'never mind – it is all right; but come what will, Pratt must be paid, for his claim is on account of a bill of sale for a mare.' Finding it impossible to overcome Herring's objection to send the cheques till he had got the money at Tattersall's, Palmer then proceeded to settle some small betting transactions between himself and that gentleman amounting to £5, or thereabouts. He pulled out a £50 note, and Herring, not having full change, gave him a cheque for £20. They then parted, Palmer directing him to send down word of his proceedings either to him (Palmer) or to Cooke. With this injunction Herring complied; the letters he wrote to Cooke were intercepted by the postmaster at Rugeley. Not having received as much as he expected at Tattersall's, Herring was unable to pay Padwick the £350; but it is not disputed that he paid £450 to Pratt.

On the same day, Palmer went himself to the latter gentleman, and paid him other moneys, consisting of £30 in notes, and the cheque for £20 which he had received from Herring, and a memorandum was drawn, and to which I shall hereafter have occasion to call attention. So much for Palmer's proceedings in London.

The Post Office, Rugeley

On the evening of that same day (Monday), he returned home. Arriving at Rugeley about 9 o'clock at night, he at once proceeded to visit Cooke at the Talbot Arms; and from that time till 10 or 11 o'clock he was continually in and out of Cooke's room. In the course of the evening he went to a man named Newton, assistant to a surgeon named Salt, and applied for three grains of strychnine, which Newton, knowing Palmer to be a medical practitioner, did not hesitate to give him. Dr Bamford had sent on this day the same kind of pills that he had sent on Saturday and Sunday. I believe it was the doctor's habit to take the pills himself to the Talbot Arms, and entrust them to the care of the housekeeper, who carried them upstairs; but it was Palmer's practice to come in afterwards, and, evening after evening, to administer medicine to the patient. There is no doubt that Cooke took pills on Monday night. Whether he took the pills prepared for him by Dr Bamford, and similar to those which he had taken on Saturday and Sunday, or whether Palmer substituted for Dr Bamford's pills some of his own concoction, consisting in some measure of strychnine, I must leave for the jury to determine. Certain it is that when he left Cooke at 11 o'clock at night, the latter was still comparatively well and comfortable, and cheerful as in the morning. But he was not long to continue so.

About 12 o'clock the female servants in the lower part of the house were alarmed by violent screams proceeding from Cooke's room. They rushed up and found him in great agony, shrieking dreadfully, shouting 'Murder!' and calling on Christ to save his soul. The eyes were starting out of his head. He was flinging his arms wildly about him, and his whole body was convulsed. He was perfectly conscious, however, and desired that Palmer should be sent for without delay. One of the women ran to fetch him, and he attended in a few minutes. He found Cooke still screaming, gasping for breath, and hardly able to speak. He ran back again to procure some medicine; and on his return Cooke exclaimed, 'Oh dear, doctor, I shall die!' 'No, my lad, you shall not,' replied Palmer; and he then gave him some more medicine. The sick man vomited almost immediately, but there was no appearance of the pills in the utensil.

Shortly afterwards he became more calm, and called on the women to rub his limbs. They found them cold and rigid. Presently the symptoms became still more tranquil and he grew better; but the medical men will depone that the tetanic seizure that afflicted him was that occasioned by strychnine. His frame, exhausted by the terrible agony it had endured, now fell gradually into repose; nature asserted her claim to rest, and he began to dose. So matters remained till the morrow, Tuesday the 20th, the day of his death.

On the morning of that day, Cooke was found comparatively comfortable, though still retaining a vivid impression of the horrors he had suffered the night before. He was quite collected, and conversed rationally with the chambermaid. Palmer meeting Dr Bamford that same day, told him that he did not want to have Cooke disturbed, for that he was now at his ease, though he had had a fit the night before.

This same morning, between the hours of eleven and twelve o'clock, there occurred a very remarkable incident. About that time, Palmer went to the shop of a certain Mr Hawkings, a druggist, at Rugeley. He had not dealt with him for two years before, it being his practice during that period to purchase such drugs as he required from Mr Thirlby, a former assistant of Mr Hawkings, who had set up in business for himself. But on this day Palmer went to Mr Hawkings' shop, and, producing a bottle, informed the assistant that he wanted two drachms of prussic acid. While it was being prepared for him, Mr Newton, the same man from whom he had on a former occasion obtained strychnine, came into the shop, whereupon Palmer seized him by the arm, and, observing that he had something particular to say to him, hurried him into the street, where he kept talking to him on a matter of the smallest possible importance, relating to the precise period at which his employer's son meant to repair to a farm he had taken in the country. They continued to converse on this trivial topic until a gentleman named Brassington came up, whereupon Mr Newton turned aside to say a few words to him. Palmer, relieved by this accident, went back into the shop and asked, in addition, for six grains of strychnine and a certain quantity of Batley's solution. He obtained them, paid for them, and went away. Presently Mr Newton returned, and being struck with the fact of Palmer's dealing with Hawkings, asked out of passing curiosity what he had come for, and was informed.

I now resume the story of Tuesday's proceedings with the observation that Cooke was entitled to receive the stakes he had won at Shrewsbury. On that day Palmer sent for Mr Cheshire, the postmaster at Rugeley. He owed Cheshire £7 odd, and the latter, supposing that he was about to be paid, came with a stamp receipt in his hand.

Samuel Cheshire, the late Postmaster at Rugeley

Palmer produced a paper, and remarking 'that Cooke was too ill to write himself,' told Cheshire to draw a cheque on Weatherby's in his (Palmer's) favour for £350. Cheshire thereupon filled up a piece of paper purporting to be the body of a cheque, addressed in the manner indicated to the Messrs. Weatherby, and concluding with the words, 'and place the same to my account'. Palmer then took the document away, for the purpose, as he averred, of getting Cooke's signature to it. What become of it I do not undertake to assert; but of this there is no question, that by that night's post Palmer sent up to Weatherby's a cheque which was returned dishonoured. Whether it was genuine, or like so many other papers with which Palmer had to do, forged, is a question which you will have to determine. And now, returning to Cooke, it may be observed that in the course of that morning coffee and broth were sent him by Palmer, and, as usual, vomiting ensued and continued through the whole afternoon.

And now a new person makes his appearance on the stage. You must know that on Sunday, Palmer wrote to Mr W. H. Jones, a surgeon, of Lutterworth, desiring him to come over to see Cooke. Cooke was a personal friend of Mr Jones, and had occasionally been in the habit of residing at his house. It is deserving of remark that Palmer, in his letter to Jones, describes Cooke as 'suffering from a severe bilious attack, accompanied with diarrhoea,' adding, 'it is desirable for you to come and see him as soon as possible.' Whether this communication is to be interpreted in a sense favourable to the prisoner, or whether it is to be taken as indicating a deep design to give colour to the idea that Cooke died a natural death, it is at least certain that the statement that Cooke had been 'suffering from a bilious attack attended with diarrhoea', was utterly untrue. Mr Jones, being himself unwell, did not come to Rugeley till Tuesday. He arrived at about three o'clock on that day, and immediately proceeded to see his sick friend. Palmer came in at the same moment, and they both examined the patient. Mr Jones paid particular attention to the state of his tongue, remarking, 'That is not the tongue of bilious fever.'

About seven o'clock that same evening, Dr Bamford called, and found the patient pretty well. Subsequently the three medical men (Palmer, Bamford, and Jones) held a consultation, but before leaving the bedroom for that purpose, Cooke beckoned to Palmer, and said, 'Mind, I will have no more pills or medicine to-night.' They then withdrew and consulted. Palmer insisted on his taking pills, but added, 'Let us not tell him what they contain, as he fears the same results that have already given him such pain.' It was agreed that Dr Bamford should make up the pills, which were to be composed of the same ingredients as those that had been administered on the three preceding evenings. The doctor repaired to his surgery, and made them up accordingly. He was followed by Palmer, who asked him to write the directions how they were to be taken. Dr Bamford, though unable to understand the necessity of his doing so, complied with Palmer's request, and wrote on the box that the pills were to be taken at 'bed-time'. Palmer then took them away, and gave either these pills or some others to Cooke that night. It is remarkable, however, that half or three-quarters of an hour elapsed from the time he left Dr Bamford's surgery until he brought the pills to Cooke. When, at length, he came, he produced two pills, but before giving them to Cooke he took especial care to call Mr Jones's attention to the directions on the lid, observing that the writing was singularly distinct and vigorous for a man upwards of eighty. If the prisoner be guilty, it is a natural presumption that he made this observation with the view of identifying the pill-box as having come from Dr Bamford, and so averting suspicion from himself. This was about half-past ten at night.

The pills were then offered to Cooke, who strongly objected to take them, remarking that they had made him ill the night before. Palmer insisted, and the sick man at last consented to take them. He vomited immediately after, but did not bring up the pills. Jones then went down and took his supper, and he will tell you that up to the period when the pills were administered, Cooke had been easy and cheerful, and presented no symptoms of the approach of disease, much less of death. It was arranged that Jones should sleep in the same room with Cooke, and he did so; but he had not been more than fifteen or twenty minutes in bed when he was aroused by a sudden exclamation, and a frightful scream from Cooke, who, starting up, said, 'Send for the doctor immediately; I am going to be ill, as I was last night.'

The chambermaid ran across the road, and rang the bell of Palmer's house, and in a moment Palmer was at the window. He was told that Cooke was again ill. In two minutes he was by the bedside of the sick man, and, strangely, volunteered the observation, 'I never dressed so quickly in my life.' It is for you, gentlemen, to say whether you think he had time to dress at all.

Cooke was found in the same condition, and with the same symptoms, as the night before, gasping for breath, screaming violently, his body convulsed with cramps and spasms, and his neck rigid. Jones raised him and rubbed his neck. When Palmer entered the room, Cooke asked him for the same remedy that had relieved him the night before. 'I will run back and fetch it,' said Palmer, and he darted out of the room. In the passage he met two female servants, who remarked that Cooke was as 'bad' as he had been last night. 'He is not within fifty times as bad as he was last night; and what a game is this to be at every night!' was Palmer's reply. In a few minutes he returned with two pills, which he told Jones were ammonia, though I am assured that it is a drug that requires much time in the preparation, and can with difficulty be made into pills. The sick man swallowed these pills, but brought them up again immediately.

And now ensued a terrible scene. He was suddenly seized with violent convulsions; by degrees his body began to stiffen out; then suffocation commenced. Agonised with pain, he repeatedly entreated to be raised. They tried to raise him, but it was not possible. The body had become rigid as iron, and it could not be done. He then said, 'Pray turn me over.' They did turn him over on the right side. He gasped for breath, but could utter no more. In a few moments all was tranquil – the tide of life was ebbing fast. Jones leant over to listen to the action of the heart. Gradually the pulse ceased – all was over – he was dead.

Scarcely was the breath out of his body when Palmer begins to think of what is to be done. He engages two women to lay out the corpse, and these women, on entering the room, find him searching the pockets of a coat which, no doubt, belonged to Cooke, and hunting under the pillows and bolsters. They saw some letters on the mantel-shelf, which, in all probability, had been taken out of the dead man's pocket; and, what is very remarkable is that from that day to this, nothing has been seen or heard either of the betting-book or of any of the papers connected with Cooke's money affairs.

On a subsequent day he returned, and, on the pretence of looking for some books and a paper knife, rummaged again through the documents of the deceased. On the 25th November he sent for Cheshire, the postmaster, and, producing a paper purporting to bear the signature of Cooke, asked him to attest it. Cheshire glanced over it. It was a document in which Cooke acknowledged that certain bills, to the amount of £4,000 or thereabouts, were bills that had been negotiated for his benefit, and in respect of which Palmer had received no consideration. Such was the paper to which, forty-eight hours after the death of the man whose name it bore, Palmer did not hesitate to ask Cheshire to be an attesting witness. Cheshire, though, unfortunately for himself, too much the slave of Palmer, peremptorily refused to comply with this request; whereupon Palmer carelessly observed, 'It is of no consequence; I dare say the signature will not be disputed, but it occurred to me that it would look more regular if it were attested.'

On Friday Mr Stevens, Cooke's father-in-law, came down to Rugeley, and, after viewing the body of his relative, to whom he had been tenderly attached, asked Palmer about his affairs. Palmer assured him that he held a paper drawn up by a lawyer, and signed by Cooke, stating that, in respect of £4,000 worth of bills, he (Cooke) was alone liable, and that Palmer had a claim to that amount against his estate. Mr Stevens expressed his amazement, and replied that there would not be 4,000 shillings for the holders of the bills.

Subsequently Palmer displayed an eager officiousness in the matter of the funeral, taking upon himself to order a shell and an oak coffin, without any directions to that effect from the relatives of the deceased, who were anxious to have the arrangements in their own hands.

Mr Stevens ordered dinner at the hotel for Bamford, Jones, and himself, and finding Palmer still hanging about him, thought it but civil to extend the invitation to him. Accordingly they all sat down together. After dinner, Mr Stevens asked Jones to step upstairs and bring down all the books and papers belonging to Cooke. Jones left the room to do so, and Palmer followed him. They were absent about ten minutes, and on their return Jones observed that they were unable to find the betting-book or any of the papers belonging to the deceased. Palmer added, 'The betting-book would be of no use to you if you found it, for the bets are void by his death.' Mr Stevens replied, 'The book must be found;' and then Palmer, changing his tone, said, 'Oh, I dare say it will turn up.' Mr Stevens then rang the bell, and told the housekeeper to take charge of whatever books and papers had belonged to Cooke, and to be sure not to allow anyone to meddle with them until he came back from London, which he would soon do, with his solicitor.

He then departed, but, returning to Rugeley after a brief interval, declared his intention to have a post-mortem examination. Palmer volunteered to nominate the surgeons who should conduct it, but Mr Stevens refused to employ anyone whom he should recommend.

On Sunday the 26th, Palmer called on Dr Bamford, and asked him for a certificate attesting the cause of Cooke's death. The doctor expressed his surprise, and observed: 'Why, he was your patient.' But Palmer importuned him, and Bamford, taking the pen, filled up the certificate, and entered the cause of death as 'apoplexy'. I hope that it is to some infirmity connected with his great age that this most unjustifiable act is to be attributed.

In the course of the day Palmer sent for Newton, and after they had some brandy and water, asked him how much strychnine he would use to kill a dog. Newton replied, 'from half-a-grain to a grain'. 'And how much,' inquired Palmer, 'would be found in the tissues and intestines after death?' 'None at all,' was Newton's reply.

The post-mortem examination took place the next day, and on that occasion Palmer assured the medical men, of whom there were many present, that Cooke had had epileptic fits on Monday and Tuesday, and that they would find old disease in the heart and head. He added that the poor fellow was 'full of disease', and had 'all kinds of complaints'. These statements were completely disproved by the post-mortem examinations.

At the first of them, conducted by Dr Devonshire, the liver, lungs, and kidneys were all found healthy. It was said that there was some slight indications of congestion of the kidneys, whether due to decomposition or to what other cause was not certain; but it was admitted on all hands that they did not impair the general health of the system, or at all account for death. The stomach and intestines were examined, and they exhibited a few white spots at the large end of the stomach, but these marks were wholly insufficient to explain the cause of dissolution. Dr Bamford contended that there was some slight congestion of the brain, but all the other medical men concurred in thinking that there was none at all.

In the ensuing month of January the body was exhumed with a view to more accurate examination, and the body was then found to be in a perfectly normal and healthy condition. Palmer seemed rejoiced at the discovery, and turning to Dr Bamford, exclaimed, 'Doctor, they won't hang us yet!'

The stomach and intestines were taken out and placed in a jar, and it was observed that Palmer pushed against the medical man who was engaged in the operation, and the jar was in danger of being upset. It escaped, however, and was covered with skins, tied down, and sealed. Presently one of the medical men turned round, and finding that the jar had disappeared, asked what had become of it. It was found at a distance, near a different door from that through which people usually passed in and out, and Palmer exclaimed, 'It's all right. It was I who removed it. I thought it would be more convenient for you to have it here, that you might lay your hands readily on it as you went out.' When the jar was recovered, it was found that two slits had been cut in the skins with a knife. The slits, however, were clean, so that whatever his object may have been in making the incisions, it is certain that nothing was taken out of the jar. He goes to Dr Bamford, and remonstrates against the removal of the jars. He says, 'I do not think we ought to allow them to be taken away.' Now, if he had been an ignorant person, not familiar with the course likely to be pursued by medical men under such circumstances, there might be some excuse for this; but it is for you to ask yourselves whether Palmer, himself a medical man, knowing that the contents of the jars were to be submitted to an analysis, might not have relied with confidence on the honour and integrity of the profession to which he belonged.

But the case does not stop here. The jar was delivered to Mr Boycott, the clerk to Mr Gardner, a solicitor. Palmer, finding that it was to be sent to London for chemical analysis, was extremely anxious that it should not reach its destination. It was going to be conveyed by Mr Boycott to the Stafford station in a fly, driven by a post-boy. Palmer goes to this post-boy, and asks him whether it is the fact that he is going to drive Boycott to Stafford? He is answered in the affirmative. He then asks, 'Are the jars there?' He is told that they are. He says, 'They have no business to take them; one does not know what they may put in them. Can't you manage to upset the fly and break them? I will give you £10, and make it all right for you.' The man said, 'I shall do no such thing. I must go and look after my fly.'

I have now gone through the painful history, yet there are some points of minor importance which I ought not altogether to pass over, as nothing connected with the conduct of a man conscious that an imputation of this kind rests upon him can be immaterial.

After the post-mortem examination, it was thought right to hold a coroner's inquest. On two or three occasions in the course of that inquiry, Palmer sent presents to the coroner. The stomach of the deceased and its contents were sent to Dr Taylor and Dr Rees, at Guy's

Hospital, who were known to be in communication with Mr Gardner. A letter was sent by Dr Taylor to Mr Gardner stating the result of the investigation; that letter was betrayed to Palmer by the postmaster, Cheshire, and Palmer then wrote to the coroner, telling him that Dr Taylor and Dr Rees had failed in finding traces of poison, and asking him to take a certain course with respect to the evidence. Why should he have done this if there had not been a feeling of uneasiness upon his mind?

I should have told you, in addition, that the prisoner had no money prior to Shrewsbury races, while afterwards he was flush of cash. Sums of £100 and £150 were paid by him into the bank at Rugeley, two or three persons received sums of £10 each, and he seemed, in fact, to be giving away money right and left. I think I shall be able to show that he had something like £400 in his possession. Now, Cooke had £700 or £800 when he left Shrewsbury on the Thursday morning. None is found. It may be that Cooke, who, whatever his faults, was a kind-hearted creature, compassionating Palmer's condition, assisted him with money. I do not wish to strain the point too far, but one cannot imagine that Cooke, who had no money but what he took with him to Shrewsbury, should have given Palmer everything and left himself destitute.

The case, then, stands thus: – Here is a man overwhelmed with pecuniary difficulties, obliged to resort to the desperate expedient of forging acceptances to raise money, hoping to meet them by the proceeds of the insurances he had effected upon a life. Disappointed in that expectation by the board; told by the gentleman through whom the bills had been discounted, 'You must trifle with me no longer – if you cannot find money, writs will be served on you!'; Cooke's name forged to an endorsement for £375; ruin staring him in the face: You, gentlemen, must say whether he had not sufficient inducement to commit the crime. He seems to have had a further object. No sooner is the breath out of the dead man's body than he says to Jones, 'I had a claim of £3,000 or £4,000 against him on account of bills.' Besides, he believed that Cooke had more property than it turns out he really had. The valuable mare, Polestar, belonged to him when the assignment had been paid off, and Palmer would have been glad to obtain possession of her. The fact, too, that Cooke was mixed up in the insurance of Bates may lead one to surmise that he was in possession of secrets relating to the desperate expedients to which this man has resorted to obtain money. I will leave you to say whether this combination of motives may not have led to the crime with which he is charged. This you will only have to consider, supposing the case to be balanced between probabilities; but if you believe the evidence as to what took place on the Monday and the Tuesday – if you believe the paroxysms of the Monday, the mortal agony of the Tuesday – I shall show that things were administered, on both these days, by the hand of Palmer, by a degree of evidence almost amounting to certainty.

The body was submitted to a careful analysis, and I am bound to say that no trace of strychnine was found. But I am told that, although the presence of strychnine may be detected by certain tests, and although indications of its presence lead irresistibly to the conclusion that it has been administered, the converse of that proposition does not hold. Sometimes it is found, at other times it is not. It depends upon circumstances. It would, indeed, be a fatal thing to sanction the notion that strychnine administered for the purpose of taking away life cannot afterwards be detected! Lamentable enough is the uncertainty of detection! Happily, Providence, which has placed this fatal agent at the disposition of man, has marked its effects with characteristic symptoms distinguishable from those of all other agents by the eye of science.

There is a circumstance which throws great light upon this part of the case. The analysis made of Cooke's body failed to produce evidence of the presence of strychnine, but did not fail to produce evidence of the presence of antimony. Now, antimony was not administered by the medical men, and unless taken in a considerable quantity it produces no effect and is perfectly soluble. It is an irritant, which produces exactly the symptoms which were produced in this case. The man was sick for a week, and antimony was found in his body afterwards. For what purpose can it have been administered? It may be that the original intention was to destroy him by means of antimony – it may be that the only object was to bring about an appearance of disease so as to account for death. One is lost in speculation. But the question is whether you have any doubt that strychnine was administered on the Monday, and still more on the Tuesday when death ensued? And if you are satisfied with the evidence that will be adduced on that point, you must then determine whether it was not administered by the prisoner's hand. If in the end all should fail in satisfying you of his guilt, in God's name let not the innocent suffer! If, on the other hand, the facts should lead you to the conclusion that he is guilty, the best interests of society demand his conviction.

The hon. and learned Attorney-General then sat down, having addressed the Court for four hours and a quarter, and the Court was adjourned for a short time, in order to enable the Court and the jury to take some refreshment. Evidence was then adduced for the prosecution....

First leading article on Friday, May 16:

The trial of PALMER now assumes a more definite aspect. The charge against the prisoner is that, having prepared, as it were, the way by means of antimony, and perhaps other poisons, he completed all by the administration of a dose or doses of strychnia. As we have repeatedly stated, we have no wish to prejudice in any way the public mind, in such a momentous case, and shall push nothing against the prisoner; but we cannot help remarking that the symptoms already deposed to are those of poisoning by antimony and by strychnia.

Of all poisons, antimony is the one that can be found longest in the tissues. There are many other poisonous compounds of antimony besides the tartar emetic, and one in particular, the muriate or butter of antimony, known to the alchemists as the fuming liquor of LIBAVIUS. We would recommend to parties concerned in this trial to keep their eye upon this fact; for in some respects the symptoms in COOKE's case might warrant a suspicion that a more acrid compound of antimony than even tartar emetic – the tartrate of antimony and potass, as it is called in chemical language – had been given.

With regard to the evidence of poisoning by strychnia, we repeat our previous observation – that those poisons which are most difficult of detection by chemical tests are providentially, we may presume, easiest of recognition by the symptoms. This fact was not, perhaps, sufficiently dwelt upon – it certainly was not made too much of – by the Attorney-General in his opening speech. The evidence of ELIZABETH MILLS, the bar-maid of the Talbot Arms, where COOKE died, speaks clearly as to symptoms resembling those of tetanus or lockjaw, and very nearly of hydrophobia. What could produce these in a healthy man except strychnia?

Elizabeth Mills

It will be observed in this case that the symptoms followed the administration of certain substances, either as articles of food or medicine – a most important fact. And – but this is a matter for the jury – that those things were administered by one individual, as far as the evidence has gone. That is to say, administered by himself personally or in his presence.

It is extremely difficult to procure convictions in cases of poisoning. The crime is necessarily a secret one; and the English law is so framed – generously, and perhaps justly – as to give the criminal every chance of escape; but at the same time neither judge nor jury should overlook the tremendous consequences to society if crimes like those in the present case, *if proved*, were to escape condign punishment.

We shall, however, give a warning with regard to the reception of medical evidence.

Some years ago a man named BELANY was tried for the alleged murder of his wife by means of prussic acid. He was a surgeon, like PALMER. That his wife died through his gross carelessness is certain – that she died through his wilful administration of the poison is doubtful. He was tried and acquitted. Dr LETHEBY (who will be a witness on behalf of PALMER) gave evidence at the trial.

BELANY's statement was that he got out of bed in the morning in order to take a few drops of prussic acid; that he could not get the stopper out of the bottle, and struck it with the handle of a knife, we believe, so that he broke the bottle, and then he poured the contents into a tumbler. He went into the next room and there sat down to write a letter, when he heard a shriek, cry, or scream, from the other room. He went back, and his wife cried, 'Oh, I have taken some of that stuff – that hot stuff,' and almost immediately fell over and expired. Now, upon this, Dr LETHEBY observed that this statement must be false, since, in animals poisoned by prussic acid, the shriek is the last effort of volition. Of course, the argument ran in this way: In animals poisoned by prussic acid, the shriek is the last effort of volition; speech is a part of volition, and, therefore, after having shrieked, Mrs BELANY could not have spoken.

Other medical assertions in this case, still more monstrous, and upon which the man was nearly hanged, we do not refer to at present. Suffice it to say that a medical gentleman showed at the time, first, that there was no evidence of a shriek at all – the question being between BELANY's *alleged* oral statement and his positive written statement, made at the same time, in which he says, 'I heard her cry for me from the other room.' Second: that he had poisoned, or seen poisoned, hundreds of animals with prussic acid, and had seen them running about, uttering shriek after shriek. That is to say, after giving one shriek, they were able to run and give another, so that volition did not cease with the shriek. Third: that we may reason, from experiments on animals, with great confidence, analogically, as regards human beings; but *speech* is one of the few points in which we cannot do so, since animals cannot speak. Fourth: that there were recorded cases of prussic acid poisoning in which human beings had shrieked, or uttered something like a shriek, and spoken afterwards.

At the same trial medical evidence equally as monstrous was given on other points, which our space prevents us from exposing at present. We therefore recommend the jury to watch the medical evidence very closely, for it does not always follow that those who by circumstances and accident are put in a prominent position in these trials are really the parties most fit for the duties.

The proceedings at the trial yesterday afternoon embraced the cross-examination of MILLS, the bar-maid of the Talbot Arms, and the evidence – direct and cross – of several other persons who were present at the final scene of the tragedy, and Dr SAVAGE, who spoke to the general health of the deceased for some time previous to his fatal visit to Rugeley.

The extraordinary manner in which 'Coroner's Quests' are sometimes conducted in this country was strikingly illustrated in the course of the day; and we trust that, after the trial is over, that subject will command a searching investigation, with a view to reform.

The able cross-examination, conducted by Serjeant SHEE and his coadjutors, was directed to neutralising or softening the effect of the evidence for the prosecution, and not unsuccessfully, it must be admitted, in the case of MILLS, the discrepancy between whose statements at the inquest and at the trial will, no doubt, be seized upon by the prisoner's counsel to damage her testimony before the jury.

It is not expected that any of the chemical witnesses will be produced before tomorrow, as the evidence of Mr PRATT and the insurance functionaries, relied upon by the Attorney-General to establish the motives for the alleged guilt ofthe prisoner, has yet to be taken.

So far, the trial – with the intelligent and patient attention of the jurors, the learned vigilance of the judges, and the decorous demeanour of the public – must strike any foreign spectator as an admirable and enviable example of the dignity and impartiality which characterises the administration of justice in the higher tribunals of this country.

CENTRAL CRIMINAL COURT,
Friday, May 16.

There is no abatement in the interest taken by the public in this most singular trial. Those parties who were fortunate enough to obtain the Sheriff's tickets of admission attend the Court daily.

This morning the Court sat at ten o'clock, and resumed in the same order as on the previous days. The jury entered first, then the judges, and, lastly, the prisoner. It was evident that Palmer's mind was not perfectly at ease, and that he begins to pass sleepless nights. His countenance today betrays somewhat of inward anxiety, and there is a nervous twitching of the mouth, seeming to indicate a suppression of feeling. He stood throughout the morning, and at times appeared to be lost in thought. Altogether, he does not exhibit the confident mien he assumed on Wednesday. Nevertheless, he watches the proceedings with eagerness. He rarely takes notes, but as points occur to him he communicates verbally with his solicitor, Mr Smith.

CENTRAL CRIMINAL COURT,
Saturday, May 17.

Long before the opening of the court, crowds of persons besieged every one of the entrances, waiting for admission. During the day large numbers of persons, unable to obtain an entrance into the court, remained standing outside, earnestly discussing the chances of the prisoner and the probable result of the trial. The interior of the court was more crowded than upon any previous day, it having been generally understood that the chemical evidence would be opened up in the course of the day. There was a large array of medical and scientific men present, sufficient of themselves to fill a very large portion of the court.

The jurors were scrutinised with considerable interest by the spectators, and probably the state of health of those individuals was never upon any previous occasion of their lives of so great public interest as at the present moment. On their physical powers of endurance a great deal now depends, for if any one of them should break down under the combined influence of the closely confined or crowded court, or by the continued strain upon their intellectual powers, the whole proceedings would necessarily have to be commenced *de novo*. The comfort and health of the jurors naturally, therefore, excite considerable attention. On Friday evening and Saturday morning they were taken out for a promenade in the Temple Gardens. The box in which they sit during the day has been widened, and made more commodious and comfortable, and they have been protected from atmospheric assaults by thick matting, which has been placed under their feet for the purpose of preventing the cold blasts which are incessantly directed into the court, and which would give the gentlemen of the jury those colds and rheumatic affections which are the sure and certain result of a prolonged visit to this court.

Mr Dallas, the American Minister, arrived a few minutes before the judges; Earl Grey shortly after followed, and occupied the same seat as on the previous days of the trial. The prisoner was looking remarkably well, and appeared more cheerful than on the previous day, and had a smile on his face. On arriving at the front of the dock, he bowed to the judges, and almost immediately afterwards entered into conversation with his solicitor. It was stated that Palmer still entertains a confident expectation of being acquitted.

First leading article on Tuesday, May 20:

As far as the medical evidence brought forward by the Crown has gone in the trial of PALMER, it seems to have proved the existence of symptoms in COOKE referable to strychnia, and that alone. We have cases of actual known poisoning by strychnia deposed to – in the human subject, too – where the symptoms were precisely such as those deposed in the case of COOKE: the suddenness of the attack, the snapping at the spoon when other substances were administered, the rigidity of the muscles of the neck, the screaming, the frightful spasms, the rigidity of the body, clenching of the hands and feet, the appearances presented by the body after death, stiffness, peculiar turning of the feet, and so forth.

The most important medical evidence yet given we conceive to be that of Mr JONES, the surgeon of Lutterworth who came to Rugeley to attend his friend, COOKE; Sir B. BRODIE; and the witnesses who depose to the symptoms and appearance in the case of a Mrs SMITH. The latter case was an undoubted one of poisoning by strychnia, administered by mistake, and the symptoms are almost identical with those in the case of COOKE, even to the expression 'Turn me over', in the last agony. There was the same desire, too, to be rubbed. JONES says – and he slept in the same room with COOKE – 'when death took place, the deceased was lying on his side, and both hands were tightly clenched, and the head and neck were bent back with quite an unnatural position, and the body was twisted back – in fact, it was quite bowed; and if the body had been placed on its back, it would have rested on the head and heels.' These are the very appearances produced by the form of tetanus called opisthotonos, the very form occasioned by strychnia; for there is another form of tetanus called emprosthotonos, in which the body is bent forwards.

The only portion of the medical evidence yet given which appears to favour the prisoner is that of Mr BAMFORD, who certified that death arose from apoplexy, evidently on slight grounds; and perhaps that of Mr DANIELL, who had seen cases of idiopathic tetanus – *i.e.*, tetanus arising not from wounds, but slight causes – it might be for instance, we suppose, from a bad tooth, and COOKE had two bad teeth and some slight affection of the glands of the mouth. But Mr DANIELL deposed that these causes of tetanus were of a slight and mild form, and analogous to ordinary tetanus, whereas COOKE's was a tremendous attack, fatal in a few minutes.

A very important part of the evidence is that which relates to the alleged purchase of the poison by PALMER. The evidence of NEWTON on this point will doubtless by objected to by the counsel for the prisoner, as NEWTON did not give the statement till some time after the coroner's inquest, nor even when examined for the Crown. It was an afterthought with him. NEWTON's statement is that he sold the strychnia on Monday evening; but ROBERTS swears positively that he sold PALMER six grains of strychnia and two drachms of Batley's sedative solution, and also two drachms of prussic acid, on Tuesday forenoon. All these are poisons in poisonous doses.

The important evidence of Dr TAYLOR was given yesterday. He deposes that the symptoms of poisoning by strychnia would be developed more or less quickly, as the poison was given in a solid or fluid state. The rabbits poisoned by him were affected in seven or ten minutes, and died in thirteen or twenty. Death would be longer in taking place, he thinks, in the human subject, because the circulation of man is less rapid. He then states that the tests for strychnia are not of that accurate character which is to be desired, and that there may be poisoning by strychnia when, from the small quantity used, none may be discovered, especially as he believes the poison to undergo decomposition in the blood. The internal organs of COOKE that were sent to him must, in their journeying to London, have been shaken in every possible way; they were in the most unfavourable condition for finding strychnia if it had been there. That fact leads us to remark that at all such investigations, a professed medical jurist should be present at the beginning, at the *post-mortem*.

Dr TAYLOR then proves the presence of antimony in the internal organs of COOKE, and states rightly that this poison, of all others, remains longest in the system, and concludes by giving a

Drs. Taylor and Rees performing their analysis

positive opinion that COOKE died from the effects of strychnia. Dr TAYLOR says, very properly, on his cross-examination, that he would allow what he heard with regard to symptoms, and so forth, to influence him so far as to serve as a guide as to what poisons he should look for, but not to influence his conclusions as a chemist from the analysis. In point of fact, as there is such an amazing number of poisonous substances, and the seeking for one may destroy the chance of finding another, how otherwise is the chemist to act?

How, then, stands the result of the medical evidence at present? Antimony is found in the body; it was proved that there were symptoms similar to those of antimonial poisoning during life; such symptoms, according to other evidence, occurred when PALMER was present; but it is not proved that the man actually died from antimonial poisoning. But it is proved, *if we are to believe the medical testimony* – that of men of the highest order – that COOKE died from strychnia, and no other assignable cause; for although no strychnia was found in the parts of the body analysed, this can be accounted for, but nothing can account for the symptoms but strychnia. We do not know, on the other hand, what is to be produced for the defence; and *audi alteram partem* is especially to be borne in mind in a case like this. Justice, no less than custom, demands that we should hear both sides before we pronounce our judgment.

TO THE EDITOR OF 'THE DAILY TELEGRAPH'.

SIR – Seeing in your leading articles a paragraph relative to the symptoms produced by strychnia, in which you ask, 'What could produce these in a healthy man except strychnia?' I feel bound to mention a fact which I do not for one moment bring forward with any intent otherwise than to do justice.

I have had under my care a patient (female) aged about twenty-four, who was suffering from violent tetanic spasms for two or three years. When the attack came on, she was frequently lifted out of bed, and the head drawn completely back to the heels, forming a hoop; the hands clenched; the spasm extended to all the muscles of the body, and the appearance was really frightful; excessive vomiting on taking food frequently brought on the spasm, which lasted from fifteen minutes to two hours. The patient has quite recovered, and is now in good health, and has been so for the last twelve months.

I have at present under my care a similar case, in a young lady of twenty. The least excitement of any sort brings on an attack, and at my last visit, during a spasm, she presented all the symptoms which we read of being produced by the poison strychnia. This disease we find in medical works under the head of *Opisthotonos*.

Should you deem this worthy a place in your valuable paper, as likely to throw any light on the present unfortunate trial, it is at your service. – I am, Sir, yours, &c.

MEDICUS.

May 17

[*The above letter is not authenticated by the name of the writer. In a spirit of justice he should have revealed himself, and we trust he will do so still, as his name might greatly enhance the importance of his communication. It will be seen that none of the medical witnesses yet examined can charge their recol-*

lection with any case presenting symptoms like those which preceeded Cooke's death excepting such as had been superinduced by the administration of strychnia. – ED.]

Wednesday, May 21:

TO THE EDITOR OF 'THE DAILY TELEGRAPH'.

SIR – Seeing a letter in your impression of today, signed 'Medicus', I feel bound to address myself through you to that gentleman. If you have not found out the name of 'Medicus', so that I may obtain his address, probably 'Medicus' would call upon me at this Court immediately he sees this, should he do so. Truth, justice, science, and human life require the fullest investigation. I trust you will think the urgency of the case sufficiently justifies the intrusion. If you have obtained the address of 'Medicus', oblige me by furnishing me with it. – I am, Sir, yours respectfully,

JOHN SMITH
Solicitor for William Palmer.
Court, Old Bailey, May 20.

[*We regret that, up the hour of going to press, no communication has been received from the party who signed himself 'Medicus'*]*

CENTRAL CRIMINAL COURT,
Thursday, May 22

Contrary to what has been the rule every day since the commencement of this important trial, the Court this morning was rather thinly attended. That may, to some extent, probably be attributed to two causes – the anxiety that was yesterday so generally manifested to hear the opening address in defence of the prisoner by Mr Serjeant Shee, who occupied the attention of the Court between seven and eight hours, till a few minutes before seven o'clock; and this morning in consequence of the very unfavourable state of the weather.

The prisoner, Palmer, on being placed at the bar, looked rather dejected, and as if he had been suffering from deep mental anxiety.

Monday, May 26:

CENTRAL CRIMINAL COURT,
Saturday, May 24

[*The entire of Saturday's proceedings were reported in our Second and Third Editions of Saturday. The Second Edition, containing the conclusion of the evidence for the defence, was published at half-past two; and the Third Edition, containing the speech of the Attorney-General, was published at seven p.m. Our Second Edition of this day will be published at two p.m., which will contain the summing up of Lord Chief Justice Campbell, and the verdict of the jury will be published in our Third Edition, within a quarter of an hour after its delivery.*]

Although this was the tenth day of this most singular, unparalleled, and important investigation, there has been no abatement in the public interest therein. For some time before the arrival of the judges, the mass of persons assembled in Court engaged in conversation, and not a few made strong comments, and ventured very decided opinions as

* It appears that Medicus either preferred to remain pseudonymous or revealed himself to Palmer's legal advisers but without impressing them. Certainly, he did not appear among the medical witnesses for the defence.

to the guilt or innocence of the accused.

A few minutes before ten o'clock the learned judges arrived, and the jury also made their appearance in the box. A few moments later Palmer was put forward, and exhibited a very cool and collected demeanour. He seemed in a thoughtful mood, but did not exhibit any symptoms of trepidation. On being placed at the bar, he cast an inquiring glance around the Court, and then seemed to scan with minuteness the features of the learned judges and those who occupied seats on the Bench. During the day he leant over the front of the dock, but occasionally wrote short notes, which he handed down to his legal advisers. In writing these notes, the prisoner's manner was remarkably collected, and certainly devoid of that nervous excitement which usually characterises persons placed in such a critical and serious position.

CENTRAL CRIMINAL COURT,
Monday, May 26,

The fact of the Lord Chief Justice summing up the evidence at the sitting of the Court this morning induced the holders of orders of admission to be on the *qui vive* at an early hour, determined, if possible, to be present, and in the best possible position they could procure. Under these circumstances, every avenue leading to the Court was thronged by eight o'clock, and it was with much difficulty that many persons who gained admission into the Court could find even standing room. So thronged was every nook and corner of the building that many gentlemen of the press were seriously incommoded from the fact that several non-professionals had usurped the space usually allotted to reporters. It is to be regretted that, notwithstanding the desire of the Sheriffs to afford to the representatives of the press every facility in their power, the accommodation has been so stinted, and that many gentlemen have been obliged to sit huddled up in a corner, take notes as best they could, whilst at the same time they were squeezed almost to death.

A few minutes before ten o'clock the jury appeared in the box, in apparently good health and strength; their long confinement seems to have agreed with most of them, and no doubt their excursion on Sunday to Wimbledon had a beneficial effect upon most of them.

Among those present on the bench was the Right Hon. W. E. Gladstone, MP. As soon as the judges had taken their seats, the prisoner, Palmer, was put forward. There certainly was a marked change in his appearance since Saturday. He was somewhat paler, and has evidently been in a state of great mental excitement; the eyes had a calm but rather dejected appearance, whilst there was a twitching about the lips which betokened that he was ill at ease, although he made every effort to conceal the workings of an agitated and troubled mind.

The usual formalities having been gone through, Lord Chief Justice Campbell began the summing up.

As the day wore on, the applications for admission increased every minute, and although the Under-Sheriffs exerted themselves to the utmost of their power to afford accommodation to all, it was totally impossible to gratify the wishes of a tithe of the people who sought to catch a glimpse of the unfortunate prisoner. The rush at the assembling of the Court after the adjournment in the early afternoon was tremendous, and not a few most respectful and influential personages holding 'red' tickets had to wait their time to obtain even a glimpse of Palmer. It is but an act of justice to say that the police officers in charge of the lobby outside the Court did all in their power to meet the wants and wishes of the vast number of persons who sought to gain an entrance. Indeed, their labours during the whole of the trial have been excessively heavy, and often have they had their patience taxed by the importunities and impetuosity of several unthinking personages who unreasonably clamoured for admission.

Some estimate of the numbers who were admitted at various times to see the prisoner may be gathered from the fact that, according to an arrangement made by the Under-Sheriffs, some of those present were not allowed to remain longer than two or three minutes, and were replaced by the crowd that thronged the lobby.

When the Court re-assembled after the adjournment, Palmer was again put forward, and it then became evident that, although he was putting on the boldest front possible, he had felt the force and tenor of Lord Campbell's remarks. Nevertheless, it seemed as if the idea pervaded his mind that the jury might possibly take a favourable view of his case.

When the Court adjourned at ten minutes past eight o'clock, Lord Campbell had not completed his summing up.

CENTRAL CRIMINAL COURT,
Tuesday, May 27.

Each day since Palmer was first arraigned at the bar of the Old Bailey, among all classes of society, from the ennobled 'peer' and influential 'commoner' down to the most humble of London costermongers, there has been one grand prevailing desire to hear the trial, and, if possible, obtain a glimpse of the Rugeley hero of poisoning notoriety.

Every morning has attracted crowds of spectators to the vicinity of the Old Bailey, and from Ludgate Hill along to Newgate Prison there was a dense crowd of people prior to the opening of the Court, who felt a pleasure in standing along the streets in order that they might obtain a glimpse of the jury. This morning, in anticipation that the trial was about to close, the crowd was exceedingly large. At their usual time, a few minutes before 10 o'clock, the jury were seen emerging from the London Coffee House, where they have been accommodated throughout the trial, treading with solemn step between two rows of police officers; each seemed fully impressed with the deep responsibility of their serious but honourable position, forasmuch as the life of a fellow being was in their hands, and it behoved them to weigh with discrimination and strict impartiality the evidence put forward for and against the prosecution.

When the learned judges entered, Lord Campbell seemed wrapt in thought, and was without a bouquet of flowers, which the other judges held in their hands.

Although one would suppose that such a protracted trial, the excitement attendant thereon, and the annoyance of being the 'butt' for gratifying a morbid curiosity, would have made a marked change in Palmer's appearance, he looked calm and self-possessed; indeed, if anything, there seemed less of anxiety on his brow than on Monday night, and his lips were less compressed.

The selfish cupidity of some characters is most unaccountable, and the coolness and indifference with which they regard a human life truly astonishing. Today the legal butcher of the Old Bailey, William Calcraft, made his appearance in the lobby outside the Court. He exhibited himself to the gaze of hundreds of respectable people, and seemed to manifest an extreme anxiety for the termination of the Judge's Charge, and his every movement indicated an ardent aspiration that he would once more be called upon, to make an official operation upon the jugular vein of the unfortunate Palmer. We question much the propriety, let alone the good taste, of allowing the common hangman to tread the precincts of a public building where are congregated none but persons of respectability, for no one could look upon that man, who, for the sake of filthy lucre, traffics in human blood, without feeling that they came in close proximity to a public character that society scouts and detests. Calcraft waited with patience, and more than once strived to obtain a view of the prisoner. Once again, we declare that it was an outrage upon decency to present this exhibition, and hope such will never again be permitted within the Old Bailey.

After the Court had been opened in the usual form, Lord Campbell continued his summing up.

As the learned judge disposed of point after point brought forward by the defence, and showed how they failed to tend in any respect to the prisoner's advantage, Palmer buried his face in his hands, and when he resumed his original position his countenance bore strong indications of the violent emotions with which he was contending. He seemed to be labouring under the impression – an opinion, indeed, which was shared by everyone in the Court – that the observations of the judge were producing a marked effect upon the jury, and lessening every moment the chance of acquittal. Strange as it may appear in the face of this statement, it is perfectly true that, as Palmer was stepping out of the dock after Lord Campbell's summing-up, he dropped a note to Mr Smith, his solicitor, stating that he felt particularly certain of an acquittal.

At nineteen minutes past two o'clock, the jury retired to consider their verdict. The Court then became crowded to excess. There was hardly standing-room, and every moment added to the numbers who craved, beseeched, and implored to obtain only a momentary admission. After the jury had been absent fifteen minutes, some parties began to express astonishment that they were not already in Court. By others this was regarded as something in favour of Palmer. At this time the appearance of the Court, to a contemplative mind, was suggestive of more than one moral lesson. Here and there were groups of persons eagerly discussing the merits of the evidence for and against the prisoner; others were freely canvassing the tenor of the Judge's charge: some said he tried his best to hang Palmer; others that he did nothing more than a judge should do, and that Palmer was worse than even Rush, Greenacre, or the Mannings.* In other parts of

* James Blomfield Rush, hanged at Norwich in 1849 for the murder of his landlord, Isaac

the Court there were those who talked of nothing but the common topics of the day; joked respecting the Derby, prophesied as to the winner of the Oaks, and were not indisposed to make bets as to the verdict of the jury.

To the credit of the female sex, we only observed that two or three ladies occupied seats in the gallery. Probably they were related in some way or the other with the prisoner or witnesses in the case; we shall not say that they were there from the desire to satisfy a morbid curiosity. At the time of which we write, outside the Court there were crowds of people standing in rows on either side of the street, three or four deep – and no one could emerge from the precincts of the Court who was not eagerly interrogated by the inquiries – 'How does it go?' 'Have the jury agreed?' 'Do you think he will be found guilty?' Any one who could give intelligence upon these points was regarded with extreme deference and respect. We may here observe that, not only in the sacred temple of justice, but also outside the Court, gaming men were not inactive; it was said that many parties had wagered heavily on the jury's verdict.

Matters went on as we have described until twenty minutes to four, when intimation of the approach of the jury was heard in the Court. The Bench at this time was crowded, and among its occupants we noticed the Reverend Ordinary of Newgate in full canonicals – a somewhat suspicious circumstance. But hark! the deep and musical voice of the crier, in almost sepulchral notes, called out 'Silence.' The judges appear, take their seats, and the names of the jury are called over. Palmer is again put forward. Alas! it is only to hear the death-knell sounded in his ear, and that a jury of his country is to stamp him a murderer of the deepest dye and most relentless character. All is now silent, and here follows what took place: –

Mr Straight, the deputy clerk of arraigns, inquired of the jury whether they had agreed upon their verdict. The foreman: We have.

Mr Straight: Do you find the prisoner at the bar guilty or not guilty of the felony and murder whereof he stands accused? The foreman: We say that he is Guilty.

Mr Straight then addressed the prisoner, and said: 'Prisoner at the bar, you stand convicted of the crime of wilful murder. Have you or know you anything to urge why sentence of death should not be passed upon you according to the law?'

The prisoner made no reply, but his face reddened and there was evidently a slight convulsive twitching about his mouth.

Mr Harker, the principal usher, then made the usual proclamation for silence.

The three judges then put on their black caps, and the Lord Chief Justice proceeded to pass sentence upon the prisoner in the following terms: –

William Palmer, after a long and impartial trial you have been convicted by a jury of your country of the crime of wilful murder. In that verdict my two learned brothers, who have so anxiously attended to every circumstance that has been

---

Jermy, and the latter's son, Isaac Jermy Jermy. James Greenacre, hanged outside Newgate in 1837 for the murder of his erstwhile mistress, Hannah Brown. Frederick and Marie Manning, executed outside Horsemonger Lane Gaol in 1849 for the murder of Marie's erstwhile beau, Patrick O'Connor.

adduced in evidence, and myself, entirely concur, and consider the conviction altogether satisfactory. Your case is attended with such circumstances of aggravation that I do not dare to touch upon them. Whether the present is the first known offence that you have committed is known only to God and to your own conscience. It is seldom that such a familiarity with the means of death should be known without a long experience, but for the offence of which you have been found guilty your life is forfeited. You must prepare to die, and I trust that, as you can expect no mercy in this world, you will, by repenting of your crimes, seek to obtain pardon from Almighty God. The Act of Parliament under which you have been tried and under which you have been brought to the bar of this court, at your own request, gives power to the court to direct that the sentence shall be executed either within the district of the Central Criminal Court or the county where the offence is committed; and, in your case, it is our opinion that, for the sake of example, the sentence shall be carried into effect in the County of Stafford. I hope that your terrible example will have the effect of deterring others from the commission of such atrocious crimes, and that it will be seen that whatever art or cunning may be exercised to accomplish such a crime, detection is almost sure to follow; and that however destructive poison may be in its effects, yet Providence, acting for the safety of human life, has given its creatures the means of detecting the perpetrators of such offences as these. Again, I entreat you to prepare for the awful change that awaits you. I will not harrow up your feelings by dwelling upon the particulars of this most foul murder, but will at once proceed to pass upon you the sentence of the law, which is 'That you be taken from the bar at which you now stand, back to the gaol of Newgate, from whence you came, and that you be afterwards removed to the county gaol of Stafford, that being the county in which your offence was committed, and that you be there hanged by the neck until you are dead, and your body be afterwards buried within the gaol, and may the Almighty God have mercy upon your soul.'

The prisoner did not seem at all affected while the awful sentence was being pronounced; but, on the contrary, there was evidently a sort of sneering expression on his countenance. The moment the Chief Justice had concluded, the prisoner turned and walked hastily away from the dock, and descended the staircase leading to the prison.

On his return to Newgate Prison, Palmer was informed that he must make preparations for his immediate departure. For a moment this seemed to annoy him, but, as it were instantly, he resumed his wonted calm and unembarrassed demeanour, and partook of some refreshments.

Extraordinary as it may appear, the spirit of Palmer remains unaffected, and his courage as undaunted as before. He shows no wincing or faltering in his bearing, and met his brother George and his solicitor, Mr John Smith, of Birmingham (not Jeremiah Smith, of Rugeley), with the same firmness and unblenched look. To his brother, who was visibly affected, and shed tears on seeing him, William Palmer spoke cheeringly, and said, 'Don't take on, George; there is a God above us that will stand between me and harm. I am innocent of the crime imputed to me. Let that be a consolation to you, my

'The Accurst Surgeon'

mother, and my boy. Act upon my word; I have never deceived you yet; and, however guilty I have been in other things, to destroy life has never entered my head.' He then tapped his brother on the shoulder and went on, 'May you sleep as sound as I do. I have had a good tea, with half a pound of steak. May you have a good night's rest as I shall. Tell my mother and my boy that I fear the grave as little as my bed.'

With that he shook hands with both. He then entered into a desultory conversation, inquiring how his boy was, saying, 'Tell Willy his father has had many troubles, but the least of all has been the accusation of murder against him.' He then said, 'Good night, God bless you! May your mind be as easy as mine is now. Don't feel low.' He then exchanged a few words of parting as he bade his brother and solicitor good-bye, to all appearance himself the least concerned of the party.

At half-past seven o'clock he was within the precincts of the railway station at Euston-square. When he arrived there, he rapidly walked from the cab to a first-class carriage. We believe that he was not only handcuffed, but also manacled. Over his dress he had a cloak and travelling cap. The only thing which annoyed him was the presence of so many persons, some of whom recognised him. Thus ends the last but one of the great scenes connected with the history of this extraordinary criminal.

First leading article on Wednesday, May 28:

It would be wrong to ascribe merely to a morbid curiosity the deep and wide-felt public interest that has hung around the proceedings of the Central Criminal Court for the last fortnight. The issues that depended upon the decision of an English Jury were of an infinitely greater importance than if they only involved the life of the prisoner at the bar, or reparation for the blood of his victims. The questions imported into the technical one – 'Guilty' or 'Not guilty'? – were of a far graver nature than any which usually demands the consideration of a criminal trial, for it amounted to this:

Is it possible that the crimes of the middle ages, by secret and inscrutable agencies, are to be introduced in the social life of the nineteenth century with impunity? Is the friend, the brother, the wife, the mother, to be hurried out of the world by some means, known only to the perpetrator and his Maker? Have the boasted discoveries of modern science resulted in this, that the hand which smooths our pillow in sickness, embraces us with affection in health, extends to us good cheer in the hours of conviviality, can mingle to us at the same time some deadly poison, which shall not only be swift in its effects, but totally baffle human investigation to discover the author of our destruction?

These were among the questions that depended upon the finding of the jury, yesterday, in PALMER's trial; and it was felt by everyone who gave an intelligent attention to the proceedings that if these questions could not be satisfactorily solved, the bonds that hold society together would have been snapped asunder, and no man could deem his life as worth a day's purchase if its sacrifice could promote the worldly objects of any villain who might snap his fingers in the face of earthly justice, and revel undetected in the fruits of his crimes.

It is, therefore, with no vulgar feeling of vengeance that we now record the fact that the man who, with unabashed front, braved the gaze of man and the anger of Heaven for the last twelve days has now been consigned, by an impartial and unimpeachable tribunal, to a death which, although violent in its character, is far more merciful than that which he permitted to his victims. But we discharge this duty to the public with satisfaction, because we feel that justice and humanity have triumphed in the jury-box at the Old Bailey, in spite of all that legal ingenuity could invent, in spite of the most unblushing perjury on the part of some of the witnesses, and in spite of the attempt to subsidise science herself and make her the handmaid, not of nature, but of murder. We fear that the impunity which for a certain time seemed to cover the atrocities of PALMER has suggested to another culprit the crime of assassination by strychnine; but the fate of the wretched convict, sent into the presence of his Maker, with his hands dyed with the blood of his fellow-creatures, will now be pointed out in the annals of guilt not as an incentive to crime but as a beacon to warn the assassin from his prey.

Towards the legitimate defence of the prisoner we consider that everything was done that legal ability could devise; and we are not disposed to blame Serjeant SHEE for the voluntary manner in which he pledged his personal belief to the innocence of his client. We trust, however, that this course will never become a practice in our courts of justice. As Lord CAMPBELL remarked in his charge to the jury, it may be attended with inconvenience; and we may add to his lordship's remark that it may sometimes be accompanied with gross injustice to a prisoner. For if a barrister – who, according to the theory of his profession, is only bound to do the best he can for his client – occasionally pledges his belief to his innocence, in cases where he fails to do so, the omission is calculated to have a most prejudicial effect upon the minds of the jury.

Laws, it has been said, have been made, not for the good, but for the bad, members of society. The former are restrained from evil by higher and holier influences than human restraint can impose. The latter have now another proof, in the expiation of PALMER's guilt, that

Murder, though it hath no tongue,
Can speak with most miraculous
organ.

We wish we could conclude these remarks by expressing any well-grounded hope that the culprit had exhibited an inclination to adopt the only means by which he can now make reparation for his offences against society by confessing his guilt and avowing his contrition. Would that we could say that this wretched man, finding the avenues to earthly clemency closed against him, had now, with broken and contrite spirit, turned his thoughts to that only remaining source of mercy – the Giver of all Good – whose laws he has so impiously defied, and whose blessings in times past he has so grossly abused. We are afraid, however, that the demeanour of the unhappy man immediately on receiving his sentence was such as to lead to the conclusion that he will die the death of the impenitent thief on the cross.

* * *

The Circulation of The *Daily Telegraph*
was yesterday
SIXTY THOUSAND COPIES.
This Journal has consequently,
within One Year, reached the
average daily circulation of the
Times.

Friday, May 30:

THE CONVICT PALMER

As everything connected with the sayings and doings of this wretched criminal is now sought with avidity, we subjoin the following gossip:

Notwithstanding the unanimous verdict of the jury, Palmer, immediately after the proceedings, complained to the under-sheriff that he had not received a fair trial. The under-sheriff observed that he had no reason to complain, and reminded him that all the judges agreed in the finding of the jury. Palmer's reply was, 'Well, sir, but that don't satisfy me.'

When informed, after the sentence was passed, that he must prepare immediately to return to his former quarters in Stafford Gaol, he asked by what railway he was to be conveyed – and, on being told that the London and North-Western was the usual and most direct route, he begged that he might be taken by the Great Western Railway, as he was so well-known on the North-Western that he would be recognised all along the line. The under-sheriff informed him that his request could not be complied with, and he acquiesced without any further observation. As it was suspected that the prisoner might attempt to commit suicide, and thus defeat the ends of justice, a new suit of clothes was prepared for him, which he was directed to put on after his return to his apartment at Newgate. Immediately after the verdict was delivered, a telegraphic despatch was forwarded to the governor of Stafford Gaol, requesting him to provide accommodation for the prisoner; and on the arrival of the train at Stafford at about eleven o'clock, a fly was waiting, in which he was conveyed to the gaol.

Mr John Smith and Mr George Palmer, the prisoner's brother, are taking steps to lay before the Home Secretary a statement of facts, mainly in connection with the medical evidence, with which they hope to induce the right hon. gentleman to recommend Her Majesty to exercise the prerogative of mercy by mitigating the capital sentence.

The jury were accommodated at the London Coffee House. A large room was prepared for them, fitted up with 16 beds, and they were 12 days 'sequestered' from their families, friends, and pursuits. The dormitory was locked at night to prevent the possibility of communicating with the outside world. The *accouchement* of the wife of one of the jurors took place during his detention, and an application was made to Lord Campbell to allow him to go home and see her, in the presence of an officer of the court. Lord Campbell, on ascertaining that the lady's health was not in danger, said he felt bound to refuse the application, as, if he granted it, he must in fairness concede a similar favour to the whole of the remaining jurors, should they make an application to visit their families.

We may observe that by the new Act under which Palmer was tried, an account of the expense of his removal and maintenance, &c, in Newgate, is to be delivered to the county treasurer of Stafford, who is to pay the same.

Friday, June 6:

TO THE EDITOR OF 'THE DAILY TELEGRAPH'.

SIR – The public mind being so much excited by the legal investigations that have lately taken place, any information on the subject of the deadly poison, strychnine, may be deemed of importance to be generally known.

A pretty exact notion of the quantity of this poison which is consumed may be formed by the testimony of the druggists, most of whom will declare that large quantities are sold by them to gamekeepers for the purpose of 'killing vermin'. But the startling fact is that in the body of the 'vermin' so destroyed, the strychnine remains unchanged, and that if the dead body of the poisoned animal be eaten up by another animal, that animal also dies. That the strychnine remains in the blood and other parts of the poisoned animal has been clearly shown by all professional chemists, except only Dr Taylor, who, because he could find none in Cooke's body, asserted that strychnine, after leaving the stomach, was decomposed, forming new compounds.

In proof of the correctness of the opinion that strychnine remains in the bodies of animals killed by it, permit me to quote a single instance which happened in a district where foxes are carefully protected. On a fox being found dead, and the proprietor of the 'covert' being blamed for it, on inquiry it appeared that some hen's eggs had been contaminated with strychnine, that a rook and magpie had both eaten of the eggs, and that these birds, after their death, had been found and eaten by the fox.

Surely the use of strychnine to kill animals calls for most serious attention, and well deserves the consideration of the Government.*

HUMANITAS

STAFFORD, Saturday, June 14:

William Palmer was executed this morning at eight o'clock, in front of the county gaol, which is situated at the end of the town, in a narrow road; directly opposite the entrance, in front of which the drop is placed, there is a wide street. Several strong barriers were placed both in the road and in the street, and 150 of the county police were present. A considerable number of special constables were also sworn in, and, indeed, every reasonable precaution was taken to avert any danger that might arise from the assemblage of so large a concourse of people as was expected on this occasion.

The inns of Stafford drove a busy trade on Friday. All day long, people flocked into the town, by road, by rail, on foot, on horseback, in gig, carriage, or on donkey. Such crowding at the railway station, such jostling in tavern yards, and tavern parlours, and coffee-rooms, such crowding and pushing in public-house kitchens and taprooms, were never seen before, for everybody wanted to get shelter, and everybody found great difficulty in securing anything of the sort. Beds had been at a premium for days before, and he who got in on Friday, hoping to secure one without having made previous arrangements for that purpose, found himself miserably deceived. There was no bed to be got – not for love, not for money, not for any consideration; and lucky were those who (content to sit up all night on a

* The use of strychnine for the killing of animals, excepting moles, was prohibited under the Animals (Cruel Poisons) Regulations 1963; the Poisons Rules 1982 permitted the use of strychnine for killing foxes in rabies-infected areas. (The Pharmacy Act 1868 prescribed precautions to be taken [e.g. a detailed entry in a poisons register] in the sale of any of fifteen poisons, including strychnine, for any stated purpose.)

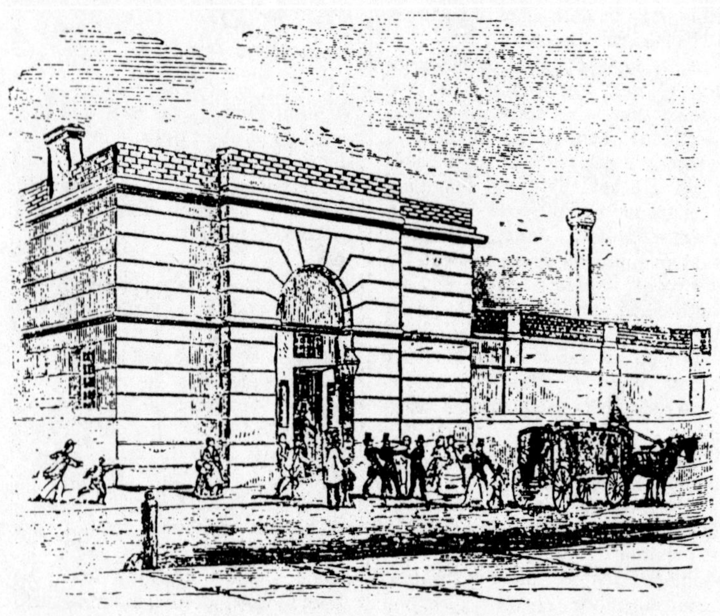

The gateway of Stafford Gaol

chair, or lie upon a table, or litter down in a hay-loft, or *share a stable with the horses*) were able to get a good supper to feed that physical strength which was necessary to withstand the mighty crush which all knew the morning must inevitably bring.

It should be stated that from the middle of the day on Thursday, down almost to the hour of the execution, the rain poured in torrents, and almost without intermission. Notwithstanding this, every train that arrived, and especially those from Birmingham, Wolverhampton, and that neighbourhood, brought enormous living freights; and on Friday evening a very large number were conveyed to Stafford by the express train from London. Most of the inns and public-houses were kept open all night, and we were informed that the charge for a bed was £1 1s. During the whole of Friday the main street was thronged. A great number of the people were well-dressed and a totally different class of persons to those who are usually at executions. It was evident that the case of the prisoner had excited a most deep and painful impression upon the public mind.

Erections were put up by private speculators in the neighbourhood of the scaffold, standings upon which were let at various sums ranging from a guinea to five shillings, and some of these were occupied as early as six on Friday evening by persons who had evidently made up their minds to secure a front place whence a good view of the ceremony could be obtained; they remained there, exposed to the rain, all night.

A number of persons connected with a religious sect, known by the name of the Primitive Methodists, made themselves very conspicuous by their proceedings on the Friday and on the day of the execution. They had large placards on which were printed the words, 'Prepare to meet thy God'. They also distributed printed papers warning of the dangers from attending horse-racing and amusements of that description, and occasionally one of the body would get upon a stool and harangue the mob in a most ranting and vehement style.

Before we proceed to narrate the facts more immediately connected with the execution, it will be necessary to state the manner in which Palmer conducted himself, and the proceedings connected with him, during the past week, promising that all the facts about to be narrated are derived from the most unquestionable sources, and their authenticity may be entirely relied upon.

Ever since Palmer has been in Stafford Gaol, his brothers Thomas and George and his sister have constantly visited him. He has another brother, Joseph, and it was stated that the reason he had not been to see the prisoner is that he is suffering from some severe spinal or rheumatic affection which prevents him going abroad. Neither the prisoner's mother nor his son had seen him since his conviction. The prisoner never manifested any wish to see his mother. He often spoke of his son in the most affectionate terms, and it is probable that he was unwilling to undergo the agony of a last interview with him. The poor child, it appears, is still at Rugeley with his grandmother; he has been informed that his father has gone to some distant part of the country, and is anxiously awaiting his return.

Palmer had listened to many exhortations that he should confess, but he always exhibited the bearing and manner of a man who had determined on the course he should take, and he never, however much pressed, refrained from declaring that he had been unjustly convicted of the murder of Cooke by strychnia, from which it was inferred that he meant to convey the impression that strychnia was not the cause of death. On Friday, Major Fulford, the governor of the gaol, being aware that Mr Smith, the prisoner's attorney, was shortly expected to arrive, went to the prisoner's cell, accompanied by the Rev. Mr Goodacre, and he addressed the prisoner, saying that if he wished to make any family or confidential communications to Mr Smith, he might rely that they would not be divulged, and that they should be kept a profound secret. Palmer immediately replied, 'What I have to say to Mr Smith I do not wish to be kept secret; but I hope, on the contrary, that you will take care to let it be made as public as possible. I have only to say that I am very grateful to Mr Smith for his exertions on my behalf, and I also thank the officers of the gaol for their kindness to me.' He then finished the sentence by using this remarkable expression – 'I also wish to say that Cooke did not die from strychnia.' Major Fulford then said, 'Mr Palmer, I hope that at this awful moment you are not quibbling as to the cause of Cooke's death. The question is not whether Cooke was murdered by strychnia, but whether he was killed by you or not.' Palmer rejoined, 'Why, Lord Campbell summed up the case as one of murder by strychnia.' Major Fulford again said, 'That is not the question. The point is whether Cooke was murdered by you or not.'

Palmer then said, 'I have nothing more to say than this, that I am quite easy in my conscience, and happy in my mind.'

The final parting of the prisoner and his relatives was very affecting. They did not leave the gaol until past 12 at night. Mr Smith accompanied them. Palmer retired to rest soon after they had left.

He slept soundly until half-past two, when he awoke, and shortly after three the Rev. Mr Goodacre, the chaplain, was admitted to his cell, and he remained with the prisoner until the last moment. Palmer remained in his bed conversing with the chaplain until five o'clock, when he got up and washed and dressed himself, and he then had a cup of tea brought to him, but he did not eat anything with it. One of the turnkeys asked him how he was, and he replied that he felt very comfortable and happy, and was quite prepared.

About three o'clock, the scaffold, which is a large, ponderous erection somewhat resembling an agricultural machine, was rolled out of the shed where it is kept to the position it was to occupy in front of the gaol.

At five o'clock, a dense mass of people had assembled, and the numbers increased down to the hour fixed for the execution, when it was computed by competent persons that there were at least 25,000 persons present. The number would, no doubt, have been much greater but for the state of the weather. Among the number there were a good many decently dressed country women, who had probably come to Stafford to attend the market, it being market day. The crowd was certainly much more orderly than might have been expected, considering the character of the district, and there were none of those unseemly exhibitions that occasionally take place at the metropolitan executions.

Shortly after half-past seven o'clock, Colonel Dyott, the high sheriff of the county, entered the prisoner's cell and asked him whether he did not think that the time had arrived when he ought to admit the justice of his sentence. Palmer immediately, and with great earnestness, exclaimed: 'No!' – then, striking one of his arms down, and with great energy, he added, 'They are my murderers.' He did not mention whom he meant by 'they', but he repeated the expression: 'I am murdered – they are my murderers.'

The executioner was shortly after this brought into the cell to perform the necessary operations upon the prisoner. He was dressed in a very clean white smockfrock; he is a remarkably thick-set, robust looking man, apparently between fifty and sixty years old. His name, it appears, is John Smith, and he carries on some little labouring trade in the town of Dudley, where he resides. Although he has only been engaged in the same capacity a few times, the last occasion being five years ago, he set about his work of pinioning the arms and wrists of Palmer, removing his neckcloth, &c, with the utmost calmness, and quite in the style of Calcraft in his palmy days. He receives no salary from the county, but merely is paid the sum of five pounds, in addition to his expenses, upon any occasion when his services are called into requisition.

When the ceremony of pinioning was completed, the high sheriff and the chaplain returned to the cell, and the Rev. Mr Goodacre again, for the last time, asked the prisoner whether he would admit the justice of his sentence. Palmer replied, in a firm, composed tone, 'It is not a just sentence.' To this the chaplain, apparently almost involuntarily, rejoined, 'Then your blood be upon your own head.'

At this moment the prison bell gave forth its mournful sound. Palmer heard it quite unmoved.

It is customary with convicts capitally convicted to allow them on the morning of execution to resume their own garments, but as the dress worn by Palmer during his sojourn in Newgate was taken away from him after the trial, and was never sent for by the prisoner or his friends, he was executed in the prison dress, which is of a most coarse description. It consists of a jacket, trowsers, and waistcoat, all composed of a rough grey cloth, the make of the garments and the material being of the same character, precisely of the same kind as that worn by paupers. At Palmer's own request, his hair had been cut quite close to his head immediately he arrived at Stafford, and this, added to his miserable clothing, very much altered his appearance, and gave him the look of a coarse, common man.

A signal being given, the procession, headed by the chaplain, moved slowly from the condemned cell. The cell was in a sort of gallery, and Palmer had to descend an iron staircase. He descended at a quick pace, and notwithstanding his arms being pinioned, he never faltered, but exhibited a most extraordinary appearance of unconcern – indeed, indifference. He made a bow to the governor of the gaol and shook hands with one of the officials of the prison, and then resumed his place in the procession.

The distance from this spot to the place of execution is considerable, and Palmer traversed the whole of it with a firm, light step – tripping, as it were, along the ground. He did not evince the least appearance of alarm when he came suddenly upon the ladder leading up to the scaffold, but at once mounted it rapidly, and having looked up and observed the spot where the rope was hanging, he of his own accord placed himself under it, and the executioner at once placed the noose round his neck. This was the only moment when he appeared to betray any emotion, and the moment the rope touched his flesh he turned deadly pale. Contrary to general expectation, the crowd did not evince any manifestation against the prisoner upon his making his appearance on the scaffold. There was a slight yell from one portion of the crowd, but the majority of those present gave no expression of feeling, and indeed almost perfect silence prevailed.

The hangman, having drawn the cap over the face of the prisoner, retired from the scaffold, and withdrew the bolt that secured the drop, which fell, and Palmer appeared to die instantaneously. There was not a single convulsive effort observable, his pinioned hands gradually dropped, and he ceased to exist apparently without a pang. His hands, which had presented a white, plump appearance, had turned blue, indeed almost black.

The awful silence which prevailed was terrible. Not a voice was raised, not a murmur was heard, and Palmer died as no great criminal had died before on the scaffold – without a word of execration, a single yell, or a single groan.

Dr Knight, the guardian of the late Mrs William Palmer, was present at the execution. He stood immediately under the scaffold.

After hanging an hour, the body was cut down and carried into the gaol, where a cast of the head was accurately taken by a gentleman named Bridges, who is connected with the Liverpool Phrenological Society, who had a special authority from the visiting justices for that purpose. The countenance of the prisoner did not exhibit any indication of his having suffered a violent death, and a sort of contemptuous smile appeared on the face.

In the course of the day the body was buried within the precincts of the gaol, in conformity with the terms of the sentence.

At Rugeley, which is being visited by great numbers of persons, the blinds of the house of Palmer's mother were closed as for a death. Palmer's former residence is shown to visitors for a fee of a shilling; and during the late fair, the small white pebbles with which the passage up to the hall-door is paved were sold to the curious in such matters for sixpence each. Someone has got possession of the rear of the house, and professes to produce very superior photographic portraits set against the background of the building, in gilt and other frames, from one shilling to a guinea. The tree overhanging Cooke's grave in the new churchyard has also been the object of a good deal of attention, and a considerable portion of it has already been carried away by visitors as mementoes of the tragic event.*

Up to the latest hour, Friday night, a strong opinion prevailed in Manchester that Palmer would not be hanged; and 12 to 1 was most freely betted and taken upon the event. In Manchester alone, some thousands have changed hands amongst the betting fraternity on the final issue of the charge against the prisoner.

It is said that Palmer's betting-books were made up to win £25,000 or to lose £400 by the last Derby. His horse was Yellow Jack, so that he would have lost.

Cooke's grave

* Upright citizens of Rugeley, concerned that most non-residents thought of the town only vis-à-vis Palmer, sent a deputation to the Prime Minister, seeking permission to change its name. 'Certainly,' Palmerston replied. 'Why not name it after me?' The idea was dropped.

1868

On May 11, the Capital Punishment Within Prisons Bill received its third reading in the House of Lords and was sent to Queen Victoria for her assent. On May 26, three days before the Bill became an Act, a twenty-seven-year-old Irish stevedore named Michael Barrett, convicted of having played a leading part in a Fenian bomb outrage at the Clerkenwell House of Detention on December 13, 1867, was hanged outside nearby Newgate by Calcraft, performing publicly for the last time. Barrett should have become the last person to be hanged publicly in the British Isles earlier than he did: his execution had been postponed for a few days, giving time for an extra-judicial inquiry regarding his contention – from the moment he was arrested and charged in Glasgow, and throughout his trial – that he was nowhere near Clerkenwell around the time of the explosion.

Tuesday, May 26:

As soon as the final decision of the Home Secretary was made known to the authorities at Newgate, preparations commenced for the execution. The timbers which have been so frequently made use of in the construction of the street barriers were drawn forth from their musty store-room. Yesterday, about noon, the iron sockets in the street were raised, the posts fixed in them, and the cross-timbers fastened together with long bolts. Some rude jests passed between the workmen and the spectators on the fact of its being 'the last job'; but there was no reference made whatever to the crime for which the convict was doomed.

The tenants of the houses facing the gaol, who had eked out their rents for many years by letting front rooms or seats at windows to see executions, raised their prices on this occasion. They talked lugubriously of one source of their profits being taken from them, and expressed a hope that their landlords would consider the fact in the future. But the last execution will be a memorable one, inasmuch as there was, at an early hour of the day, quite a run on the best places. Ten pounds for a small room on the second floor, the admissions limited to three, were asked in several cases; while single seats ranged from 10s to 25s. 'I've nothing under a guinea,' said one woman. 'But why such a price?' she was asked; 'your window doesn't face the scaffold.' 'That may be so,' was the reply, 'but then the convict always looks this way.' There was, how-

SENTENCE of DEATH
ON
MICHAEL BARRETT
FOR THE
Clerkenwell Explosion.

The trial of William Desmond, Timothy Desmond, Nicholas English, and Michael Barrett, for the murder of Sarah Hodgkisson, and four other persons, arising out of the Clerkenwell explosion, was concluded on Monday, the 28th April. The case of *alibi* set up for Barrett failed, and the jury returned a verdict of Guilty against him, and acquitted the other prisoners. The prisoner reviewed the evidence that was brought against him, and warmly citicised the conduct of Mullany and other witnesses. The judge then passed the usual sentonce of death upon the prisoner.

Throughout the kingdom, among high and low,
A great excitement has long been caused,
Of a dreadful crime—horrible to tell,
The fatal explosion at Clerkenwell.

Out of the seven they for the crime did try,
One Michael Barrett is condemned to die.

Patrick Mullany was a witness made,
A military tailor he was by trade;
To save himself, he evidence gave,
Which be his neck has saved.

The dreadful affair was at Clerkenwell,
In a neighbourhood where poor folks did dwell,
Caused great destruction—it many killed;
Houses fell—some wounded—and much blood
was spilled.

The informers swore, and others beside,
When the prisoners, all at the bar was tried;
That by Michael Barrett the deed was done,
And from the spot did to Scotland run.

He was taken in Glasgow and to London brought,
He says of the crime he never thought,
He would not be guilty of such a deed,
But he was convicted, as we my read,

When before a jury he had been tried,
That he was guilty he strongly denied;
And to the judge he aloud did say,
They had wrongfully taken his life away.

But Barrett's pleading was all in vain,
He could no mercy at all obtain;
The judge said, Taken back you must be,
And from thence be hanged up to the tree.

Now Michael Barrett is doomed to die
For the crime of murder on a tree so high;
He says Mullany caused his downfall,
May God have mercy upon his soul.

The jury said, when they did retire,
That Michael Barrett did the powder fire;
Convinced they were that he did the work,
To rescue two prisoners, Casey and Burke.

Though Michael Barrett is condemned to die,
The dreadful deed he strongly does deny,
There is One above who a'l secrets know,
He can tell whether Barrett is guilty or no.

The witnesses were examined strict,
By their evidence they did him convict;
And for wilful murder he is doomed to die,
In the front of Newgate on the gallows high,

We hope all men will a warning take,
And long remember poor Barrett's fate;
We find it difficult throughout the land,
For man to even trust his fellow-man.

A dreadful tale we'll have long to tell,
The fatal explosion at Clerkenwell.

W. S. FORTEY, Printer, Monmouth Ct., London, W.C.

A broadsheet

ever, one exception to the rule, in the case of a respectable shopkeeper, who, in spite of most tempting bids for his front rooms, modestly responded, 'I haven't fallen so low as to let my windows to see a fellow-creature strangled.' In every case where a seat was taken, the hirer was earnestly enjoined not to be later than three in the morning, because after that hour the place could not be reserved, notwithstanding that payment was taken in advance.

At three o'clock this (Tuesday) morning, everything was orderly, and, indeed, no attempt at disturbance is expected.

Wednesday, May 27:

To anybody with the doleful experience of two or three Old Bailey executions to fall back upon, for a comparative standard, the smallness of the crowd in front of Newgate, yesterday morning, might have seemed remarkable. It *was* remarkable. As a cheerful but not personally prepossessing gentleman, touting either on his own account or on account of some Old Bailey householder, said, with much unction, a few hours before the time appointed for Barrett to suffer death, 'This is the last public exhibition you'll ever have a chance of seeing.' Making a little allowance for the speaker's enthusiasm, which led him, in his supreme regard for one kind of 'public exhibition', to ignore all others, his words were the words of truth. Is it to risk a charge of egregious optimism to assert that the cause lies mainly, if not altogether, in the growth of self-respect, of decent thoughtfulness, decent feelings, true manly refinement, nay, even in a real love of law and justice – which would not brook the spectacle of either being made a mockery – among the English people?

An observer new to the scene might have thought the assemblage a very huge assemblage, even for the occasion. But, if he had possessed free right and power of passing to and fro, and in and out, and if he could have seen, but half an hour before the enactment of that grim spectacle on the scaffold, how many people within hail of the spot were quietly bent on other business than looking at an execution, he would scarcely have missed an agreeable surprise.

Over the bridge, hard by, came, it is true, a straggling and motley procession, whose grotesque figures the etching-needle of Callot could scarcely have caricatured. The 'beggars were coming to town' – over the bridge. There was the wretched raggedness, there were the dirt, sloth, scurvy and cretinism of rural vagabondage, trooping over the bridge. The sallow professor of epilepsy, in drab rags and a slouch hat, who divides his valuable time pretty equally between feigning fits on door-steps, hawking groundsel and chick-weed for singing-birds, and driving the parochial mind to the verge of madness or beyond it by smashing panes of workhouse glass, and tearing up the fantastical tatters which are facetiously called his 'clothes', shambled, with jerky, paralytic gait, over the bridge.

The door at Newgate through which came condemned persons to their execution.
(From an etching by Sir D. Y. Cameron, R. A.)

But on the bridge, pausing as they went to their daily toil, labourers surveyed the progress of the work on the western side. No thought had they, no thought had scores and scores of foot passengers who went that road, of going a step out of their track to see Barrett swung from the gibbet in the Old Bailey.

As for the eligible places opposite the drop, they almost went begging. Attempts to run up their price failed as much as did attempts, in some instances, to sell them at any price at all. The touts were hopelessly busy all night long. One spectral old scarecrow, who, as Sir Charles Coldstream has it, 'looked too dirty for a ghost', and who, indeed, was clad in what seemed to be a full suit of dried mud, with a mask of the same to match, was conspicuously eloquent in his recommendation of a 'nice comfortable seat' at a third-floor window, and lowered his price from fifteen to five shillings with the rapidity of a Dutch auction, but without finding bidders. If any persons there were who paid the prices quoted on the previous evening, they were such as had more money than wit, and were easily parted from both wit and money. The greater number of windows were blank and void when St Sepulchre's bell began to toll. Nor were they half filled when the hour of eight struck, and the man came forth to die.

It had been a fine night, still and warm, with no signs of rain except that poetical weather-omen, 'the new moon with the auld one in her arms.' Availing themselves of the mildness of the night-season, women, girls, boys, and a few men, sat or reclined on the pavement, or in the shadow of doorways, or in any corner they could find, as the dwellers in stifling alleys are wont to do on hot Sunday afternoons when the indoor closeness becomes intolerable. There were other and very different groups standing or moving about near the nail-studded black door, with its gracefully surmounting festoon of leg-irons. The two or three men thus congregated were recognisable as belonging to the disaffected class or band, whose title, self-bestowed, is that of Fenians.

When the faint darkness of the fine spring night was giving place to day, a rumbling in the great yard of the dingy prison, and a rattling of iron bolts on the gate, aroused the sleepers outside to a dreamy semblance of interest. The creaking portals opened, and, for the last sad and horrible time, out came the black, heavy case on four dwarf iron wheels. The bringing forth of the cumbrous machine, and the placing and fixing of the structure ready for its work, attracted a considerable crowd of sottish men and bedraggled women, who amused themselves by staring at these preparations until the opening of the public-houses at four o'clock.

By seven, the crowd of intending spectators at the Newgate-street end of the Old Bailey – now cramped and confined by the works of the Holborn Viaduct, and by the hoarding in front of St Sepulchre's Church – as well as in the narrow funnel which runs down towards Ludgate Hill, had increased, and settled into a compact mass, which, nevertheless, did not fill half the space usually occupied. Not only was the assemblage less in number than was ever before known, but it was also a quieter crowd. Hats of the chimney-pot or truncated drainpipe shape, which somehow symbolises respectability, were to be seen here and there; and wonderful as it may seem, the wearers generally escaped the bonneting process which would formerly have been visited on any being bold enough to

Preparing for a hanging at Newgate

enter such a throng with his head surmounted by a high-crowned hat.

The square open space about the scaffold was lined by the City police; and a double file of these well-disciplined men, armed with revolvers, was drawn up close beneath the shadow of the drop. It was noticeable that, look which way one might, not a soldier was to be distinguished by his scarlet tunic among the black or colourless coats of the crowd. Pickets had, indeed, been sent out to collect all stragglers the night before; and the only suspicion of a military element was in the rumour that soldiery had been stationed in St Paul's Cathedral and in St Sepulchre's Church, to be ready in case of need.

Eight o'clock drew nigh. The voice of one solitary street-preacher was heard to mingle with the tolling of the church bell; and there was little noise beside. It was worth while to watch more than one manly young face that grew very much graver each time that it was turned towards the church clock, and then to the ugly beam and chain over the way. A handsome, well-grown man, little past the age of a lad, who would have dashed at the head of his company up to the guns of a fort, shrugged his shoulders, and bit his lips, and lost the courage that champagne or brandy had given him, when the long-hand of the clock pointed five minutes to eight. It was really no bad thing to see this youth turn coward, by perhaps the only possible means open to him for such a conversion.

More noticeable, because somehow attributed, rightly or wrongly to relationship to a victim of the bombing, was the behaviour of a young woman who clung to the barrier at the edge of the footway opposite the scaffold, and behind the line of policemen. She was accompanied by two female friends; or, for that matter, she may simply have been supported in her anguish by women who till then were strangers to her and to each other, for sympathy is of a wider and more spontaneous growth than the over-refined among us are apt to believe. Indeed, the feeling of pity for this poor soul was not confined to those of her own sex; inasmuch as two or three fellows of most unpromising aspect kept a little space for her, by word or blow, till she sank with a scream as the bolt was drawn for Barrett's fall.

When Calcraft had drawn the thin white cap over the culprit's face, the features and even the dark orbits of the open eyes being plainly visible through the veil, he adjusted the cord, and then the sounds from the crowd became at once more audible and more unmistakably significant. Among the cries were, 'Shame!' 'Goodbye, Barrett!' 'Bravo!' 'Yah, yah, murderer', and 'Down with him!' Calcraft, before going down to draw the bolt, shook the culprit's hand, and spoke a few words to him, apparently by way of caution to remain steady in his place on the drop. He then left the culprit standing face to face with the priest, and in a few moments more the bolt was drawn, the body fell, and a shriek of women rose from the crowd.

At first it was thought that Barrett had fallen stone dead; but the convulsive heaving of his chest and shoulders and the quick motion of his legs, horribly apparent after a few seconds to those who were near the half-lifeless body, gave the denial to this supposition. His death, however, was speedy, the pallor of the neck showing infallibly when it had taken place. Almost as soon as the rattling fall and the dull shock were heard, a policeman fainted, and was taken inside the gaol.

Leading article:

For the last time in our National History, it is to be hoped, that most detestable British upas tree*, the gallows, has been reared in the Old Bailey, and has borne its black fruit for all the rascaldom and felonry of a great city to witness.

A generation hence, it will be well-nigh incredible to our children that, in the midst of the reign of the good Queen VICTORIA, men and women should have been publicly strangled, in a narrow lane connecting two of the most populous

* A fabulous Javanese tree that poisoned everything for miles around.

thoroughfares in the British metropolis. Was it possible, our successors may ask, that in the days when the Holborn Viaduct was being built, and Ludgate-hill was spanned by a stately railway arch, a fragment of mediæval barbarism was permitted to linger in the Old Bailey, with the sanction of the State and the direct participation of the Corporation of London, whose salaried officer CALCRAFT still continues to be?

To us in these days it may seem equally inconceivable, equally incredible, that since the accession to the throne of the House of BRUNSWICK, men and women have been publicly hanged in Fleet-street – that at the execution of SARAH MALCOLM, over against the Middle Temple gate, the crowd was so dense that a boy is said to have walked on his hands and knees over the heads of the crowd, from the Temple to Chancery-lane. It may seem not less inconceivable that men and women have been hanged on Snow-hill, in Shoe-lane, and in Bloomsbury-square; that a woman, CATHERINE HAYES, was publicly burned alive; that, in the press-yard of Newgate, BLUESKIN suffered the *peine forte et dure*, and was literally pressed to death; and that, within the memory of men still living, miserable creatures, by the half score, were hanged almost every Monday morning for such offences as stealing sheep and horses, or goods above the value of forty shillings, and for such misdeeds as forging one-pound notes or the Excise stamp on hats. As for the pillory set up, now on Cornhill, now in Spring-gardens, now at Charing-cross, with some quivering wretch garotted in it, to be pelted with filth and rotten eggs, or to have his eyes knocked out of his head and his teeth knocked down his throat with sharp stones flung by the pitiless mob – as for the cart rumbling along Cheapside or the Oxford-road, with some half-naked thief or wanton made fast to its tail, and the hangman with his scourge, following to lash the wretches' shoulders raw – as for vagrants sitting in the stocks in St Martin's-lane: those were everyday occurrences, and accounted as trivial as the ducking of a pickpocket and the nailing of his ears to the pump at the Royal Mews, the mobbing of a Frenchman in Leicester-fields, or the baiting of a bull in the Poultry.

Yet there is one little error against which it may be as well to warn our descendants. The conversion of the Old Bailey into a Golgotha was a barbarism not entirely of a 'mediæval' kind. It was quite a modern device. In remoter ages, Smithfield, which was really the town-green of old London, served as a commodious spot on which to burn witches and heretics, boil poisoners, and pour melted lead down coiners' throats. Later, Tyburn became the regular place of execution for ordinary criminals; while those who were reserved for the more especial mercies of drawing and quartering were mangled and seethed in pitch on that broad, open common which is now Kennington Park. For centuries the thoroughfare by Holborn towards St Giles's – where the culprit was indulgently permitted to complete the intoxication which he had commenced in the condemned hold – and so towards Tyburn, was known as the 'Heavy Hill'. The sages of the Georgian era took fright at the fact that the ignorant multitude were accustomed to regard the grisly procession up this 'Heavy Hill', with the convict sitting on his coffin, and the hangman smoking his pipe, as a triumphant cavalcade – that they were given to shouting, singing, and dancing round the patient as he took his last draught at St Giles's – that they were addicted to screeching themselves hoarse with delight when he was slung off the ladder or flung out of the cart at Tyburn – and that, on the whole, 'Hanging Day' was made a festival and a fair.

It was considered a great advance in civilisation to replace the 'triple tree' by two uprights and a cross beam, and the cumbrous cart and ladder by a shutter, allowed to fall by the withdrawal of a bolt. It was thought highly indecent for JACK KETCH to get astride of the sufferer's shoulders, and twist his cervical vertebrae round. It became the decorous thing to go underneath the scaffold and pull the dying man's legs. And this revolting practice has continued down to our own times.

Finally, in order to put a stop to the saturnalia of Hanging Day, the philanthropists of the last century elected to put their black sheep to death in the midst of one of the narrowest and most inconvenient thoroughfares in London; and, the Old Bailey being close to a large meat market, market mornings were prudently selected as the most appropriate for human sacrifice. At this distance of time it is difficult to tell whether the plan was adopted through sheer stolid ignorance or through a desire to edify or recreate the carcase-butchers and the outlying rascality of Field-lane, West-street, and Saffron-hill.

With the disappearance of the gallows from the public street will speedily come, we trust, the adoption of some more decent and efficient means for the extinction of human life, so long as imperfect laws shall decree that human life is to be extinguished. The mere infliction of so much torture on a criminal is not, we suppose, an object with economists of the Draconic kind; otherwise it might be expedient to flog the criminal, or put his legs in the 'boots' and his digits in the thumbscrews, before we hanged him.

The guillotine has been adopted by every other civilised country in Europe, save two. Russia abides by the gallows, but, for all crimes save regicide, has abolished capital punishment, and has even substituted hard labour in the mines for the knout; and Spain holds by the *garote*. The guillotine, we presume, would be scouted as 'un-English'. It was very English, however, in the days of the Gibbet Law of Halifax; and it was at least British when Scottish noblemen were decapitated by the 'Maiden'.

An esteemed contemporary recommended recently that capital criminals should be shot. The author of the recommendation had probably never witnessed a military execution, nor was he aware how often it is necessary for the sergeant-major to go up to the poor wounded wretch, writhing on the ground, and give him his *coup de grâce* by blowing out his brains with a pistol.

To give the condemned man a dose of prussic acid or some other strong poison would seem about the quickest and surest way of despatching him; but we are quite ready to admit that, so long as capital punishment is retained as a punishment, it should be surrounded by some circumstances of ignominy; and there is no ignominy in dying as SOCRATES died.

Still we hold that it has become necessary to devise a simple apparatus which shall supersede the gallows as it at present exists, with its clattering drop and its occasional necessity for tugging at the culprit's legs. In many of the American

States such an apparatus is in use; and the mere touch of a spring, or the mere liberation of a counterweight, is enough to run the criminal swiftly up to a great height, and break his neck instantaneously. By the adoption of such machinery, the Americans have been enabled to rid themselves of one intolerable pest and nuisance to a civilised community – the existence of JACK KETCH. The pinioning is done by the prison warders. The act is mutual, and no individual odium is incurred. One touch of the sheriff's foot does the rest. We do not venture to suggest as to what particular gaol official such an easy task might be confided in England; but it is surely high time that we were rid of Mr CALCRAFT as a recognised member of the body-politic.

Leading article on Thursday, May 28:

Locking the stable door after the steed is stolen is proverbial; but what can we call rewarding the stable-boy on such occasion by way of encouragement to future neglect? The Clerkenwell explosion was among the most astounding instances of the wonderful unwisdom displayed by the directors of the Metropolitan Police; yet, just as we have completed the final act of the tragedy – just as we have hanged the chief culprit – a bill is brought into the House of Commons containing a special clause for adding to the emoluments of the Assistant Commissioners. It is a Government bill, and its third clause enables the Treasury to allot a sum not exceeding £300 a year as an allowance for house rent to each of the three Assistant Commissioners of Police! Why, nobody can tell. If having allowed BARRETT to commit his crime deserves an addition of nine hundred a year to the salaries of the chief managers of the force, it is difficult to calculate how much the 'dauntless three' would have deserved had they, by a little exercise of common sense, saved us from the shock and pain of that terrible event. Or if the Government admits that the police *did* neglect their duty on that occasion, how great must be their not-generally-known merits to outweigh such a deadly sin!

The 'butcher's bill' of the explosion affords a lasting evidence in this case: six persons were killed on the spot; eleven died afterwards from injuries directly or indirectly caused by it; two women, one a mother, are maniacs; forty women were prematurely confined; twenty children died from the shock; one hundred and twenty persons were wounded; fifteen are permanently injured with loss of eyes, legs, arms, &c; and the material damage is estimated at £20,000.

The commonest care, the simplest intelligence, could have prevented the calamity; and yet, a few months after the occurrence, with the recollections of it brought painfully and freshly before us by the scene of Tuesday, the Government will reward the directors of the police by adding to the salary of each Assistant Commissioner £300 a year! The other day a sergeant of constabulary who, against the orders of his superior officer, had subscribed for a forbidden newspaper, was summarily dismissed; but, for permitting Clerkenwell to be blown up, three of the men primarily responsible are rewarded with an extra £300 per annum. At this rate, if the Houses of Parliament are blown up, the officers will deserve two or three thousand a year.

The facts of the Clerkenwell case are extremely simple. When ORSINI exploded his bombs at the Opera-house in Paris, it was said that the Emperor severely rebuked the chief of the police for his ignorance of the coming event. But the London event was distinctly foretold to the authorities in Scotland-yard, and they took what they considered precautions. They were warned that an explosion was planned, and they posted their constables around the gaol. The policemen saw the barrel placed near the wall, but, according to the official excuse, it was suggestive of nothing save beer. One may see in a pantomime a simplicity of that kind affected by the Clown; but in real life surely nothing so grossly idiotic ever occurred before.

Another excuse given is that the police expected an explosion from below; they were prepared for a mine, but not for a lateral attack. But surely, over-officered as our police are by ex-military men, the veterans in Scotland-yard must at some period or other of their soldierly career – many years ago – have heard of gates and walls blown in by bags or barrels of powder. It would seem not, or else they have, in the lapse of years, or in the decadence of their intellects, utterly forgotten the nature of powder, the various manners of explosion, and also the simplest rules of common sense.

It is plain to anybody that five or six men patrolling outside the prison could have watched the whole exterior wall and that, unless they shut their eyes, they must have observed the death-bearing barrel, and might have conjectured its contents.

Of two things one: either the Commissioner, Sir RICHARD MAYNE and the Assistant-Commissioners gave the sentinel police no information of what was expected, and, if so, grossly neglected their duty; or they selected for the work the most marvellously stupid men in the force – policemen in comparison with whom DOGBERRY rises to the level of VIDOCQ.

We are inclined to believe that the first is the more probable alternative. There is a cardinal principle in English service that private soldiers, constables and subordinate civil servants are not to be told or trusted too much – they are simply to obey their instructions. If the Commissioners merely said to the policemen, 'Watch the prison walls, and note anything suspicious', we can well understand the subsequent catastrophe. The policemen would have arrested a man with a dagger or a revolver, but a barrel suggested BARCLAY & PERKINS [brewers] and the consequent inference – 'not suspicious'. In any country but England, the gentlemen who so disgracefully mismanaged the business would have been dismissed on the spot. In England we are asked to give them an extra £300 a year.

If the Home Secretary thinks that Sir RICHARD MAYNE and his three Assistant Commissioners deserve something handsome for their admirable conduct in Clerkenwell, let him move Her Majesty to confer an honour on those heroic men who remained snugly in Scotland-yard, and left Clerkenwell Prison to be guarded by four or five of their worst constables.

Why should the ratepayers of the metropolis expressly reward an inaction which, to put it mildly, they do not appreciate? Fancy the feelings of a Clerkenwell rate-paying artisan when the tax-collector comes to him and virtually says, 'Your children were killed; your wife is a maniac; you have lost the sight of your right eye. For permitting this, which they might have easily prevented, the three Assistant Commissioners of Police are to get an extra £300 each a year, and Parliament has decided that you are to bear the expenses; please pay at once.' Of course, the taxpayer will pay: JOHN BULL may grumble, but there are few things he cannot be made to endure – and pay for.

Leading article on Monday, August 10:

For the first time, Englishmen are about to witness a private execution in their own land. Men have been done to death ere now, in this country of ours, with no spectators to behold their doom. But hitherto such killings within prison walls have been performed stealthily, and centuries have passed away since even the suspicion was raised that a prisoner who died in durance had perished by other than natural means. Henceforth no criminal who incurs the last penalty of the law will leave his prison alive.

On Thursday next, Maidstone will be the scene of an event new to our English annals. On that day, THOMAS WELLS will be hanged within the precincts of the county gaol.*

Concerning the unhappy man himself, there is nothing to be said. Against punishment by death there are many and weighty arguments; nor can it be denied that the tendency of the age is opposed to the maintenance of the gallows as a national institution; and undoubtedly many of the advocates of private hangings have supported the change from a belief that it would conduce to the ultimate abolition of all capital punishment. Meanwhile, we cannot doubt that the reform will prove to be in itself a gain, whatever may prove to be its ulterior results.

Nor is it quite correct to describe as 'private' such executions as that by which this man WELLS is to die. One of the common arguments in

* In the late afternoon of Thursday, April 30, Wells, who was eighteen and had been employed for a year and a half by the London, Chatham & Dover Railway Company as a porter and carriage-cleaner at the Priory Station, Dover, was given a ticking-off by the station master, Edward Adolphus Walshe, for firing a pistol, 'an old smooth-bore, single-barrelled piece', at birds pecking at seeds he had planted in the little garden that he was allowed to cultivate at the station. As Wells's response was 'pert and rude', Mr Walshe told him that he would report the matter to his own immediate superior, Superintendent Henry Cox, and that there would be a disciplinary hearing next morning. During the rest of Wells's work-shift, till 8 p.m., several of his colleagues heard him, at different times, muttering threats against Mr Walshe, whom he repeatedly, monotonously, referred to as 'that old bugger'.

Early on May 1, he bought fourpennyworth of gunpowder from one ironmonger and twopennyworth of percussion caps from another. At the hearing, conducted in the station master's office by Superintendent Cox, with Mr Walshe standing beside his own desk, Wells refused either to admit the firearm offence or to apologise for being rude to Mr Walshe. Superintendent Cox 'told him to go away for ten minutes and try to come back in a different manner, and if I found he was then in the same humour, I should feel it my duty to report him to the *District* Superintendent, recommending that a small fine should be inflicted. I enquired of Mr Walshe if he had experienced problems with Wells favour of the former system was that, if the criminal were put to death within the gaol, the populace would never believe that the sentence had actually been carried out; but, in reality, no such difficulty occurs. In New York, for instance, the most inveterate sceptic would find it hard to raise a doubt whether an execution had taken place. The sheriffs, the officials of the prison, and some of the civic functionaries are expected to be present as a matter of duty. The reporters of the public papers are admitted *ex officio*. Moreover, the sheriffs have a certain number of tickets at their disposal, and, ghastly as the spectacle is, there is sufficient morbid curiosity among mankind to ensure that there shall be no lack of applicants for admission. Thus every so-called private execution is witnessed by a hundred or more of independent spectators, whose report is a sufficient guarantee for the due fulfilment of the sentence.

In order to secure additional testimony to the fact that the punishment has really been inflicted, our legislators have provided that a coroner's inquest shall be held on the corpse of the condemned within four-and-twenty hours of death, and that the verdict of the inquest shall be formally published. There appears something like a mockery about such an investigation in the case of a man whose body has just been cut down from the gallows; but we admit the urgent necessity, if we are to have executions at all, of convincing the public that there has been no tampering with the due course of justice.

Nor can we assume that the effect of the example will be destroyed by the veil that is thrown over it. Where everything is terrible, it is difficult to argue about degrees of terror; but we are inclined to think that, to the culprit himself, hanging within the prison must be more dreadful than the old 'gallows-dance' in the presence of a great multitude. In the horror of facing, when on the scaffold, the thousands of upturned faces, sensitive natures may have found another pang added to the bitterness of death. But murderers, as a rule, do not possess extreme sensitiveness; and we suspect, horrid as the statement may appear, that the publicity of their last appearance on earth has in many cases tended, if anything, to

---

in the past, and he said that he had once asked him to carry some manure to my flower-garden, but he had refused to do it, saying that it was not part of his work. At the expiration of the ten minutes, Wells came back into the office. I asked him if he was prepared to apologise to Mr Walshe. He made no reply, but was kept in the office for some further ten minutes in consequence of someone speaking to me. I saw him leave the office. After he had left about two or three minutes, the door was re-opened from the outside. I heard the explosion of a firearm, and Mr Walshe fell lifeless, a large wound almost obliterating his face. The next thing I saw of Wells was when he was apprehended by police officers in a carriage on the siding about half an hour later.'

At the end of Wells's trial at Maidstone Assizes, lasting most of Thursday, July 23, the jury, after a brief absence, found him guilty of murder; despite evidence from his parents and from a friend of the family, a licensed victualler named Absalom Hicks, that ever since Wells had 'got squeezed in the stomach between carriages once last August, rendering him insensible for several hours,' he had been 'full of nonsense' and 'very flighty', the jury made no recommendation to mercy; 'to the usual enquiry as to whether the prisoner had anything to say why sentence of death should not be passed upon him, Wells made no reply, and the judge [Mr Justice Willes], who was much affected, passed the sentence in the usual form.'

mitigate the agony with which such men have regarded their end. To see the full light of day, to know that he was the object on which a thousand eyes were looking, about which a thousand hearts were thinking, to form the principal personage in a pageant, ghastly, no doubt, but a pageant still – all such theatrical accessories contributed in no small measure to the bold bearing and careless carriage with which many a criminal confronted a shameful death. To 'die game' has often been the ambition of a ruffian too hardened to be accessible to any higher influence than a vulgar greed for the admiration of such as himself.

But there is no pride in 'dying game' when no crowd of comrades, mates, and lookers-on is present to mark how the desperado dies, when he sees nothing before him save the dull prison walls, when he hears no murmur round him of a multitude, when there is nothing to break the silence of the hour, when the few pale faces towards which his eyes inevitably turn are strange, unknown, indifferent. If the choice were given to criminals whether they would be hanged in public or in private, ninety-nine out of a hundred would choose the popular pageant; and that fact alone is sufficient to establish the superiority of the new system.

The one sole plea in favour of punishment by death is that it deters criminals from the commission of crime to an extent which no other penalty can effect. The plea begs the whole question; but if we let it pass for the day, the more clear becomes the conclusion that we increase the popular terror of the gallows, and so augment its deterrent influence, when we shut out the loud multitude, and veil the last moments of the condemned in cold seclusion.

Nor can any doubt be entertained as to the effect that private executions produce upon the imagination of the public. In America no information is given beforehand of the exact time at which a criminal will be hanged. All that is known is that, at some minute within a period of three or four hours, he will suffer death. By some odd attraction, a considerable crowd generally collects about the prison when men are aware that an execution is going on within its walls. There is nothing to be seen, nothing to be heard. The mob knows only that behind the doors the hangman is carrying out the sentence of the law – that somewhere in a dreary, dark courtyard, surrounded by high stone walls, which nearly shut out the light of the sky, a human being is writhing in the last bitter death-struggle. The knowledge of the unseen reality sobers and awes even a rowdy gathering; and, except the voices of the street preachers plying their work amid the crowd, not a sound is heard until the black flag is raised above the walls, and the signal shows that all is over.

Here, as in America, the private infliction of capital punishment will be unaccompanied by the demoralising saturnalia of ruffiandom which has hitherto taken place at every public execution. The cut-throats, thieves, and bullies of our great towns will no longer march together in regiments to the foot of the scaffold; and ordinary people will not henceforward be brutalised by the spectacle of a dying man's agony.

The strange thing is that the old foul practice of strangling human beings to death in the public streets, in the presence of men, women, and children, should have been allowed to exist so long. Some day we may learn to look on all capital punishment with as much disgust as public executions now inspire.

Friday, August 14:

THE FIRST PRIVATE HANGING

Yesterday morning, between half-past ten and a quarter to eleven o'clock, the murderer, Thomas Wells, was hanged in the interior of Maidstone Gaol. It would be as indecent as inappropriate to say that the results of the arrangements made on this occasion by the prison authorities were in any way 'satisfactory' – to all concerned, indeed, who were of right feeling, the entire affair must, from its very nature, have been productive of unmitigated horror and inextinguishable disgust; but there was not the slightest ground for complaint as to the manner in which the hideous apparatus of slaughter was bestowed, or in which the hangman did his office, and the officials their duty; and, taking the whole ghastly transaction as an experiment, it must be in justice admitted that it was completed without hitch or flaw, and that those whose painful and thankless task it may in future become to repeat such a deed in other parts of the country could not do better than follow, to their closest details, the 'mode' exhibited at Maidstone on Thursday, the 13th of August, 1868.

The privacy surrounding the execution was, with the exception of those whose public duties absolutely compelled them to be present, entire and complete. The visiting magistrates might have claimed the privilege of their position to survey these sequestered shambles; and, also in virtue of their official powers, they might have granted – as is too frequently the case in America – tickets of admission to their own personal friends and acquaintances, but from the first course they humanely, and from the second they most wisely, abstained. If there were any visiting justices in the gaol at the time of the execution, there were none on the place of death itself. The High Sheriff of the county was likewise absent; but he was represented by one of his deputies, Mr Under-sheriff Turley. The ordinary and the governor of the gaol were of course on the spot, with the surgeon, and a sufficient staff of warders.

These, with the culprit, the hangman, and his assistants, made up the actors in the tragedy. As spectators there was a working carpenter, who had superintended the erection of the gallows, and who was allowed to remain while it worked to remedy any shortcomings which might arise in the machinery; and there were just ten newspaper reporters – five from the metropolis, and five attached to the local press. The demands of morbid curiosity, if any were made, had been rigorously refused; the 'artist' attached to some 'illustrated' police paper had not been permitted to penetrate to the interior of the gaol; and the execution was thus, to all intents and purposes, strictly 'private'.

The handsome and prosperous town of Maidstone did not exhibit on Wednesday evening one single foreshadowing of the tragedy which was to be enacted on the morrow; on the contrary, Maidstone seemed rather to be holding high festival than otherwise. It was the weekly drill day of the local volunteers; and at sunset the citizen soldiers were gaily marching down the High-street, preceded by a brilliant brass band, and followed by the usual shouting crowd of boys. Another brass band, and a noisier one – that of the Kentish militia – had just returned from a trip to Hampton Court, and gave a final *al fresco* performance in front of the Mitre Hotel. A third brass band, the most blatant of the three, was installed in an area at the bottom of Middle-row, where a kind of fair was being held. This band belonged to Wombwell's Menagerie, which, with a conjuring booth, and a few stalls for the sale of fruit and gingerbread, made up the entire attractions of the fair as aforesaid. They were sufficient, however, to draw together a motley crowd of canal boatmen, brick-makers, hop-pickers, and cavalry soldiers, with the usual complement of romping boys and girls.

It did not seem to enter into the calculations of anyone that in the forenoon of the next day a human being – a fellow-creature for all his crimes – was to be put to death within a stone's throw of their pleasure ground, and within ear-shot of the drums and trumpets of the three brass bands. There was no substantial reason, perhaps, why the honest townspeople of Maidstone should pause in their hilarity and put on doleful faces because a criminal, who had undeniably deserved death, was to undergo his doom next day in a place to them wholly invisible and inaccessible.

And as the fairground was thronged, so was the area before the prison totally deserted that Wednesday night. The gaol, with its adjacent court-houses, forms an imposing pile, which in the calm starlight looked massive almost to grandeur. There was no riotous, screaming mob congregated before the high stone walls. There was no screaming of ribald ballads. There were no chapmen and hucksters vending their wares. There was to be no show, in fine, such as in old days would have brought crowds of

Maidstone Gaol

sightseers from Chatham and Rochester, from Canterbury and Ashford. At midnight on Wednesday the space fronting the gaol was wholly deserted. In the casement of the entrance-gate, only, glimmered a solitary light – evidence that there were those within who were waiting and watching – suggestive that ever so many yards and corridors off, there might be Somebody in a cell who for days had been tasting of the bitterness of death, and who, ere the hands of the clock had made another round, was to drink the cup of mortality to the lees.

Nor, on the morning of execution itself, did Maidstone offer, externally, the slightest symptom of interest in the grim drama which was to take place at half-past ten o'clock. Mr Charles Dickens, in the notable letters published many years since [in *The Times*, November 1849], and in which he first pointed out the impolicy of public executions, pictured, with his own unrivalled graphic force, the aspect of a city when a private hanging was taking place in a gaol. The sullen flapping of the black flag against its staff, the sonorous tolling of the church bells, the shops all shut, and awe and terror in the faces of the citizens: all these adjuncts to the solemnity of the unseen punishment he powerfully dwelt upon; but all, with the exception of the flag, which, in accordance with the law, was hoisted over the entrance-gate when the deed was done, and the bells of the prison and one adjacent church, which tolled funereally for half an hour before and half an hour after the execution, were conspicuous by their absence. No shops were shut; people went cheerfully about their ordinary business; and from first to last there were not a hundred persons gathered before the gaol.

Those who were there formed the mere shadowy phantom of 'an execution crowd': a few gaping paviors and bricklayers, who had, perhaps, knocked off work for an hour on the chance of 'seeing something' – they knew not what; a few depraved and bleary-looking tramp-women; an old pauper with sore eyes, blinking at the jagged posts of the gate, as though it were that of a workhouse, where they hanged people in lieu of starving them, and a scattering of ragged, callow, viciousfaced boys and girls, the vilest dregs and offscourings of the vagrants of the countryside. But all these made up but a frayed and feeble fringe of low humanity. There were no boisterous, ribald, blasphemous groups. There were no public houses choke-full of screeching raff and scum. There were no white kid gloves and opera glasses at the windows. The Show had been put down for good and all.

He who for many years has been a prominent performer in those horrible spectacles contrived to pass into the gaol almost unobserved. About a quarter to ten, a cab, coming from the railway station, was rapidly driven towards a tavern, called the New Inn, close to the prison. From the vehicle a passenger alighted; the door of the tavern, which had been opened for a moment, as though the visitor was expected, was cautiously closed; but, in a minute or so, the passenger came out, and walked rapidly and nervously, close to the walls of the prison, till he seemed to be clinging to the stonework like a lizard, in the direction of the entrance gate – an old man, of low, stunted stature, with a pale, keen face, and a long white beard; decently clad in somewhat faded black, and on his head a tall, shabby black hat; a handsome

Dr William Palmer

Note written by Palmer to his counsel during the trial

I wish there was 2½ grains
of Strychnine in old Campbells
acidulated draught solely because
I think he acts unfairly -

Samuel Herbert Dougal:
'one of the most notorious criminals of the century'

Dougal's executioners

Dougal's headstone

George Joseph Smith, whose lethal exploits gained him representation in wax at Madame Tussaud's. The bath is the one in which he dispatched his final victim. *(Courtesy of Madame Tussaud's, London)*

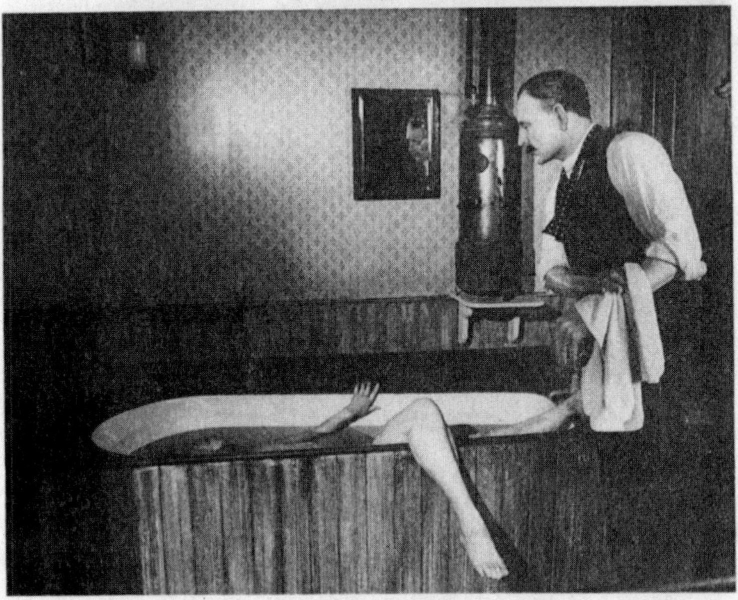

Smith's three known victims: (clockwise from top left): Miss Bessie Mundy, Miss Margaret Lofty and Miss Alice Burnham

Frederick Bywaters and Mrs Edith Thompson. Below: Bywaters with the Thompsons in the garden of their house at Ilford

Thomas Pierrepoint, who hanged Bywaters, with his nephew and protégé Albert

John Ellis, who hanged Mrs Thompson

Mrs Alma Rattenbury and her lover George Percy Stoner

The Villa Madeira, scene of the murder of Francis Rattenbury

Where Mrs Rattenbury died

gold watch-chain crossing his vest; in one hand he carried a threadbare carpet-bag. This was Calcraft, the hangman; in the bag was his hanging 'tackle', his straps and buckles. Some of the crude and evil-faced brats loitering about the gate seemed, as though they had been carrion crows, to have instinctly smelt out this minister of death, and they set up a shrill hoot as the gate was opened to receive the hangman, and closed behind him with a clang.

Shortly before ten, the representatives of the press were admitted to the gaol, and conducted to the 'round house', or guard-room of the warders – an apartment whence a view of the principal exercising yards of the prison could be gained. It was in another and much smaller yard that the hanging was to take place. In this 'round house' the reporters spent one of the deadliest half-hours it is possible to conceive. A grim silence reigned, broken only by the occasional clanking of keys as the gates were unlocked to allow an official to pass through, or the hurrying in of a warder, with a pale face, from the condemned cell. The culprit was breaking down, it was whispered, and water and restoratives had been sent for. All this while the prison bell was tolling. If the spectators cast their eyes for a change into the larger exercising ground, an exceedingly unpleasant object met their gaze in the shape of Calcraft, walking up and down, laughing, and apparently joking with his assistant; one Smith of Dudley, who is spoken of as an 'amateur' hangman, and as the probable successor of Calcraft when the old man with the beard shall retire on his black laurels.*

A minute or so after half-past ten, the reporters were summoned into a vaulted corridor, where they waited until Calcraft had pinioned the unhappy criminal. Then another grated door was unlocked, and the little group of spectators, many of whose faces were whiter than the whitewash on the walls, were led into the place where Thomas Wells was to be killed.

It was a small, oblong yard, thirty feet by twenty perhaps. Along one of its longer sides ran a wooden barrier breast high; and in front of this barrier those privileged to see the sight were ranged. There was ample room for all to see. At the opposite extremity of the yard, against the wall, had been built a long, low shed. By the fresh appearance of the walls on either side, they seemed to have been built up to prevent the possibility of any view of the proceedings being obtained by those without. A pit or trench some five feet deep had been dug in the ground beneath the roof of this shed, and over the trench were the gallows and the drop, the latter nearly level with the paving of the yard. The gallows was composed of the usual uprights and cross-beam, and the drop was the one in habitual use when executions at Maidstone were public; but neither gallows nor drop was painted black. Scaffold there was none.

Policemen were not required. The warders wore their usual uniform; but the governor, a nonchalant gentleman of military mien, was in civilian garb, with a wide-awake hat and a natty cane. There was no

* When William Calcraft retired in 1874, after forty-five years' service, he was succeeded by William Marwood. (A popular conundrum: *If Pa killed Ma, who would kill Pa? – Marwood.*)

black drapery about; no corporate functionaries with robes and wands. The officiating clergyman only, the Rev. Mr Fraser, whose ministrations to the unhappy wretch under his spiritual charge are said to have been, during the last few days, well-nigh incessant, wore his surplice and hood. The vestments of the priest excepted, the matter in hand might have been of no more moment than the flogging of a garotter.

The doomed man was already on the drop, already under the beam, when the spectators ranged themselves at the barrier. A smart shower of rain had followed a leaden, sultry morning. All were of course uncovered. The culprit's face had not yet been concealed by the cap. He was pinioned, and his hands were convulsively clasped. He was clad in the velveteen suit of a railway porter. His neck, so shrugged up were his shoulders, seemed obliterated. Hunched, and crouched, and huddled together, and the limp body surmounted by a great, flat, motionless face – more livid than blanched, the eyelids closed, but the eyeballs evidently turned upwards – the whole form of this miserable wretch looked like some monstrous stuffed figure with a scarecrow mask. The face was simply that of an idiot; the grey-blue lips parted – in all else vacuity.

The good priest was clasping the culprit's hands with one of his own, bearing him up bodily, while he read the concluding passages of the Burial Service; at a short distance at either side, a warder stood to support Wells if he fainted. Behind the victim, in the shadow of the shed, hovered Calcraft, ready to pull down the cap and adjust the noose. A little lower than the ground, on the steps of the pit, was the hangman's assistant waiting to assist in drawing the bolt. It was a dusky, shadowy group seen through the rainy mist; but more distinct than the surplice of the priest, gleamed out of the shadows the white idiot face with the parted lips.

Presently Wells began to sing. It was some incoherent fragment of a hymn. He had been practising the same hymn, the Ordinary said, for days. It was an old, dim, Sunday-school reminiscence, perchance – one of the vague and fitful memories, as of a long-forgotten language, which will surge up round a death-bed. In the midst of his vocal quavering piping, the cap was drawn over his face, but beneath the covering, even, this fearful psalmody was feebly audible. Then the drop fell with a great clatter and rebound, and all was over.

No; not quite all. The authorities were sternly and scrupulously determined that the public should know, through their representatives, that this murderer had been precisely and exactly dealt with according to the law, and that, just as no one hair of his head would have been harmed without proper warrant, so in the manner of his slaying the behests of the law had been undeviatingly carried out. The undersheriff, with grave courtesy, invited the spectators to approach the brink of the pit and inspect the miserable wretch on whom justice had been done. This was almost immediately after the drop fell.

The victim did not jerk; his knees were not drawn up; but the body swung completely round – once and twice. Then convulsive movements of the hands, which became a deep purple in hue, and some swaying of the shoulders and bendings of the neck were all the signs of suffering perceptible. It was very dreadful to look upon him there, trussed and pinioned, hanging, his nightcapped head all on one side, in that pit, and to know that but a few weeks since he had been a hale, hearty lad of eighteen, earning an honest livelihood. It was frightful to look upon him, hanging as he was, with his velveteen jacket, and *a flower in his button-hole*; but his limbs had stretched to their normal length, and, although dead, he looked more human, with all his troubles over, than when he had crouched under the drop with his blank face buried between his shoulders, and quavering that unearthly stave. The gaol officers said he had given no trouble, and, according to the clergyman, he died penitent.

So was this ruffianly young assassin of the Dover stationmaster put to death, literally in a hole and in a corner. Thus much details would not have been bestowed on a most appalling and sickening transaction but for the fact that this, the first private execution in England, marks the beginning of a new and most important chapter in the history of English civilisation, and that the record of what was actually done on the 13th of August, 1868, will, in process of time, become of moment to those who study the manners and customs of a nation. May God grant that, when the time comes for this page to be tilled by students still perhaps unborn as evidence of what has been, it shall be no more possible in England to hang any man, be he a murderer as vile as he who suffered yesterday in the hole at Maidstone.

1881

Wednesday, June 29:

At Windsor yesterday, the forty-third anniversary of Her Majesty's coronation was observed with the customary honours, the bells of the Royal borough and St George's Chapel ringing at intervals, while salutes of twenty-one guns were fired from the artillery in the Long Walk and Virginia Water. At the naval and military stations throughout the kingdom, the day was similarly celebrated.

* * *

EXTRAORDINARY OUTRAGE ON THE BRIGHTON LINE

On Monday afternoon, the Brighton express train steamed slowly out of Croydon station, on the southern outskirts of London, and in a first-class carriage were seated two persons, one an elderly gentleman, a stockbroker, travelling back to his home at Preston, near Brighton – the other a murderer.

The elderly gentleman, Mr I. F. GOLD, may have been reading his paper, or simply looking out of the window, when, before he had time to do anything, to seize the alarm-bell handle and pull it, or to shout for assistance, a sudden and desperate attack must have been made upon him. From the state in which the unfortunate man's body was subsequently found, as well as the condition of the carriage, it is perfectly evident that he was repeatedly stabbed, and that two shots were fired at him as well. Yet this did not prevent him from making a determined struggle for his life. Two or three hours later, Mr GOLD's body was found lying in Balcombe Tunnel.

In one respect, the present murder is even more alarming than that committed by the notorious MÜLLER, because this tragedy was perpetrated in the afternoon, in broad daylight, when murderers might be supposed to be careful and honest people to be tolerably safe from their evil designs, whereas it was at night when Mr THOMAS BRIGGS was foully done to death and hurled from his carriage on to the North London line some seventeen years ago.

As far as can be at present known, we are justified in supposing that the motive of the person, whoever it was, that assassinated Mr GOLD was simply and solely plunder. It seems to have been the custom of Mr GOLD to travel up to town for purposes of business. On the occasion when he met with his death he was known to have proceeded to London in the morning to cash some coupons, and was expected back by the express leaving London Bridge at two o'clock. This is a train which does not stop between Croydon and Preston Park.

When the express arrived at the latter place, a man was found in a first-class carriage apparently wounded and covered with blood. He gave his name as LEFROY, and the story he told was certainly remarkable. He stated to the railway officials that shortly after leaving Croydon he heard a shot fired and felt a blow on his head, upon which he became insensible, and only recovered consciousness on arriving at Preston Park. His travelling companions, he alleged, were an elderly gentleman and a person having the appearance of a 'countryman'. The elderly gentleman was undoubtedly the unfortunate Mr GOLD, whose body was discovered some hours after in Balcombe Tunnel, and LEFROY's account leaves it to be inferred that the 'countryman' was the person who fired the shot and who commited the murder.

LEFROY, there is no doubt, appeared to have been wounded when he got to Preston, and his wounds, which, it is stated, were of a very slight character, were dressed at the County Hospital at Brighton; the surgeon there will be able to state whether the injury on his head was produced by a shot or not. It seems incredible that a shot fired at close quarters should produce a wound which would render a man insensible for an hour and then allow him to walk about as if nothing had happened. If LEFROY's account be true, how did the murderous countryman, who first stunned LEFROY himself and then proceeded to deal with Mr GOLD, manage to escape! He must have jumped from the express train while it was running at a high rate of speed – some forty or fifty miles an hour; and, though there is nothing absolutely impossible in such a feat, the chances of a man coming off unharmed who tries it are exceedingly small. Yet no trace of the supposed perpetrator of the crime has been discovered.

Meanwhile, where is this so-called LEFROY? By what looks like an incredible piece of stupidity on the part of a policeman, he was allowed to go off to his home at Wallington, not far from Croydon. On the discovery of Mr GOLD's lifeless body in the tunnel, a telegram was at once despatched to detain him, but by then – some time on Monday evening – he had taken off his bandage, changed his clothes, and disappeared. While we desire to say nothing that should prejudice opinion against even a strongly suspected man, it would be idle to ignore the inference that will be drawn from this and other indications, and it is sincerely to be trusted that LEFROY will either voluntarily or otherwise be shortly forthcoming. If he is an innocent man, he may be said to be suffering under very serious suspicion, so much so indeed that the police have issued a notice intimating that he is 'wanted for murder'. If it be actually proved, as stated, that the murdered man's watch was discovered in LEFROY's boot by the guard of the train, that his neck was badly scratched and his collar torn off, and that his wound on the head was a sham injury, apparently self-inflicted, then there will be reason to regret that LEFROY was ever for a moment allowed to get clear away. At present the police are on his track, and they will, we hope, before long succeed in discovering his whereabouts. It is a fact of the deepest significance that Mr GOLD's pocket-book has been found, but that no notes or cash were contained therein, whence it seems certain that the murderer first killed and then plundered his victim, throwing the body afterwards out on to the line.

This atrocious crime will cause a thrill of alarm and horror throughout the length and breadth of the land. That an ordinary business man, journeying by train on his professional duties, should be savagely assaulted in a first-class carriage in broad daylight, shot at several times, stabbed brutally, and then thrown out upon the line in a dying state or dead, is enough to shock the nerves even of veteran travellers by rail.

At such a juncture it may be worth while to recall what took place in the remarkably similar tragedy when the German tailor, FRANZ MÜLLER, attacked Mr THOMAS BRIGGS on the 9th of July, 1864. The nine forty-five train from Fenchurch-street had got as far as Hackney Station, when a gentleman, stepping into a first-class compartment, called the guard's attention to the state which the carriage was in. No sooner had he entered and placed his hand on the seat than he found it covered with blood. Further examination revealed the startling fact that not only the seat, but the sides, windows and floor of the carriage were all smeared and splashed with the same ghastly evidence of crime. A hat, a walking-stick, and a small leather bag were all that was found besides in the carriage. On the line, however lay the unfortunate victim, chief clerk to a banking firm in the City, who had been brutally murdered and subsequently robbed as he was sitting in his first-class compartment. When discovered, this hapless gentleman was still breathing, but he was described as being covered with blood, and his head much disfigured, 'as if by blows inflicted by some blunt instrument', and he very shortly succumbed to the terrible injuries which he had received. A gold watch, with an Albert chain, had been stolen from his person, and the waistcoat bore marks of these articles having been wrenched away with violence. How his murderer was hunted down and captured as he was disembarking from a steamer at New York is matter of history.* The story is a strange one, but to all appearances not stranger than that of the murder of Mr GOLD on Monday last, and we can only hope that in this case, as in that which it so closely resembles, the perpetrator of a foul and cruel crime will be speedily brought to justice.

ANTECEDENTS OF LEFROY

A correspondent forwards the following statement:

The description first published of the supposed murderer, Percy Lefroy, is somewhat misleading. Lefroy is not a labourer in the common sense of the term, and it is difficult to say what he is. For some time he went by the name of Mapleton, but only latterly has been known as Lefroy, his private cards bearing that name and his letters that signature.

In some reports he has been spoken of as a 'reporter', whilst he described himself as an author and journalist. So far as can be ascertained, he never was employed professionally as a reporter, although he contributed to the local press of the neighbourhood in which he resided, as the files of the *Wallington and Carshalton Herald* will show. His writings took the form of biographical sketches of local celebrities, and these were supplemented by a series of theatrical notices. His tastes decidedly inclined towards dramatic authorship, and he repre-

* The murder of Mr Briggs was the first committed on a British train (thirty-nine years after a locomotive first plied publicly). Despite German efforts to save Müller (one by the King of Prussia, who telegraphed a plea to Queen Victoria), he was executed outside Newgate on November 14, 1864.

sented himself to be the author of a number of most successful burlesques and opera-bouffes played in Australia and America.

Lefroy, in the neighbourhood of Wallington, has latterly borne the nick-name of 'Ananias', and in some quarters he was equally well known as 'Sloomy'. During the last few days of his residence in Wallington, where he resided at a young ladies' boarding school kept by one of his cousins, he pursued a plan with nearly every person with whom he could claim more than a passing acquaintanceship. He invited them to dine with him at a restaurant in the Strand, there to meet some celebrated people. If his invitation was accepted, he immediately tried to negotiate a loan of a few shillings.

In regard to Lefroy's personal appearance, the official description is not a good one. He has always represented his age to be twenty-two. In that respect the report seems to be correct, but he is nearer 5ft 9½in than 5ft 8in. His extreme thinness and the length of his face, adorned by very slight whiskers and moustache, might, perhaps, incline one to think him taller than he really is. His eyes are grey; his teeth and gums are fully exposed when he smiles. In matters of dress he was usually negligent, and invariably had on a light-coloured overcoat of thin material, which hung irregularly upon his shoulders; his trousers were of a thick, coarse-patterned material. Ordinarily, he did not display much jewellery. A small diamond pin or else a large crystal one commonly decorated his scarf, in the centre of which it was rarely if ever placed. On one hand he had a ring, but the writer never remembers seeing him refer to a watch.

In company, Lefroy had a manner of ingratiating himself that was remarkable, and in conversation he possessed a power of narrative that was essentially dramatic, not to say sensational. He is very abstemious. Cricket seemed to be his principal diversion. On a quite recent occasion, he got up an eleven at a cricket match, his contingent being understood to be colonial journalists, while on the other side were several well-known theatrical gentlemen. Lefroy's eleven lost, and when the wickets were drawn and he was required to pay his quota towards the expenses, he excused himself on the ground that his bag had been cut open and his purse extracted. It was subsequently found that other bags had been cut in a similar way, but whether anything was missing from them is uncertain.

During the last general election, he was employed as clerk to the local Liberal Association, and he appeared to be very grateful for the financial help this engagement afforded him.

On account of his delicate health, he was only sent to school for a short time, a private tutor sometimes being called in to educate him. His relatives desired that he should not enter upon any business or profession until he was twenty-one years of age, thinking that by that time he might shake off his consumptive habit, and get rid of the troublesome cough that had never left him. About three years ago, his relatives induced his trustee to advance him his small inheritance, between £200 and £300, and with this they gave him a complete outfit, and sent him off to Australia. Letters of introduction were given to him to prominent persons in the Colony. He, however, only remained in Australia about one year, returning two years ago to reside with his cousins, the Claytons, in Wallington. His father died just after his return. By his mother's family, Lefroy, or Mapleton, is connected with people moving in good circles, many of them being in prominent official positions. His maternal grandfather held a high rank in the army. His father was a staff-commander in the navy, and was for many years a magistrate in one of the colonies, retiring from the service with a captain's pension. His father's sister is a lady of independent fortune, who resides in a city in the West of England. It is well known that his father at his death suffered from softening of the brain, and that his grandfather was insane.

Thursday, June 30:

All through yesterday, the police were engaged in following up the real or supposed clues they possessed likely to lead to the hiding-place of Percy Lefroy. A full description of Lefroy has been circulated throughout the country, and the description has been telegraphed to various places abroad to which it is thought he may have made his escape. In London a watch was kept at all the railway stations and steamboat piers and wharves; and at Wallington, a similar sharp look-out was maintained. The house of Mrs Brickwood, Lefroy's sister, in Southend, Essex, was searched, but to no purpose. Mrs Brickwood states that she knows very little of her brother, as she has seen him only rarely. Efforts were made, but without success, to obtain a photograph of Lefroy.

Friday, July 1:

The Government and the London, Brighton and South Coast Railway Company have each offered £100 reward for information leading to the apprehension of the murderer of Mr Gold.*

Matthews, the cabman, whose evidence led to the apprehension of Müller, has been in the neighbourhood of Wallington, possibly with a view of ascertaining if his experience can lead to the arrest of a criminal of the same stamp.

A correspondent, a City solicitor, reminds us of a curious incident contemporaneous with the Müller outrage. He says: 'I was in the habit of going home by rail at that time, and I carried a strong umbrella as the best means of protection. On one occasion I got into a carriage without noticing that the only other occupant had what seemed to be a roll of paper in his hand. As the train commenced to move, I thought he held it in an attitude of readiness for attack, and I accordingly sat equipped with my umbrella, prepared for any emergency. I was sure he had a bludgeon concealed in the harmless-looking roll of paper, and he certainly looked excited enough for a deed of violence. Need I say that I breathed more freely when I reached my destination. I sent a letter, which was published, to a morning newspaper, detailing my 'narrow escape'. Next day I read in the same journal a letter from my fellow-traveller stating that he was really the aggrieved person, that my watchful, suspicious air, and the position of my weapon of defence, my umbrella, made him uneasy,

* The 1993 purchasing power of the 1881 £ is reckoned to be about £42.

and that his roll of paper was simply a cucumber which he was bringing home to his family.'

Subjoined we give a sketch portrait of Lefroy by a gentleman who knew him and had frequent opportunities of noting his characteristics. It has been attested as an excellent likeness by several persons with whom Lefroy came into close contact.

Subjoined we give a sketch por... ...leman who knew Lefroy and had frequent op-portunities of noting his characteristics. It has been attested as an excellent likeness by several persons with whom Lefroy came into close contact.

The police have issued the following further notice:

Murder.—Percy Lefroy Mapleton, whose apprehension [is] sought for murder on the Brighton Railway, left the ...w Hospital, at Islington, at 9.30 on the morning of ...day, June 28. Description: Age 22, middle height, thin, sickly appearance, scant ...

This was the first time that a British newspaper published a picture of a fugitive from justice. A few days later, the police reproduced the picture on 'wanted' notices. Surprisingly, Lefroy's profile was not unique. During the week or so following the *Telegraph*'s publication of the picture, hundreds of Lefroy look-alikes were spotted in divers parts of the British Isles, also in France, and, if not fleet of foot, were either arrested by policemen or impelled into police stations by civilians made courageous by the thought of the reward-money.

From various editions of the *Telegraph* till July 8:

The interest which has been excited has shown itself throughout the entire country, and there seem to have been few considerable districts in which some one has not been arrested or placed under suspicion on account of a supposed resemblance to Lefroy. The police continue to assert that the capture can only be a question of a few hours. It is not, alas! an uncommon thing for murderers to escape; but for a person who is known and under suspicion for such a crime to continue long at large undiscovered is happily a rare occurrence. Charles Peace eluded pursuit longer than most known murderers;

but that was done by the aid of marvellous disguises such as few other men could assume. . . .

Late at night, the news went abroad somewhere about Bexley, Kent, that a man closely resembling Lefroy was seen tramping to Gravesend. An inspector of the Metropolitan Police tracked the man mile after mile for a long distance, but at length the officer got off the scent. It was excusable, for the man had already been taken into custody on suspicion. He turned out to be a decayed gentleman who had the misfortune to resemble the supposed perpetrator of the railway tragedy. The local police were not long in setting him at liberty, making amends by the hospitality of a good breakfast and the present of a shilling with which to pay his railway fare onwards. He did not, however, take to the train, but to the highway, and thus met the inspector who had originally started in search of him, and was re-arrested, only, however, to be again shortly afterwards set free. . . .

A suspicion is gaining ground that Lefroy has committed suicide. . . . In some quarters a belief is current that Lefroy has assumed feminine attire. . . .

Yesterday an American gentleman called at one of the metropolitan stations, stating that he was firmly convinced that he very much resembled the man wanted, that he was continually being watched, and that he should eventually find himself in custody upon the murder charge. The gentleman therefore begged that he might be allowed to take up residence at the station. It was evident to the inspector on duty that he was under the influence of excitement. The divisional surgeon, who was sent for, certified that the gentleman was suffering from 'over-consciousness'. He recommended him to take some days' rest in the country. It was only after a great deal of persuasion that he was induced to take his departure. . . .

'Victim to a Busybody' writes: 'Having just recovered from a severe illness of three months' duration, and still being compelled to use two sticks when walking, I last Sunday morning managed to reach Hyde Park. While resting myself upon one of the seats, my appearance seems to have attracted the attention of a busybody, who constituted himself an amateur detective by informing a constable of his suspicions that I was the missing Lefroy.

The constable rather abruptly requested me to stand up, which, after some hesitation, I consented to do. He then told me to take off my hat, and before I could comply saved me the trouble by removing it himself. I was quickly surrounded by between 200 and 300 persons. The constable, after questioning me as to a cut on my neck (caused by a careless barber about an hour previous), and one or two other matters, asked for my name and address, which I gave him, although I had previously been recognised by one of the onlookers. Not satisfied with this, an inspector, who had arrived, ordered an officer to follow me home, accompanied by the usual twenty or thirty curious members of the British public. My rate of progress is considerably under two miles an hour, but the constable lost sight of me *en route*, and upon arriving home I found Constable 192A making inquiries. Now, Sir, I wish to ask if the police authorities do not think it would have been as well to prove the accuracy of my address without putting me (in my present state of health) to the pain and annoyance of a cross-examination before a London crowd?'

Monday, July 4:

ATTEMPTED MURDER OF PRESIDENT GARFIELD

We publish this morning, with the profoundest regret, the intelligence that Mr James Abraham Garfield, President of the United States, has been shot by an assassin, and dangerously, if not mortally, wounded.

On Saturday morning the President went to the Baltimore and Potomac railway station, Washington, intending to travel, with a portion of his Cabinet, by the limited express for New York. They arrived at the building at about twenty minutes past nine. While the President and Mr Blaine, the Secretary of State, were walking side by side from the carriage into the station, Charles Guiteau took aim with a large-sized revolver, and before anyone could prevent him, fired at the President. The President fell. Guiteau was at once arrested. The President was conveyed to a private room in the station, and surgical aid was at once summoned. Within an hour, the President was removed back to the White House. It appears that he was shot in two places. The first bullet entered the right arm; a second ball entered above the right hip in the region of the kidneys. The physicians have probed for both missiles, but hitherto without success.

Intense excitement prevails throughout the country. At Washington the military have been called out to preserve order.

Leading article:

President GARFIELD has narrowly escaped – if he has escaped – the fate of the first and greatest CAESAR, of HENRY of Navarre, of WILLIAM the Silent, of ABRAHAM LINCOLN, and that latest victim of the political murderer's hate, ALEXANDER of Russia. From all accounts, the would-be assassin, CHARLES JULIUS GUITEAU, a native of Illinois, between thirty and forty years of age, is – whether he be mad or sane – a distinct product of that stupid and mistaken dogma of American politics which allows that electoral activity is entitled to the reward of place. The fellow is said to have run through the career of unsuccessful lawyer, fugitive lecturer, preacher of Second Adventism, general adventurer, and, last and worst, of office-seeker. Unfortunately the United States teems with such useless and dangerous citizens – men who become professional politicians in their eagerness to escape the burden of honest labour. It is understood that Guiteau was a delegate to the Chicago Republican Convention, and a disappointed man. Having applied for the post of United States Consul at Marseilles, and been refused, he is said to have nourished a grudge against the chief dispenser of patronage.

How far the theory that GUITEAU is a madman may or may not be substantiated by facts it is not as yet our province to inquire. But it is certain that if the words attributed to him after he had fired at Mr Garfield be truly reported – those words being, 'ARTHUR is now Presi-

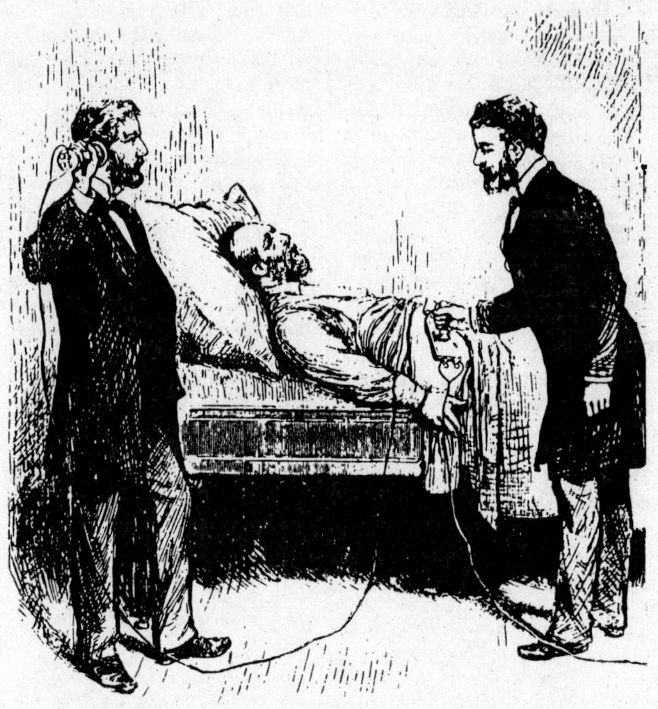

Trying to locate the bullet

dent' – there will be wide-spread suspicion in the United States that the crime may have been the result of a political conspiracy. There is no country in the world where suspicion finds more advocates ready to receive it with easy credulity than America, and, as is shown by books and newspaper articles which still appear, a belief is extensively held, alike in the North and the South, that ANDREW JACKSON had something to do with the assassination of ABRAHAM LINCOLN, to whose chair he succeeded. We should, ourselves, hesitate to call in question such a groundless suspicion, involving a libel upon a prominent American statesman, were it not that public comment in the United States, accustomed to mistake licence for liberty, will assuredly deal with this aspect of the case. Inquiry will, however, probably discover that the crime had nothing whatever to do with politics in a party sense, but was the individual act of an undisciplined vagabond driven to homicidal mania by a combination of uncontrollable greed of office and despair of gain. America will find – better sooner than later – that the cancer of place-hunting must be cut out, or it will eat away the healthy life of the body politic.

Blood is thicker than water. The American people and we come of a common stock and speak a common language. We are brethren in the heritage of freedom and of genius, and as brothers we offer them the comfort of brotherly love today. The banners they like to set fluttering on the Fourth of every succeeding July – because in our bad quarrel they proved themselves English to the backbone – will droop from their poles this morning or lie all unfurled. The wonted laughter will not be heard, nor the wonted healths be pledged. Instead, American men and women, with bowed heads and bended knee, will pray for the safe passage through the Valley of the Shadow of Death for the Chief of their State. Our QUEEN, readiest in all these isles to soften sorrow with sweet sympathy, was quick to send her message of kindliness under the seas. What more can be said than that this British nation, clasping a brother's hand, bids America be of good cheer and of good hope?

President Garfield lingered till the night of Monday, September 21. 'The President's last words were "It hurts", after which he passed into a state of unconsciousness. Hypodermic injections of brandy were given, but without avail.' A few hours later, Vice-President Chester Arthur was sworn in as the twenty-first President. A jury found that Guiteau was sane, and at noon on Friday, June 30, 1882, after a lavish meal, he mounted the scaffold and, with a clergyman acting as lectern for a Bible, read aloud fourteen verses from Matthew 10, starting with the words, 'And fear not them that kill the body but are not able to kill the soul.' He then told the assembled reporters: 'I am now going to read some verses which are intended to indicate my feelings at the moment of leaving this world. If set to music, they may be rendered very effective. The idea is that of a child babbling to his mama and papa. I wrote it this morning about ten o'clock.' He proceeded to recite in a high-pitched voice: 'I am going to the Lordy, I am so glad,/I am going to the Lordy, I am so glad,/I am going to the Lordy,/Glory hallelujah! Glory hallelujah!' . . . and so on . . . and on . . . and on. The minute he finished, the black cap was placed over his face. He dropped the manuscript. 'Glory, ready, go,' he said loudly, and the hangman pulled the lever.

MURDER.

£200 REWARD.

WHEREAS, on Monday, June 27th, ISAAC FREDERICK GOULD was murdered on the London Brighton and South Coast Railway between Three Bridges and Balcombe, in East Sussex.

AND WHEREAS a Verdict of WILFUL MURDER has been returned by a Coroner's Jury against

PERCY LEFROY MAPLETON,

whose Portrait and Handwriting are given hereon,—

Dear Sir

I much regret having been unable to call upon you the last week having been away from home since Thursday week last in fact not seeing your letter until to-day. But I need hardly say that any night next week you care to name with the exception of Monday I shall be only too happy to call upon you Dear Sir

Yours faithfully
Arthur Lefroy

and who is described as being 22 years of age, height 5 ft. 8 or 9 in., very thin, hair (cut short) dark, small dark whiskers; dress, dark frock coat, and shoes, and supposed low black hat (worn at back of head), had scratches from fingers on throat, several wounds on head, the dressing of which involved the cutting of hair, recently lodged at 4, Cathcart Road, Wallington, was seen at 9.30 a.m. 28th ult., with his head bandaged, at the Fever Hospital, Liverpool Road, Islington. Had a gold open-faced watch (which he is likely to pledge), "Maker Griffiths, Mile End Road, No. 16261."

One Half of the above Reward will be paid by Her Majesty's Government, and One Half by the Directors of the London Brighton and South Coast Railway, to any person (other than a person belonging to a Police Force in the United Kingdom) who shall give such information as shall lead to the discovery and apprehension of the said PERCY LEFROY MAPLETON or others, the Murderer, or Murderers, upon his or their conviction; and the Secretary of State for the Home Department will advise the grant of Her Majesty's gracious PARDON to any accomplice, not being the person who actually committed the Murder, who shall give such evidence as shall lead to a like result.

Information to be given to the Chief Constable of East Sussex, Lewes, at any Police Station, or to

The Director of Criminal Investigations, Gt. Scotland Yard.

JULY 4th, 1881.

(4313) Harrison and Sons, Printers in Ordinary to Her Majesty, St. Martin's Lane

Saturday, July 9:

CAPTURE OF LEFROY

A feeling of profound satisfaction will everywhere be experienced at the news that Percy Lefroy Mapleton, the supposed murderer of Mr Gold on the Brighton Railway, was captured last night at Stepney, in the East End of London. Notwithstanding the strength of the circumstantial evidence against him, it is only right still to call him the supposed instead of the actual assassin. Indeed, at this moment more than at any previous period, the proud maxim of British law must be remembered – that a man is always to be considered innocent until he has been found guilty. Until the trial, it is absolutely necessary, in the sacred interests of justice and fair play that, despite the weight of damnatory evidence against Lefroy, we should suspend our final judgment.

Inspectors Jarvis and Swanston are the fortunate officers of the Metropolitan Police Force who effected the capture, at about half-past eight o'clock last night, and there is no doubt that the portrait published in *The Daily Telegraph* has been, to a great degree, instrumental in procuring the apprehension of Lefroy, it being through this likeness that the suspicions of the persons who gave the information to the police were first aroused.

The arrest itself seems to have been due to private information furnished to the police by some persons in the neighbourhood of the house where Lefroy was lying hid. This house was No. 32, Smith-street, Stepney. We know as a fact that, the Tuesday morning after the crime Lefroy called at the Fever Hospital in the Liverpool-road, where his sister was residing, in order to borrow a few shillings, and thence he must have gone off and taken these quiet, out-of-the-way lodgings on the following Thursday. What he did and where he went in the interval is not known; but for more than a week he has been living at Stepney, under the assumed name of Clark, and his landlady, Mrs Bickers, who appears to be a hospitable and kindly woman, does not seem to have entertained a suspicion that her mysterious lodger was the hunted man on whose head the reward of two hundred pounds was fixed.

When arrested, he was found to be without money, and his bill for lodging had not been paid. If he succeeded in getting anything out of Mr Gold's pockets besides the watch which was found in his shoe at Brighton, he certainly did not obtain much ready money. No opposition whatever was offered by him to the officers. There sat the man, 'wanted for murder', perhaps the most notorious Englishman existing today, in an upper room, with his tightly buttoned coat hiding such underclothing as it was desirable to conceal. He is said not to have left that one room, except for a short interval occasionally at night, for eight whole days. It would seem that Lefroy's behaviour at the moment of his capture was as cool and collected as it had been all through the varied scenes of this dreadful tragedy. Charged with being the real Lefroy, or Mapleton, he at once confessed to his identity, but at the same time added that he was 'not guilty' of the murder of Mr Gold. This is a point which will very soon be put to a practical test.

The accused man was taken to Scotland-yard, thence to King-street, and today he will be brought before the magistrates within whose jurisdiction the crime was perpetrated.

Monday, July 11:

FROM LONDON TO LEWES

It was seven o'clock in the morning of Saturday, and the morning was fine. Word had been sent round that Lefroy would be taken by the ordinary half-past seven a.m. train from Victoria to East Grinstead – that being the petty sessional division of the district in which Mr Gold met his fate, as the coroner's jury have said, at the hands of Percy Lefroy Mapleton – there to confront the dignity of the law in the shape of the local magistrates.

The weather was beautiful – perfect holiday weather – but sadly out of harmony with the grim business in hand. A light wind chased some gauzy clouds along the sky, and blew the smoke sideways from the chimney-tops across the yard of the railway station.

There was neither hurry nor bustle; nor, with the exception of a little crowd of policemen drawn up inside the station to the right of the first entrance, were there any visible signs of preparation. Outward-bound holiday-makers, bent Brightonwards, took their tickets unconcernedly, not dreaming that they were to be fellow-travellers of the suspected murderer. Some workmen and persons employed about the station, knowing who was expected to arrive, were on the watch for the four-wheeled cab, which presently, at a smart pace, drove into the yard.

Suddenly the group of policemen displayed extraordinary activity. Keeping together, they pushed about the passengers, driving them back like chaff before the wind. Some of the passengers, in ignorance of the arrival or intended arrival of Lefroy, remonstrated with the police, begging to be allowed to proceed peaceably on their several journeys. One individual, seemingly of some consequence, said, 'Do you know who I am?' To which the active and somewhat too zealous superintendent thus addressed made answer, 'No, I don't; but I know my dooty'; and imitating the 'dooty' of his brother constables all along the line, assaulted the seemingly important individual, both rudely and violently. While this – to the police – possibly pleasant diversion was going on, Inspectors Swanston and Jarvis had hurried their man into a first-class compartment of the Brighton train, and drawn the blinds. Beyond some unnecessary violence on the part of the police, and some strongly worded remonstrances by the roughly-used passengers, no harm had been done. True, both might have been spared, for there need not have been the slightest occasion for either.

No sooner was Lefroy settled in the carriage, in the middle seat, with his face to the engine, than he commenced to talk in an unconcerned manner with his captors. His ennunciation is that of a fairly well-educated man, and he speaks deliberately, as one who forms his sentences with care. A little quiet crowd gathered outside the carriage windows, but kept a respectful distance. By and by, he grew more cheerful, and in the dim light of the shut-up compartment might easily have been mistaken for an ordinary common-place traveller.

But had he known what would happen at East Croydon, he might not have enjoyed the cigarette he was allowed to smoke. There were a great many people upon the platform of that station, many of them very rough and indulging in all kinds of horseplay. The blinds of the carriage were drawn, but the window was down, and seeing this, and noting there were no police present, some of the bolder by-standers got upon the footboard, and drawing aside the blind, stared and jeered at Lefroy, who, appealing to his caretakers, requested that they would not suffer him to be made an exhibition of.

He had been talking pleasantly enough until the train steamed into Merstham tunnel, when he became silent and disturbed, first folding his arms across his breast and drooping his head, next lifting his head, thrusting his neck forward, and with his right hand stretching out his under lip, and letting it contract again and again.

When Redhill was reached, it seemed as if all the town, learning the news, had come upon the platform. A noisy mob gathered round the windows, laughing and jostling. One cried, alluding to the drawn blinds, 'They want to keep the sun off him'; and another, pretending to believe that those inside the carriage were asleep, knocked on the panel, and called out, 'What time in the morning do you want your hot water?'

Although the police, acting on instructions, had taken their tickets to East Grinstead, by the time the train reached Three Bridges it was known that our destination had been changed from head-quarters, and that the prisoner was to be taken, via Hayward's Heath, to Her Majesty's prison at Lewes. At Hayward's Heath, which was reached at ten minutes past nine, we changed carriages, and Lefroy was walked from a backward compartment of the Brighton train along the platform, possibly 150 yards, to a forward compartment of the Lewes train. Marching thus between the two detectives who captured him, one of them carrying a bundle of blood-stained clothes done up in a soiled white handkerchief, Lefroy, seen by me for the first time in the strong light of the morning, looked a wretched object.

Some touch of pity came into the hearts of those who watched him, crouching in the carriage, with tears in his eyes, passing through Balcombe Tunnel; but his appearance upon the platform at Three Bridges did not induce compassion. Crowding by the windows of the train in which he had ridden, the people hooted and yelled at him as he went by. He evidently felt his degradation deeply. His face worked convulsively, his fingers clenched, and then opened, and his arms twitched in the grasp of his captors. A crumpled billy-cock hat, a seedy-black ribbed cloth Chesterfield overcoat, a pair of rough Scotch tweed trousers – buff with narrow red lines, some distance apart at right angles – and a pair of worn-out shoes completed his costume. With narrow, sloping shoulders, a round back and long, thin neck, he stands apparently five feet ten inches high. Although his whiskers and moustache had been cut off, his face was not shaved. In complexion he looked sallow, of the colour of worn parchment, and his skin stretched tightly to his face, bringing out, in considerable prominence, the bone of the lower jaw at the articulation under the ear. The hair is cut short, dead black, and poor in quality. He had the weary, fearsome look of a starved and hunted creature, and as he went by, the people cursing and groaning at him, his brows more than once contracted and his upper lip was raised, showing the gums and the eye teeth pressed together – a very painful sight.

Why so many persons along the line should have made a holiday of the procession to gaol of a wretched, friendless lad accused of a shocking murder is not easy to understand.

We were kept waiting nearly an hour at Three Bridges, and during that time the miserable youth, sitting back in the compartment, trying to cover his face with his hand, and breathing heavily, seemed to suffer terribly. It was found that one of the side blinds of the new carriage would not draw down to the bottom, so that it was possible to see very well from the outside what was going on within. This was made the most of by the ladies and gentlemen at Three Bridges. Assembled in force, awaiting their turns, each came up to the window, took a long look, as at a peep-show, and gave way to the next comer. An affectionate father, anxious to please his pretty golden-haired, blue-eyed little daughter, lifted her up in his arms, until her face touched the window-pane; and as he put her tenderly upon the ground she clapped her hands joyfully, prattling in her childish treble, but doubtful as to the identity of the accused creature on view. Thus for nearly an hour the platform was kept as a promenade of sightseers, speaking their minds freely about Lefroy within hearing of that wretched man, so that, looking from the crouching, frightened figure inside to the good-humoured, excited, and manifestly delighted, mob on the other side of the carriage-door, I could hardly help wondering at the seeming absence of compassion, even among the women, who appeared to laugh loudest.

When, at length, we got clear away from Three Bridges, and the detectives, now joined by Superintendent Berry, talked among themselves, Lefroy's spirits quickly revived. He gossiped lightly with Mr Berry, who has been in Australia, on theatrical and literary affairs in the colony, displaying great volubility and an apparent knowledge of the subject. Could it be possible that this was a carriageful of plain-clothes policemen guarding a man accused of murder? Rather it seemed a pleasant party of friends gossiping about books and the play. But the rustics, with sunburnt faces, open-mouthed, standing leaning on their scythes, at Keymer Junction, told a different tale. No sooner did the train draw up to the platform than they clamoured round the carriage door, with imprecations and shouts of 'Hang him!' 'Tear him to pieces!' Their cries for vengenace sounded strangely under the blue sky in the warm summer air, and it was with a sense of relief that we left Keymer behind.

Lewes was reached by half-past ten o'clock, and Lefroy, having been transferred from the train to a cab, was hurried along up the steep streets to the constabulary office, where a halt was made. It was thought that he might be brought before a magistrate in the town; but as no official of the kind was about at the time, he was carried at once to the new county gaol. He walked firmly, even lightly, up the broad steps, and the great doors being shut behind him, he was lost to view.

Unfortunately, Captain Crickett, Governor of the prison, was away on a holiday, and the establishment had been left in charge of the head turnkey, of whom Superintendent Berry, presenting his prisoner, wanted to know whether he could have him back again, should he require him for purposes of examination. The turnkey replied that he could not. Now, according to the terms of the coroner's warrant, Mr Berry's duty was, for the time being, finished, when he had consigned Lefroy to the care of Captain Crickett; but, as that officer was out of the way, the Superintendent started off into the town to fetch a magistrate. Gentlemen in the commission of the peace, it happens, are not plentiful at Lewes, and the Superintendent was a long time before he came back with one – Mr Molineux, a banker in the town. Meanwhile, I took up a position in the warder's lodge, a neat apartment about twelve feet square, furnished with an unpainted deal table and a few chairs, and set off by some pots of geraniums in the window, and still further embellished with written and printed rules and regulations of the establishment, which, since May 26, has become an alternative prison with that at Maidstone.

Presently the head turnkey appeared, and I suggested to him that as an inquiry was about to be held, I desired to be present as an auditor. The head turnkey, however, declined to grant the required permission. Certainly for many reasons it was to be regretted that Captain Crickett was not there on this day, of all days in the year, when his presence seemed most needed. In due course, however, the prison doctor put in an appearance. He looked at Lefroy, asked him how he felt, and tapped his chest, saw that the wounds on the head were quite healed, and that the hair had been cut and was commencing to grow again. Then the doctor came forth from the prison, and mounting his chaise, drove off.

The magistrate, when at length he arrived, accompanied by the clerk's clerk, was for allowing the press to be present at the inquiry; but the head turnkey overruled him on the ground that he could not act without the governor's permission, or, better still, an order from the Home Secretary. The reporters were in a quandary. They sent civil messages asking to be allowed to come in, but the head turnkey was obdurate. The clerk's clerk, however, promised through the porter that they should see the depositions later on. Lefroy was, therefore, examined within the prison walls in secret in the presence of Mr Molineux, the head constable, the head turnkey, and the police witnesses, called in one by one. The magistrate wished to remand the prisoner until Tuesday, when the knife – with which some of the wounds on Mr Gold are supposed to have been made – will be produced, but Lefroy said he would prefer that the remand should extend to Friday, and the magistrate gave way.

Tuesday, July 12:

The station superintendent at Three Bridges writes to say that the train which conveyed Lefroy to Lewes on Saturday morning was detained there only for a short time, and suggests that the reported delay of nearly an hour occurred 'at some other station lower down the line'.

It is stated that Lefroy wrote a long letter on Saturday to his sister from Lewes Prison, detailing his circumstances, and asking for assistance to enable him to make a defence to the charge of murder that has been made against him; also informing her that he is in need of many articles for personal comfort. His sister yesterday communicated with several of the family relations of the prisoner, informing them what she proposed doing, and asking their advice and co-operation.

It is understood that it has now been definitely arranged that the examination of Lefroy shall be taken before the magistrates at Cuckfield. Lefroy will therefore be removed from Lewes on Friday morning in the custody of some of the gaolers, and will be lodged in a cell at the police-station at Cuckfield, in which town he will remain until the conclusion of his examination. Special arrangements for his safe custody are being made. The police-station is situated about 200 yards from the Talbot Hotel, where the magistrates hold their sittings, and there will be an increased police force in the town, to prevent any molestation taking place.

Saturday, July 16:

Cuckfield, seated in the midst of fields and farmyards and, if the nose may be depended upon, of pigsties as well, is unused to pageants of any kind, and the arrival of a prisoner charged with a horrible murder caused, yesterday morning, such a thrill of excitement to permeate through the town or village – for it lays claim to both titles – as cannot be remembered by the very oldest inhabitant.

Long before the examination of Lefroy could by any possibility take place, the villagers had gathered in great and gratified crowds to gaze at the windows of the Talbot Hotel, familiar enough to them heretofore, but now endowed with a new and pleasing interest. Within the edifice would presently sit the suspected author of the Brighton Railway murder; through those windows the prisoner would gaze upon the Cuckfield roofs, and there was just the possibility that if they waited long enough, a glimpse either of the prisoner or of somebody connected with him might possibly be caught, if only a close watch was kept. Happy, then, were they who could take up a commanding position on the pathway or in the road and watch the front of the hotel unceasingly. Happier, of course, those who hoped to obtain presently admission to the court.

There the preparations were complete. In a long room, probably used heretofore for festivities of various kinds, three long tables had been placed – one at right angles to the two others, and covered with green baize. Thereat the magistrates would presently sit. At one of the two others it was intended that the lawyers, and at the other the members of the press, should be placed. Seats ranged at the back of the tables round the walls sufficed, with these tables, to fill up half the room, across which a stout barrier of timber was drawn. Beyond that partition appeared a well-sawdusted floor and no seats. Here the Cuckfield public were to assemble.

It was an impressive sight to see the population of this rural spot advance to the scene of trial. The magistrates had taken their places – a group of patriarchs – at the head of the table. Lefroy Mapleton, preceded by a county policeman and followed by one, had comfortably sunk into an arm-chair; the reporters and lawyers had taken their places: and then came the crowd. Their faces were a 'three-volume story', their behaviour was a study. They could only see by either crowding up to the barricade or leaning over each other's shoulder, yet, broiling hot as the day was, and almost suffocating as was the odour of pigsties which came in through the half-opened windows, they cheerfully rushed up, ready, apparently, to die of suffocation rather than lose one twitch of the prisoner's face or one glimpse of his counsel. "Ee's a wisperin',' said one, singularly like Lefroy in appearance. 'His hair is very rough,' lisped a pretty, delicate girl, as she looked pityingly over the barricade. 'Why don't they 'ancuff 'im?' asked a man with a red face, who looked like a butcher. 'Wich is the murderer?' roared out a farmer's boy. Cuckfield was evidently having a great treat, for Lefroy Mapleton was in full view. There was a decrepid old man who could scarcely toddle and there were lads in their teens, some farm labourers, and, for all I know, the most remarkable people in the district, all as full of excitement at witnessing the spectacle before them as though each had been the proud possessor of the reward which had been offered for the capture of the accused.

There he sat, a direct contradiction of every phrenologist and physiognomist in the world. I can safely say I have seldom seen a more thoughtful, harmless face, with a broad and deep benevolent forehead, quiet, meditative eyes, a cranium that showed none of the supposed characteristics of the murderer; a pallid countenance that might have been merely 'sicklied o'er with the pale cast of thought', and that kind of indecisive mouth which those who are always open to convincing argument are popularly supposed to possess. Lefroy Mapleton seemed to be a man in whose presence any old gentleman might safely place his handkerchief over his head and take a nap in a railway carriage. True that he had a retreating chin, but therein he showed the principal characteristic of higher humanity, for have not Darwin and his disciples shown that with advancing civilisation has come a receding and diminishing chin, and that a day will arrive when very intellectual, benevolent, and well-conducted people will have little or no chin at all? The fact that Lefroy Mapleton has but a small chin was consequently a point in his favour, and had a phrenologist been on the bench in place of the venerable gentleman who presided over the Cuckfield Court, I am not sure that he would not forthwith have released the prisoner, and arrested someone else in his place.

I have said Lefroy wore a thoughtful look. His demeanour during the earlier part of the examination and while the details of evidence against him were read by Mr Pollard was that of a man with a critical air, as though he had been asked to pronounce an opinion on an essay which the lawyer had written and in which, by the bye, he took no particular interest.

The whole scene and the demeanour of the prisoner carried me strangely back to a very similar spectacle enacted in the summer of 1878 in the city of Berlin. There too, seated in a chair, coolly listening to evidence which was being produced minute after minute to prove him an assassin, sat Hoedel, the man who had fired at the Kaiser. A poor

T. W. Best

TALBOT FAMILY HOTEL,

Commercial and Posting House

CUCKFIELD

Commodious Apartments. Families Boarded by the week.

Horses and Carriages for Hire

neck it was which in a few days was to be cleft by the executioner's axe, and a thin meagre body which the court, as it sat, was intent upon placing in the grave. Yet there was the same calm, quiet, sometimes careful, sometimes abstracted air which marked Lefroy, the same benevolent cast of features, the same inoffensive face. Seated like Lefroy's examiners, sat also Hoedel's judges, at a long, baize-covered table, wearing no wigs or paraphernalia of the courts, but for all the world just such a set of country gentlemen as the administrators of Cuckfield justice. The public, too, was behind a barrier, and the reporters sat at a table; so, for a few minutes, I felt that I might once more have been listening to the evidence given by witnesses of Hoedel's trial, and waiting for the verdict that was to consign him to death.

Mr Pollard, the Solicitor to the Treasury, is a man of engaging manner and jovial mien, and had he been addressing a meeting of intimate friends upon a most pleasant and agreeable subject, he could not have unfolded the charge against the prisoner with more comfortable or amiable an air. Every word he uttered, if proved, was a nail in the coffin of the man who quietly reclined in the armchair at his side, and yet he proceeded with all the air of a man who would not for the whole world give the slightest trouble to anybody in the place – who had a little statement to make that was, perhaps, on the whole, worth listening to, but which, on so hot a day, must necessarily be a little tedious, and consequently could only be delivered in a half-apologetic tone. There was nothing of the tone of a prosecutor about the orator, still less of a public prosecutor demanding justice for an outrageous crime.

Lefroy, as I have said, seemed to be one of the least interested in the discourse; the ladies and gentlemen crushed against the barricade were far more demonstrative in the attention they paid. 'Een't 'ee a-givin' it to 'un?' said one from whose nose and forehead the perspiration streamed in large drops. The quiet manner of Mr Pollard had evidently no misleading effect on him.

Yet calm and soft as was the manner of the prosecutor, the scene was grim enough in all conscience. Close to the constable who guarded the prisoner sat a keen-visaged

THE BRIGHTON RAILWAY TRAGEDY – PERCY LEFROY MAPLETON BEFORE THE MAGISTRATES AT CUCKFIELD

detective, Inspector Jarvis, with a black bag containing damning evidence of a foul deed. Opposite was the chief of the detective department of Scotland-yard, the astute Superintendent Williamson – no agreeable neighbour for a criminal. There were witnesses at hand with all sorts of unpleasant details bearing upon the narrative which Mr Pollard unfolded. The machinery of the law was represented by the magistrates on the bench and the clerk of the court; the constables who guarded the doors and the lawyers who watched the case were all in full working order. The order of the place was undisturbed quiet; but it was the kind of quiet that often accompanies death.

Wednesday, July 20:

One warm day in Calcutta, the Prince of Wales and suite stood in a small room, interested spectators of a striking scene. A cobra that had bitten a dog and killed it almost instantaneously was wandering about the floor, defiant in air, reckless in bearing, to all appearances caring for nothing, when suddenly a visible change came over its conduct. No blow had been struck at it, no weapon hurled at it, and yet in an instant it was cowering and almost shivering – regarding a something which so far was visible to scarce anyone or anything but the snake. That something was much more harmless in look than the snake itself; it was only a quiet, ferret-like creature, interested for the moment in matters quite foreign to the snake which was now crouching in the corner. Yet to the cobra, venomous, deadly as it was, the look of that mongoose was as the sight of death, for its instinct told it that the quiet rodent would presently clasp it in a deadly embrace, and it was for this that the mongoose had been brought.

My recollection yesterday morning at Cuckfield Court was irresistibly carried back to that curious scene. Lefroy had taken his seat, and was making himself comfortable in the old armchair which he had occupied last Friday, expecting, no doubt, the same – to him – tedious and monotonous kind of examination to which the Court had been subjected by the placid, good-humoured Mr Pollard, when suddenly there appeared in the doorway of the Court, accompanied by Mr Superintendent Williamson, the lithe form and keen visage of Mr Harry Bodkin Poland, the Senior Counsel to the Treasury. From the lawyer came no glance of recognition, no long piercing look at the individual who lounged in the armchair, and yet the moment the occupant of that armchair descried him, his behaviour altogether changed. The listlessness had gone as by magic, the 'bored', unamused attitude had changed, as the eye of Lefroy rested anxiously upon the celebrated lawyer who had appeared on the scene. It was the first look of apprehension and nervousness I had as yet noticed on the part of the prisoner; but it was one that told a singular tale.

Justice standing blindfolded, impartially holding the scales, when skilfully carved in good marble, or well depicted on canvas, is an impressive spectacle; but Justice with its hat cocked on one side, possibly because Justice, as embodied in the persons of three Cuckfield magistrates, is afraid of catching cold in its head from a ventilating window, does not come up to the standard of dignity required by historical scenes.

Yet if the appearance of the

'For the Crown.' A caricature of Harry Bodkin Poland by 'Spy' (Leslie Ward), which appeared in Vanity Fair, *March 3, 1886.*

Bench lacked something, the attitude of that most unhappy of police officials, Detective-Sergeant Holmes, who allowed Lefroy to escape on the day of the murder, was fifty times less imposing. It is not given to every man to possess a brain capable of grasping what is in the mind of a lawyer who is cross-examining him, and Holmes, half bewildered by the sense of blunders made, and quite puzzled as to what Mr Dutton, the prisoner's counsel, might be driving at, as he questioned and re-questioned him, got at last into a state of helpless confusion. A more pitiable spectacle has seldom been seen in a magisterial court. Mr Poland, it is true, put this unfortunate detective a little at his ease; but his uprising was the signal for a renewal of the nervous movements of Lefroy, who at this time sat twitching his chin with his finger and most anxiously listening to the piercing questions and remarks made by the clever lawyer.

Nothing but the somewhat irritating character of some of the cross-examinations sufficed, apparently, to sustain the court in its severe trial under the oppressively hot weather. It converted what might have been fainting into simmering. The witnesses and the Court appeared, as the afternoon wore on, to be tired and sleepy, so much so that one witness had to be made to stand up before his intellect seemed capable of acting freely; by the time he had done, nearly all the Court was dozing. Even the chairman was at this period so overcome with the general drowsiness that some time had to be expended in explaining to him the exact meaning of the evidence.

But there is this to be said for the chairman – he is a very venerable man. A bottle of eau-de-Cologne and some iced water, with glasses, helped to brace the Court up at this time, but the intense heat soon had it all its own way again. The interest excited by the inquiry into a singularly horrible crime was not proof against the dulling influence of a powerful sun and two comets.*

Thursday, July 21:

Murder is dirty work. I remember some years ago finding myself seated in a Milan theatre, at which a piece called, if my memory serves me, *The Exquisite*, was to be performed. The hero of the piece was a carefully attired but languid personage who, with the very worst intentions of all kinds in the world, seldom did much harm, for the reason that the crime which presented itself to him was either too troublesome or otherwise objectionable. At length, however, a supreme temptation arrived. It was to assassinate an acquaintance.

For the individual who should be the victim, the Exquisite had no compassion; he would have regarded the corpse with infinite pleasure. And the death of the man would bring all kinds of most satisfactory and engaging pleasures to the gentleman, who re-arranged his delicate lace ruffles and smoothed down his silk velvet jacket as he thought of the possibilities in store for him if he would only go through

* Since the start of the month, England had sweltered under the worst heat-wave ever recorded by trustworthy thermometers; on most days, the temperature rose above 90°, and on some of those days got close to 100°. And 1881 was 'the year of the comets'; of the seven observed from different parts of the world, two were visible to the naked eye in England during June and July.

the formality of a murder. But at length, after sufficiently meditating upon the matter, the Exquisite decided not to butcher his friend. 'I could not do it,' he slowly lisped, 'without making such a mess that it would be positively inconvenient.'

There was a gentleman sitting next to me in the theatre who received this remark with derision. He would have been happy to kill anybody he knew for the sake of a little rum, Parmesan cheese, or macaroni, and he intimated as much.

The murderer of Mr Gold must have been a person strangely different in character from *The Exquisite*, and very much more like my neighbour in the theatre. For the tale told of Mr Gold's appearance when the body of that unfortunate gentleman was found in Balcombe tunnel, was sickening in the extreme.

It did not seem to annoy the prisoner, as he sat and heard how the old man's face was cut to pieces by a small knife, or how a bullet had been fired into the base of the helpless victim's brain. The spectacle that carriage presented in which the struggle took place was appalling in the extreme. On the floor was without doubt an aged man holding his head close to his neck in order to prevent someone who knelt upon him from cutting his throat. The old man's hands were meanwhile employed in trying to catch hold of his assassin, clawing at his neck, indeed, while the murderer gashed at his face just above the chin in default of getting at his throat. Such a *mauvais quart d'heure* was probably never exceeded in horror on a railway, for the struggle must have lasted very nearly till the distance between Merstham and Balcombe tunnels was traversed. It was certainly a dirty business, and the idea of the Italian author of 'The Exquisite' was a right one. There was no one in the court who listened to the horrible details given yesterday who could have come to any other conclusion.

The only person in the court who exhibited anything like cheerfulness was Mr Poland, but then his case was proceeding so well under his most businesslike hands that it would have been a difficult matter to repress that satisfaction which the progress of justice evidently gives this accomplished prosecutor.

Mr Hall, the acting house-surgeon at the Brighton Hospital, is a smart-looking young doctor, though the hesitancy of his answers scarcely supported this impression. He very properly examined the wound which subsequently turned out to be caused by the pistol by cutting out the surrounding flesh and searching for traces of gunpowder.

Like an English surgeon, a similarly practical young gentleman, who in 1877 chanced to be with the Turkish troops on the Danube, Mr Hall made a considerable discovery. 'Can you tell me,' asked the then active but now dead Aziz Pasha, 'why so many of the Egyptian soldiers lose the forefingers of their right hands, and so are incapacitated from further active service?' 'Let me look at the wounds,' quoth the young surgeon. The men were paraded. 'You see,' said the doctor, 'that these finger stumps are filled with grains of powder, and it will therefore be plain to your Excellency that the rifles that did the mischief must have been held quite close to the injured hands, as otherwise the grains of powder would not be here. The men have blown off their own fingers to escape further fighting!' 'Mashallah!' exclaimed Aziz Pasha to the young Giaour,

'Allah hath given great wisdom. Let every man who comes in without a forefinger on his right hand in future be shot forthwith.' And from that day few Egyptians lost that finger.

Mr Hall, by carefully looking at Mr Gold's wound, proved the ready work of the pistol, and the distance at which it was discharged. His recognition of Lefroy, or rather Lefroy's recognition of him, was almost theatrical, for the prisoner evidently did not enjoy Mr Hall's appearance, and strove hard to hide his emotion at first, though when the witness eventually got a little mixed up in his evidence, Lefroy began to regard him quite favourably.

Meanwhile, the Chairman of the Court went on, as was his wont, making the most voluminous notes of the evidence. 'Wot's ee a writin' of?' asked a Cuckfielder. ''Ee's gitin' ready for 'is summin' up,' was the reply. It can hardly be that the magistrate entertained a like conviction. Neither a summing-up nor the tedious, irritating cross-examination of the various witnesses seemed, however, to be needed, for, after all, a magisterial investigation is not a court of assize, and Lefroy has yet to go before a jury of his peers. Still, as the Chairman did not stop the cross-examinations, they went on. 'Did you say,' asked Mr Dutton, for the hundredth time, 'that the prisoner told you there were two persons in the carriage with him?' 'Yes,' was the inevitable reply; whereupon the Chairman leant earnestly forward, asked in a solemn tone, 'Two?' and then once more wrote that down very carefully.

The whole business grew tedious as the afternoon wore on. The attempts of Mr Dutton to show that Lefroy, at the time of his visit to the Brighton Hospital, looked insane, perhaps enlivened the situation a little, but, on the whole, it may be said that the proceedings waxed tamer and tamer till they ended.

Friday, July 22:

On Wednesday night a strange scene was witnessed at the door of the Talbot Hotel, Cuckfield. Four policemen were being got into line, while four others were being formed up in such a way as to compose the sides of half a square. 'When the prisoner comes,' said the sergeant who was getting the men into position, 'you will let him go into the hollow and then march.'

The Cuckfielders gathered round, eyes wide open and mouths agape, for they felt something of surpassing interest to them was about to happen. That 'something' was at hand. In another minute a tall, thin, cadaverous young man, tightly held by the left arm by a sturdy policeman, supported, too, on the other side, by another constable, and followed by four men in a line, passed through the door of the hotel, entered the hollow of the half-square, which, being closed up by the newly-arrived policemen, was consequently formed into a square, and moved off down the street, followed by the natives of the place as though it had been the most entrancing spectacle ever witnessed.

It was not 'entrancing', yet it was distinctly painful. The wretched appearance of the central figure in that procession as it moved slowly down the principal thoroughfare of the dull village was such as was capable of moving the most careless mind. Charged with a barbarous murder, in the clutch of the police, surrounded, in fact, by the myrmidons of justice, Lefroy presented a picture such as is, happily, but seldom to be seen in a civilised country. There was no attempt at mobbing him; there were no shouts uttered; the unhappy prisoner was, if not exactly pitied, at least to a certain extent regarded with a feeling akin to commiseration – his looks were so depressing.

Scarcely less saddening were they yesterday morning when he entered the Cuckfield Court once more and re-took his seat in the armchair. The appearance of the court, with the venerable gentlemen, who are the habitual inspectors of the county lunatic asylum, taking perpetual notes; the Cuckfield population beyond the barrier; the array of weary reporters, and the group of police and lawyers, was not calculated, perhaps, to raise the spirits of anybody who had to enter it. But beyond that, however successful the defence of Lefroy may eventually be – a point upon which I desire to express no opinion whatever – the evidence of the proceeding days had not been of a character to render him happier than he ordinarily was or more at his ease. It may therefore be taken as not at all surprising if, on this the fourth and last day of his examination, the prisoner seemed a little 'low'. If he had exhibited any cheerfulness under the circumstances it would have indeed been astonishing. All the high spirits of the court seemed to have concentrated themselves in Mr Poland alone. That experienced lawyer was evidently in his element.

What a miserable thing is poverty! The witnesses of the early morning had been heard, and the Court had adjourned for a comfortable lunch, when Sergeant Tobutt having been called, a list of the pawntickets found by him in Lefroy's bloodstained overcoat pocket was read out. Strange indeed was the record. A metal watch, a suit of dress clothes, four plated spoons, two coats and trousers – what a bundle of articles for a man who at the time was professing to be the recipient of £1,000 a year! The prisoner would not have pawned the clothes – he may have wished, for various reasons, to get rid of the plated spoons – unless he had been in dire want. Yet there he was at the pawnbroker's, striving hard for a few shillings. The incident suggested many thoughts of a serious nature, but none more so than the idea that, had Lefroy never been in such dire want at the time of pawning these articles, his friends might not have been put to the expense of these proceedings at Cuckfield.

Inspector Swanson is one of the keenest and, if the term can be used, most detective-like Scotchmen that it would be possible to find. Lefroy may have received him in 32, Smith-street, Stepney, with coolness, but the appearance of such an officer of police was not certainly calculated to inspire a suspected man with confidence. I am afraid that Mr Swanson's manner of announcing himself as he entered the room was not quite that of the most agreeable visitor. His attitude as he stood opposite Lefroy yesterday did not at any rate suggest that. There are many people in the world whom a person hiding from general observation would prefer to see rather than Inspector Swanson. The business-like way in which he proceeded with his evidence suggested what his manner was when he was in the room. He had actually taken down the prisoner's words in a memorandum book at the very moment when Lefroy was in his grasp. No wonder that Mr Dutton refrained from cross-examining him.

Inspector Jarvis, who had accompanied Mr Swanson to the house, was a very fit companion indeed. As they stood side by side, while the depositions of Mr Swanson were being read over and Mr Jarvis was waiting to give his evidence, they certainly appeared patterns of what two such men should be. The chances of escape remaining with anyone who was in their hands would be very slight.

Mr Jarvis also created no very favourable impression upon Lefroy, who probably remembered pretty vividly the close searching to which this sharp detective had subjected him. If he did not recollect it before, he certainly had good reason for doing so when Mr Jarvis produced the bloodstained clothes which he had discovered in the locked-up drawer and the false whiskers and moustache. What Lefroy had intended to do with a pair of great bushy brown whiskers and moustache half a dozen shades lighter than his hair, I do not pretend to say. In a French court they would have tried the whiskers on to see what effect would have been produced, but this was not done in Cuckfield.

The production of a collar saturated with blood and a piece of a woollen shirt from which a great deal of the top part had evidently been torn away caused Lefroy to begin writing notes for his counsel with much energy, as such things well might. Mr Poland's manner at this moment, as he measured the bloodstained collar, and compared it carefully with the others found in Lefroy's possession, can only be described as one of unqualified satisfaction. When the collar was at length placed upon the table, a more sensitive lawyer gingerly pushed it away from him by means of a roll of paper, and refreshed himself after the effort by sniffing at a bottle of eau-de-Cologne. Mr Poland was far too business-like, however, for this, and took charge of the collar forthwith.

The clear and concise evidence of Mr Jarvis, followed as it was almost immediately after by the positive identification by the pawnbroker's assistant of Lefroy as the man who pledged the revolver, and besides as the pledger of the other articles, tickets for which Sergeant Tobutt found in Lefroy's coat, very fairly justified Mr Poland, shortly afterwards, in bringing the examination to a close.

Enough had been adduced to warrant the magistrates in sending the prisoner for trial before Her Majesty's judges, and this course was ultimately taken with the due formalities.

Saturday, July 23:

There appears to be an impression that, in accordance with his express wish, Lefroy will be tried at the Old Bailey, but in no case can a change of venue be made unless it is declared that there is a positive prejudice existing in a county to such an extent that a prisoner would not be fairly dealt with in a legal point of view by the jurors empanelled and others concerned. If the accused were removed to Newgate, it would be under Palmer's Act, but in the ordinary course he will take his trial at Maidstone Assizes in the autumn, he having been committed to Maidstone Gaol.

Wednesday, November 2:

MAIDSTONE, Tuesday Evening.

The opening of an assize in a county town is a matter of considerable interest. It fills the hotels; it brings into the place the gentry of the neighbourhood who are summoned upon the grand jury; it witnesses the arrival of those who are to be tried for offences more or less thrillingly horrible; and it is accompanied by all the pomp and circumstance of the Judges' entry.

The town snatched a hurried repose on the advent of the morning which was to witness the gaol delivery. Then came a somewhat early awakening, and a bustling about in preparation for the looked-for event, and by nine o'clock so much of Maidstone as could find its way to the front of the gaol in which the law courts are situated assembled, and braving the piercing cold and wind, patiently waited the coming of the Judges.

Inside the court, where the assize was to be opened, a curious picture presented itself. It wanted still nearly two hours to the time when the representatives of justice should arrive. Yet already the 'public' had put in an appearance. What possible interest the majority of those who had thus gathered together could take in what was going forward it was difficult to conceive. There were, for instance, a very old lady and a little girl who had not yet reached her teens, a sergeant of infantry and a couple of very young ladies, and an old gentleman so deaf that when a policeman begged him to move to another place he was unable to catch a word that was said to him, and a few youths who ought to have been at school.

These and more of such sort were the 'public' assembled to welcome the envoys of the Queen, and there they were, perched up in a gallery, staring round, and probably wondering what was going to happen. Down in the well of the court had been packed, in an enclosure, the petty jury, and in another the grand jury,* the latter endeavouring to solve the problem of how twenty-three gentlemen could be placed in seats scantily measured off for eighteen; while clustering round the clerk of the court were reporters armed with bulky note-books, and clinging as tenaciously to their seats as though they expected at any moment to be seized and summarily ejected.

If inside the court, however, the hours of waiting dragged slowly, outside the very minutes must have seemed to be days long. It is true the populace assembled had the satisfaction of witnessing the fixing of telegraphic apparatus specially conveyed thither for the reporting of the Lefroy trial, true also that on the arrival of the various witnesses against the man charged with the murder of Mr Gold there was a certain excitement, but the cold wind must have severely taxed the determination of the wistful throng for all that. It is not given to everybody to disregard a thermometer which stands at nearly freezing point and an air which is laden every now and again with thin flakes of snow. Still, a great treat

* Since the Assize of Clarendon, 1166, bills of indictment had to be laid before a grand jury of from twelve to twenty-three persons. If, in a particular case, the grand jury found a true bill against the accused, the bill became an indictment and was presented to the petty jury. An Act of 1933 abolished grand juries except for the counties of London and Middlesex (chiefly for offences committed abroad), and the Criminal Justice Act, 1948, abolished them altogether.

The Session House, Maidstone

was in store for those who could wait – a treat which was made up of gorgeous carriages and a sight of two Judges in full-bottomed wigs and scarlet and ermine robes, of a High Sheriff in full uniform, and, last but by no means least, a wonderful apparition as of a functionary in light blue, carrying a cocked hat astride his brow, and bearing aloft a long silver trumpet with which to blow three blasts as Justice alighted from the carriages and entered the courts. There was this happiness for those who tarried, and glad were they who, being able to bear up with the cold, heard at last the trumpet's sound, saw him of the light blue uniform and enormous hat, gazed upon the gold chain of Lord Chief Justice Coleridge, and witnessed the alighting of the High Sheriff.

The actual entry into the Crown Court was accomplished with but little excitement. Is it an indictable offence to say that the proceedings might have been designated sleepy? The calling over of a long list of grand jurors, beginning with Sir William Hart-Dyke, and ending with an unknown esquire, awakened no enthusiasm, and even the 'Proclamation against Vice', strictly enjoining her Majesty's lieges not to play cards on Sunday, and always to go to church, failed to draw from the listeners any sign of emotion. To the bulk of the audience, the declaration that dice-throwing on the Sabbath must not be permitted in even private houses seemed, I regret to say, a matter of the very slightest importance. I had never heard the proclamation before, and imagined till the date 1860 was read out that it had been indited by William Rufus, and would finish up with some reference to the curfew bell. It strangely enough ended 'God save the Queen', so that I gathered the ceremony to be one of modern make; but I fear no such reflection ever crossed the minds of the majority of the Maidstonians who heard it.

At length these preliminary proceedings were over, and the grand jury standing up, Lord Coleridge began the practical business of the assize. I do not propose to follow his lordship through his charge to the twenty-three gentlemen who leaned forward, apparently regarding all he said with the deepest interest. With the address of the Lord Chief Justice, the grand jurors retired, and then the court suddenly emptied.

Outside were still the witnesses in the Lefroy case grouped together, waiting to be called, and round them the Maidstone populace. And at the moment I am writing, the crowd still lingers, now recognising prominent personages connected with the trial, and now pointing out people who have nothing whatever to do with the case, glad, at any rate, to find themselves the spectators, if not of one of the last scenes in the Brighton Railway tragedy, at least of the circumstances attendant upon the trial of him who is accused, and who, if report be correct, confidently hopes for an honourable acquittal.

The trial of Lefroy began on the morning of Friday, November 4, and ended in the afternoon of the following Tuesday:

The jury retired at twenty-five minutes to three o'clock.

At a quarter to three, they returned into court and answered to their names. As all eyes were turned upon the prisoner at the bar, still seated as of yore, the Clerk of the Court demanded the verdict, 'How say you – Guilty or not guilty?' The foreman rose, his face crimson with emotion, and while one or two of his colleagues showed signs of almost breaking down under the excitement of the moment, replied, 'Guilty'.

Up rose Lefroy at a touch from the gaolers who now gathered around him, and, placing his hands behind him, advanced to the rails of the dock. The Clerk asked him, 'Have you or have you not anything to say for yourself why the Court should not pass sentence upon you?'

The Prisoner (in a firm voice): 'Merely to thank the jury for the careful – '

The remainder of the prisoner's remarks, if there were any, was lost in the proclamation of silence while sentence of death was pronounced.

Throughout the whole trial, one dreadful object has ever and anon appeared in view. On the first day of the case – as far back as last Friday – it could be seen, nestled snugly under the lea of the edge of the desk at which the Lord Chief Justice sat, partially hidden too by the lavender gloves of his lordship, and now almost disappearing from view as the books with which the judge dealt were pushed hither and thither. Then it came nearer, and was presently to be found, not placed against the wood-work as before, but between the note-book which his lordship had filled and the one on which he was writing – still nearer, yesterday getting under his lordship's elbow, till this morning it was to be seen mixed up with the papers on which the judge had made the notes for his speech. From there but one more movement was possible; it must either disappear altogether, or be placed upon his lordship's head. And it was there – the Black Cap – that I saw it, when, on glancing from the pallid prisoner in the dock to the flushed jury in the box at a quarter to three this afternoon, I turned to hear the Lord Chief Justice pronounce the sentence.

The silence of death prevailed; the prisoner was about to hear his doom, and yet there he stood, apparently altogether at ease, pallid perhaps, but for all that collected and self-possessed. There was a moment when he grasped the rails in front of him, and swayed as though he were about to fall; but that was only for a second – he was quickly himself again, and, folding his arms, turned his gaze once more from the Judge, when, the sentence being finished, he took hold of the rails again with one hand, while with the other outstretched in the direction of the jury, he said, in a firm tone of voice and with a theatrical air, 'Some day you will learn, when too late, that you have murdered me!' Another instant and he had disappeared through the floor to the cells below, surrounded and jealously guarded by turnkeys, and so passed away to that place where he is to be excuted and buried.

He was conveyed during the evening from the county prison at Maidstone to the South-Eastern Station, under a strong escort of local constabulary. A large number of persons had assembled to witness his departure, but there was no demonstration from the public. The condemned man, having reached Lewes, was at once conveyed to the prison in a cab, attended by two warders. A large crowd had gathered, and greeted him with groans and jeers. It is stated that the execution will take place in Lewes Gaol on the 29th inst.

Saturday, November 12:

Although the memorial has not yet been drawn up asking for a remission of the sentence upon Lefroy, it is understood that a considerable quantity of evidence is being got together, showing that not only was the family of the convict tainted with madness, but that he himself has shown at times distinct indications of unaccountable delusions. The case is consequently not being abandoned. Meanwhile, Lefroy continues to declare his innocence. He himself denies the charge of insanity, and would only ask for respite on the ground that the evidence given against him was untrue and insufficient for his conviction.

Monday, November 28:

LEFROY CONFESSES

THE MURDERS OF LIEUTENANT ROPER AT CHATHAM, AND MR. GOLD.

EXTRAORDINARY DETAILS.

HOMICIDAL MANIA.

REPRIEVE REFUSED.

ANOTHER PETITION YESTERDAY.

On Saturday last, the convict Percy Lefroy made a confession to the governor and chaplain of Lewes Gaol and subsequently to his relative Mrs Brickwood that not only was he guilty of the crime for which he has been convicted, but that he was also the murderer of the late Lieutenant Roper, of the Royal Engineers, who, it will be remembered, was shot in Chatham Barracks on Feb. 11 last, and over whose fate a cloud of mystery has hung ever since that date. The convict has furthermore given the chaplain a written history of his life, wherein, besides these two great crimes, he avows the commission of others, which, if his own condemnation can be believed, must rank him henceforward among the greatest malefactors of the age. Much suspicion must, of course, attach to such of these statements as are unsupported by collateral facts, since the convict has shown so constant a habit of falsification; but there are those among them to which a comparison of dates and particulars lends serious confirmation.

In regard to the murder of Lieutenant Roper, the body of this officer was found lying at the head of the stairs leading to his quarters, pierced by a bullet. Nothing had been taken from his pockets or his apartment. The deed seemed to be that of a robber surprised and hastening to escape, or of an assassin animated by personal motives.

After all these months of mystery, it appears that Lefroy has declared himself the author of this tragedy. In the light of so terrible an avowal, slight facts which are recalled by his relations assume a new importance. They remember that at the date of the assassination Lefroy did, indeed, visit the neighbourhood, and that he returned from it haggard, pale, and dreading pursuit; giving contradictory accounts of his proceedings and awakening suspicions now confirmed. Explanation is alleged for the cruel deed in a quarrel which the convict had with Lieutenant Roper on the subject of a well-known actress, Miss Violet Cameron, for whom the condemned youth cherished, it seems, an imaginative passion. His story about the quarrel is so far corroborated that his cousin Mrs Clayton distinctly remembers that one night early in the year he came home and told her that he had had a great row in Piccadilly about Miss Cameron.

This lady's name has been more than once mentioned by the convict, and he certainly appears to labour under a perfect delusion to represent to his relatives, indeed, that he was actually married to her, and it was said he carried her portrait about with him. Prior to his trial, he persisted in assuring his solicitor that she was the companion with whom he had arranged to travel to Brighton on the day of Mr Gold's murder; and so recently as Friday last he made a statement respecting Miss Cameron which, if uttered by a perfectly sane person, would be accurately characterised as an impudent falsehood. He assured his solicitor that having written to the lady expressing sorrow for his conduct in vilifying her name, he had just received from her a reply, granting her forgiveness and enclosing him some flowers. It is almost needless to add that whether on Lefroy's part this be a delusion or a wilful misstatement, Miss Cameron has never written to the convict nor sent him any flowers.

As regards the murder of Mr Gold, his account is sufficiently full to show that no mystery here remains. The criminal has cleared up every point of doubt, and if he has been as accurate in regard to the assassination of the Engineer officer at Chatham, a veil which seemed impenetrable has been withdrawn from an equally awful occurrence, while those who sympathised with the convict on account of his youth must now regard him as old in crime, and presenting such a specimen of perverted humanity that it would be indeed a relief if we could think him mad.

It is not even certain that these two frightful crimes exhaust the terrible account of heinous sin which Lefroy is about to explain. He himself has added to the crushing load statements which seem to indicate that he tried to rob one of his friends, Captain Simmons, and perhaps to poison him with prussic acid, which the miserable youth had obtained. There are also very suspicious circumstances – it is said – which go to suggest that Lefroy has had something to do with the disappearance of a third person named Clarke, which name, it may be remembered, he assumed when hiding from the officers of justice at Stepney.

The Home Secretary has rejected the petition of the friends who openly declare Lefroy mad from his youth up, the offspring of mad ancestors, always acting a part, always lying, always, as he himself says, 'behaving like two people in one'. The solicitor of the convict has since urged these new confessions as proofs of 'homicidal mania'. No serious doubt could have been entertained at the Home Office as to the propriety of carrying the law into effect. There is not much likelihood of his having further disclosures to make such as would justify a postponement of the execution.

Leading article on Wednesday, November 30:

LEFROY paid the extreme penalty of the law yesterday morning, and, with his shameful death, public interest in all that concerned the story of his crime will naturally soon fade away. The memory of criminals, unless they be at the same time great historical personages, is happily short-lived, yet, by what might seem a paradox, every detail in the life of a notorious culprit is, for the time, full of interest for his contemporaries.

This appetite of the mind for particulars of great crimes and criminals has been stigmatised as vulgar. It is only vulgar in so far as it is universal, the common attribute of every age, people, and clime.

The Athenians, who, thrice each year, at the festival of BACCHUS, gathered, thirty thousand strong, in their vast theatre to listen to the magnificent trilogies of the earliest and greatest dramatists, 'supped full of horrors'. Where in life or literature can be found a story more terrible than that of SOPHOCLES' *Oedipus the King*, in which the hero kills his father and marries his mother JOCASTA? In much the same manner, the British public take an extraordinary interest in the career of such a deplorable character as LEFROY, not by any means, as we think, out of a morbid love for the commonplace details of a murder done for the greed of gain and bare of one single noble or redeeming trait, such as Sir FRANCIS BACON calls the wild justice of revenge, but because it is, like all other striking crimes, a suggestive episode of the great human tragedy in which everyone plays his part.

BACON also says: 'There is no man doth a wrong for wrong's sake; but thereby to purchase himself profit, or pleasure, or honour, or the like.' Thus when a human being does a wrong altogether out of the common, his fellow creatures are impelled by an irresistible and natural curiosity to study his diseased nature and to trace his misguided motives to their source.

The mere narrative of how LEFROY murdered Mr GOLD in a first-class compartment of a railway carriage proceeding from London to Brighton is subordinated in thought to the long mental process of corruption and the course of circumstances and events which led up to the fatal deed. Facts and details are only in so far interesting as they explain the sin and the passion, the dark necessity and the nefarious desire. By this, in many instances, unconscious study, many a mind may usefully perceive that LEFROY's primary motive was egotism. A perpetual, diseased love of self led his footsteps by slow degrees towards the gallows. He was ready at all times to render subservient to his own wants and desires, without remorse or scruple, the property, the reputation, the confidence of his fellow creatures, and at last even human life itself.

The curiosity and interest excited on behalf of such a psychological study need not necessarily be morbid. The feeling is eminently natural and profoundly human. Public attention dwells on the life story of a great criminal as it hunts out the moral of a literary or pictorial satire. In both cases the analytical faculty stimulates the intellect to an exhaustive inquiry. Men follow the career of a LUCRETIA and of an 'Idle Apprentice' with as abiding a relish for the lesson conveyed as if BULWER and HOGARTH had founded their teachings on reality instead of fiction. LEFROY, on the other hand, is the visible villain of a human drama, and, therefore, so much more interesting, because so much more real, than any possible creation of the fancy.

Whenever an execution of some remarkable criminal takes place, the question of capital punishment is sure to crop up. Opinion is greatly divided as to the justice of the death penalty – at present never enforced but in extreme cases. Between fifty and sixty years ago, the annual average of executions in England amounted to nearly one hundred, but with the passing of milder laws, the number has happily decreased. A glance at the statistics of murder in England and Wales, compiled from the returns of coroners' juries, will show how comparatively seldom the hangman is now called for. For twenty years past, the number of culpable homicides from year's end to year's end has maintained a remarkable equal average.

Attribute the fact to what cause we may, draw every possible deduction from the figures, and the result remains that every succeeding twelve months produces almost the same number of homicides. During the past fifteen years, education has been gradually spreading over the land, material prosperity and refinement have vastly increased. The spirit of gentleness and of culture has permeated downwards until an ordinary mob of today is far less brutal than a similar crowd in the third quarter of the century; but still, the annual interval between the beginning of spring and the end of winter-time produces its comparatively equal tale of murders.*

How is this sum to be lessened?

* This remained true (though there was an enormous increase in the volume of other types of crime – by over 300 per cent from 1930 to 1959) till the Murder (Abolition of Death Penalty) Act 1965 was made permanent in December 1969.

Offences initially recorded as homicide

	Annual average	Per million population
1900–09	306	9.0
1910–19	275	7.5
1920–29	284	7.3
1930–39	321	7.9
1940–49	353	8.2
1950–59	315	7.1
1960–69	336	6.5
1970–79	512	10.4
1980–89	687	12.4

That, and that alone, is the problem with which statesmen and philanthropists have to deal. Tenderness towards the murderer is clearly a matter of secondary consideration. When someone suggested to ALPHONSE KARR that it was wrong of men to take life which they could not give, he replied agreeing with the proposition, but suggesting that the assassins should set the example. Society is its own master, and, inasmuch as we in Great Britain are ruled by majorities, directly the electoral majority expresses itself in favour of the abolition of capital punishment, such terrible and saddening scenes as that witnessed at Lewes Gaol yesterday morning will cease to exist.

There can, however, be only one justification for doing away with the death penalty, that of increasing the general safety against individuals of homicidal tendency. Public executions, as previously conducted, shocked the national sense of propriety. Condemned as brutalising, they were duly abolished. Private executions may possibly some day be doomed to a like fate, but, even while the death penalty continues to be enforced, they might perhaps be conducted with a greater degree of humanity than at present marks the last ministrations of the law. Founding its right on the Mosaic doctrine of 'an eye for an eye, and a tooth for a tooth', Society says to the potential murderer: If you kill another, you shall be killed in turn, the object being to make the death penalty deterrent. Revenge, however, in any shape, should be unknown to the law. In some parts of the world, in Switzerland for example, capital punishment was done away with in favour of perpetual imprisonment; but in course of time the Swiss found it advisable to recur to the simpler and, as in their case it proved, more efficacious deterrent of death.

Assuming Society to be possessed of an inalienable right to take the life of any citizen whose continued existence would be a source of public danger, the question arises under what circumstances should such right be enforced? That depends on the degree of culpability of the condemned criminal. Confirmed insanity is held to be a condonation of murder, hence we have a Criminal Lunatic Asylum at Broadmoor, where many undoubted murderers have passed the remainder of their useless and worthless lives, not altogether in discomfort, if forgotten by the world. But how shall we define the difference between homicidal mania, which reprieves from the gallow, and homicidal intention, for which there is no such excuse? 'Anger,' says the sage, 'is a brief madness'; and the law occasionally allows something for homicides committed under the influence of passion.

On the other hand, if we take a career like that of LEFROY, though it seems to display an abnormal condition of mind amounting to a monstrosity, yet no sufficient excuse was thought to be offered for a stay of execution. It would, however, appear that his grandfather and his father were both tainted with insanity. He was the offspring of old age. His physique was poor, and his mind from childhood upward out of balance. Nevertheless, he was gifted with intellectual faculties above the average, his education had not been neglected, nor his manners left destitute of polish. In his case, natural and acquired advantages were not lacking, but with all and above all the lad – for he was little more than a lad – was afflicted with a very palpable mental deformity. It seemed as if he could not speak the truth – as if, the ways of honour and dishonour being at the same time open to him, some familiar spirit of evil compelled him to take always the crooked path. He revelled in the practice of deceit, begotten of an insatiable egotism, as uncontrollable as the hunger of a wild beast. Gifted with a not unready pen, with a smooth tongue and plausible manners, he might easily have followed some honourable employment. He, however, wilfully chose the devious paths of fraud and crime, paths which finally and fatally led him – who so valued applause – to infamy and death at the hands of the common hangman.

Weighed in the balance of ordinary apprehension, LEFROY was no doubt sufficiently sane. To have excused him, Justice would have had to allow that all great badness is the same as madness. This wretched youth has passed to his last account bitterly expiating his false and wicked life; but public sentiment is assured of the wisdom and necessity of the stern sentence of the law. The miserable convict LEFROY – done to death on the very threshold of manhood – now lying stark and cold in a prison grave, thought to succeed without truth, virtue, or pity. Deceiving others, he cheated himself at last, fell from sin to sin, until conscience was dead, and the promptings of his wicked mind sounded like the voice of the evil one. What could be a sterner lesson of morality, or better worth pondering by youth? No sermon, however eloquent, could paint a moral more fraught with warning, terror, and reproof!

1903

Leading article on Wednesday, June 24:

Yesterday SAMUEL HERBERT DOUGAL was, at the Chelmsford Assizes, found guilty of the murder of Miss CAMILLE HOLLAND after a two days' trial. The evidence against him was overwhelming. What could be urged in his defence was too slight and trivial to stay for a moment the inexorable course of justice. But rarely have the mills of Heaven ground so slowly, and never perhaps have they proved so conclusively their power of grinding so small.

It was four years ago – in May, 1899 – that Miss HOLLAND was shot through the head and her body hidden in a ditch close to the Moat Farm; only a few weeks ago were her remains discovered, and the

May 1, 1903. The scene at Clavering during the inquest on the body of Miss Holland

halting foot of Justice began to limp to its goal.

The story itself is curious and interesting, albeit full of the details of a sordid intrigue and the workings of the coarsest greed. In the autumn of 1898, Miss HOLLAND, a lady apparently of cultivation and agreeable manners, who after her aunt's death was possessed of property to the value of six thousand pounds,* was visited at Elgin-crescent, Bayswater, by a man who was identified as DOUGAL, and for the next few months the man and the woman lived together as husband and wife at Hassocks, near Brighton, at Saffron Walden, and finally at the Moat Farm.

The last house, close to which was the scene of the murder, is an exceedingly lonely spot, at Clavering, Essex, approached by a narrow farm road, with no inhabited places in the vicinity, and far from the railway station. There was a ditch leading from the farmyard to the road, which DOUGAL began to fill up soon after commencing his tenancy, sometimes working with his own hands, sometimes directing the labourers in his employ. The work was not completed on the day when the prisoner decided to take the unhappy woman's life, and therefore afforded a ready-dug grave when the fatal shot was fired.

At Moat Farm DOUGAL and Miss HOLLAND lived for the early weeks of May, 1899, with only one servant, who had on more than one occasion to complain to her mistress of the soi-disant husband's behaviour. It must be remembered that the Moat Farm was taken on the strength of Miss HOLLAND's money, and, indeed, the life of the pair at this time was only rendered possible because the lady, who was about fifty-six years of age, had been foolish enough to be attracted by the prisoner, and to allow him to spend her money for her. Doubtless then rapidly came the moment of disenchantment and disagreement, and DOUGAL grew to be tired of his paramour, and to resent his position of dependence upon her bounty. Common libertine as he was all along – as the servant's experience proved – he soon conceived the black design of ridding himself of his companion, and on the 19th of May, according to the theory of the prosecution, became an actual murderer.

On that day Miss HOLLAND, dressed for a drive, was seen by her servant, to whom she said that she should not be long away, in a pony-cart with DOUGAL, apparently intending to do some shopping or attend to some other business which would not involve a protracted absence. She was never seen again. The prisoner seems to have put a weapon to her head, and shot her only a few yards away from the farm, hiding her body in the ditch before alluded to, where nearly four years afterwards it was found as damning evidence against the man with whom she had lived, and on whom she had squandered her money.

That no one else save DOUGAL could have committed this dastardly crime was rendered clear in the course of the trial. He was her paramour; he lived with her at the Moat Farm; he went out driving with her on the last day when she was seen alive; he was the man who immediately benefited by her death,

* The 1993 purchasing power of the 1903 £ is reckoned to be about £48 – therefore, the value of Miss Holland's 'dowry' was equivalent to well over a quarter of a million pounds in 1993.

and, as a matter of fact, he was first apprehended on a charge of forging her name on a cheque. The motive for the crime was therefore manifest. Nor, again, was there any doubt that the body found in the ditch was that of Miss HOLLAND. Her clothes were identified, especially her boots, made on special lasts by a shoemaker in 1897, for feet remarkably small. Rarely has evidence more conclusively pointed to the guilt of a prisoner. Although no eye saw his cowardly crime, and although for so long he had managed to escape even the breath of suspicion, DOUGAL found himself at last enmeshed in the toils of that avenging law which remorselessly tracks down the criminal.

The world is well rid of a man who, living in the companionship and on the money of a bright, clever, well-educated woman like CAMILLE HOLLAND, rewards her affection for purposes of vulgar greed by foul and brutal murder.

Miss Holland

A CAREER OF CRIME. REMARKABLE STORY.

Dougal's career stamps him as one of the most notorious criminals of the century. He is a man of smart military appearance, pleasant of speech, and polite of manner, attractions which have enabled him apparently to win the affections of undiscerning ladies both in America and in England, whom he has lured to their ruin.

While in the Army, he was stationed some time at Halifax, in Nova Scotia. He is a man of considerable education, and was chief clerk at the time to the commanding officer of the Royal Engineers. When Dougal first landed in Halifax, he was accompanied by a wife, who suddenly became ill and died. She was buried the following day. Three weeks after the death of the lady, Dougal sailed for England, and returned five weeks later with another woman, whom he introduced as his wife. It was stated in Halifax that this lady had a considerable fortune. She seemed on arrival to be in excellent health, but shortly afterwards she had fits of vomiting and coughing. In fourteen days the lady was dead, and on this occasion also the remains were buried the following day.

It is not disputed that when Dougal left Halifax, he persuaded a young woman to accompany him, and according to the latter's story the man had promised to marry her. It is also true that she returned to Halifax still single.

The man is next met at Aldershot, whence he wrote to friends in Halifax that his talents had been rewarded by a commission. Shortly afterwards he was appointed to some minor office at Dublin Castle, and amongst his duties was that of banking money. While employed in Ireland, he forged the cheques of two well-known members of the aristocracy. One refused to charge him, but the other did, and he was sentenced to twelve months' imprisonment. A considerable portion of this term was spent in a lunatic asylum.

In August, 1894, he made the acquaintance of another young lady. A matrimonial paper was the means of the introduction, and the scene of the first meeting, as in the case of Miss Holland, was Camberwell-green. He made love to the young lady, who is described as twenty-six years of age at the time, and good-looking. She possessed a little ready money and certain brewery shares. He induced her to sell the latter, and together they went to live in a country house on the outskirts of the village of Watlington, in Bucks, with the avowed intention of 'chicken farming'. Incubators and agricultural implements were bought, and the lady removed her furniture and pictures to the new home. Suddenly, in December, 1894, the man went away to London, and returned with another lady, whom he described as 'his wife'. The first lady seems to have continued to live at the house until February of the following year, when things became intolerable. She is known to have applied to the magistrates for protection, and alleged that she went in fear of her life. That day a policeman accompanied her home, and the following day, after borrowing money in the village for her journey, she left Dougal.

It is remarkable that at Watlington, as at Clavering, Dougal's arrival on the scene was warmly welcomed, and the first impression he made was invariably in his favour. On Sundays he attended the village church, and the local charities benefited by his subscription. He was a good shot and an enthusiastic patron of athletic sports.

An attempt will be made to secure the condemned man's reprieve on the present occasion, on the ground of his alleged lunacy while in prison for the forgery charge.

Wednesday, July 15:

Just before Samuel Herbert Dougal was executed in Chelmsford Gaol yesterday morning, the chaplain, after reciting the service, leaned anxiously forward to the culprit with an invitation to confess his crime. William Billington,* the executioner, paused. Dougal turned to the chaplain in blank amazement, as if he did not understand the question. Still more anxiously, the chaplain repeated his inquiry, which was really an exhortation: 'Dougal, guilty or not guilty?'

There was a moment's silence; then the doomed man answered, quietly, 'Guilty'. In an instant his life was over.

Dougal recently cried like a child half a dozen times a day. His breakdown began with the execution of Howell, the Colchester murderer, on the Tuesday previous. Howell had shared his seat in the chapel, had exercised with him, and smoked with him. Dougal's last day was spent in earnest preparation for the end. He went to chapel, and he gave up his usual morning exercise in order to draw up and execute, in the presence of the chaplain, his will and testament. It is believed that he bequeathed most of whatever he may be found to possess to his wife, who wrote pathetic letters to him during his confinement, and to the little daughter, to whom he appeared to have been much attached.

Yesterday morning, the condemned man rose at six o'clock, after a good night's sleep, and breakfasted an hour later on an egg, bread and butter, and tea. At 7.57 officials, together with the executioner and his assistant, proceeded to the condemned cell. The door opened, and Dougal was seen standing awaiting his visitors. Save for the absence of hat and collar, he was dressed in the same fashion as at Saffron Walden, before the justices, and at the Chelmsford trial. A warder advanced with brandy in a bottle, and Dougal drank from the tin can proferred him. Officers, bare-headed, lined each side of the short route of the solemn procession. Dougal walked unassisted to his doom. It was to be noticed how faultlessly he had polished his boots.

* The elder surviving son of James Billington, who was a Public Executioner on a regular basis from 1892 till his death in December 1901. During the first few years following his succession, William was usually assisted – and was in the execution of Dougal – by his brother John.

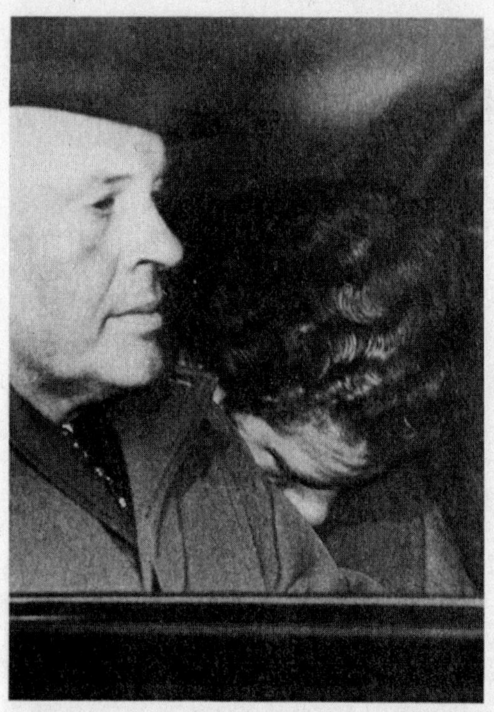

Derek Bentley being taken from Croydon Police Station on November 3, 1952, and Christopher Craig, below, on his way to the magistrates' court

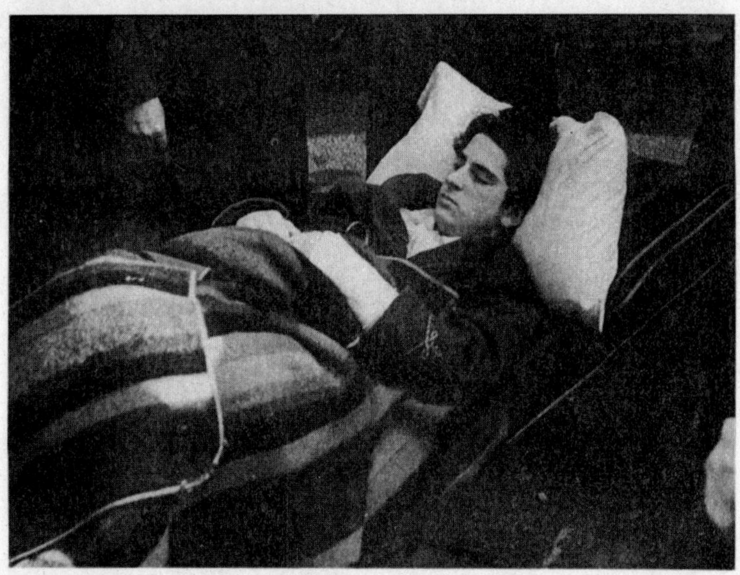

Lord Chief Justice Goddard, who presided over the trial of Craig and Bentley. Below: Christmas Humphries (the son of the judge in the Rattenbury-Stoner case), who led for the Crown

Francis Cassels and (below) John Parris, who represented Bentley and Craig respectively

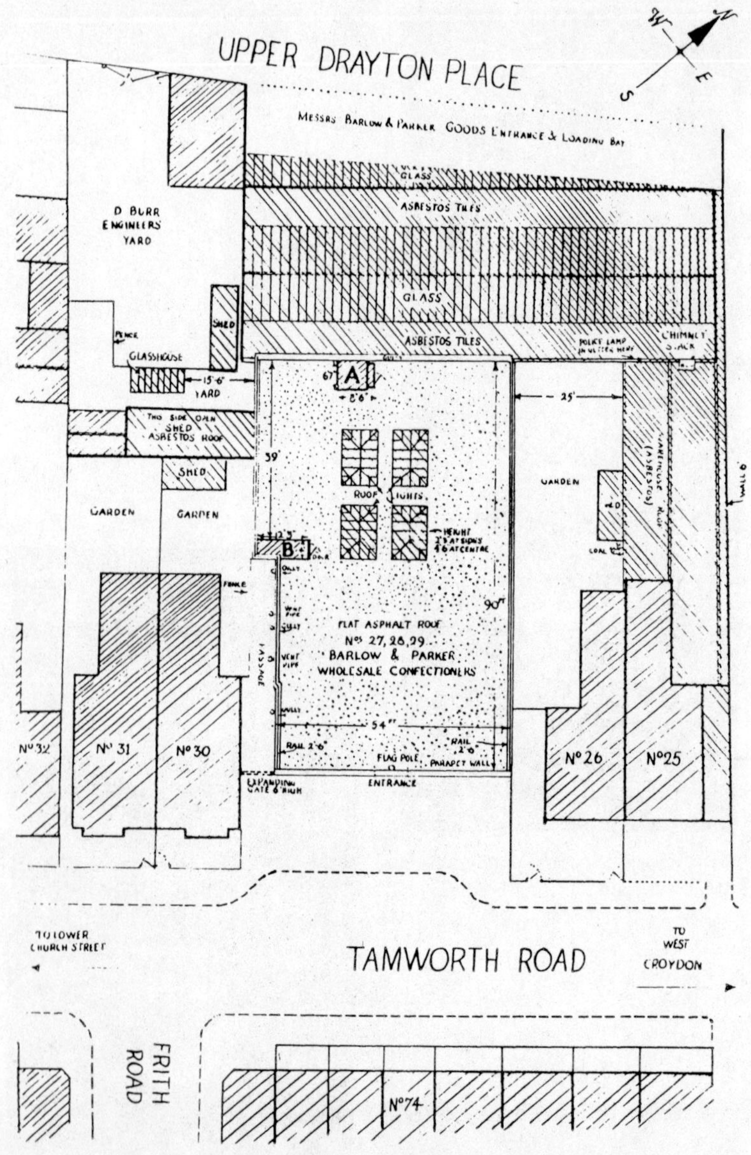

Plan of Barlow & Parkers premises, where the gun battle took place. 'A': head of lift-shaft. 'B': head of staircase. A trial exhibit

The roof, showing the head of the staircase, the lift-shaft (with the glass and asbestos roof behind), and the glass roof-lights. A trial exhibit.

Craig and Bentley

Mrs. Violet Van der Elst, campaigner against capital punishment, complaining at being moved on

The four policemen who received awards for their actions in the Craig and Bentley case: Detective Sergeant Fairfax and PCs MacDonald, Harrison and Jaggs

Police photographs of Peter Allen

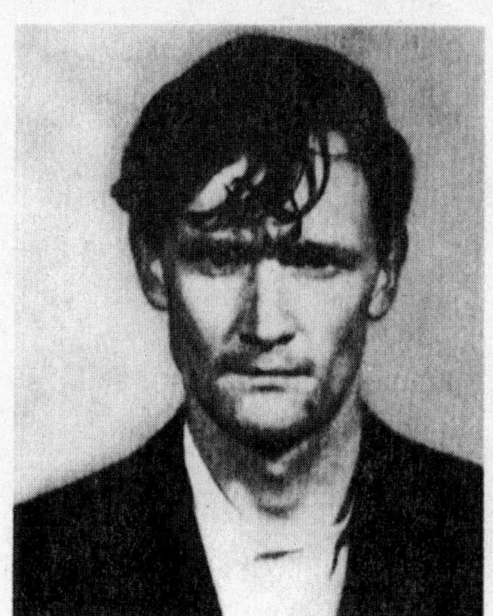

and Gwynne Evans

Albert Pierrepoint, following his retirement as executioner

Harry Allen celebrating his appointment as executioner in 1956

1915

Wednesday, March 24 (thirty-three weeks after the start of the Great War):

DEATHS IN A BATH

Not for many years has there been a case of alleged murder surrounded by such extraordinary circumstances as were revealed at Bow-street Police-court yesterday. The prisoner, a man named George Joseph Smith, aged 43, had previously been before the Court on a minor charge, during the hearing of which important developments had been foreshadowed, but the full story, as opened by Mr Archibald Bodkin, counsel for the Crown, was a truly amazing one.

Arrested on February 1, the prisoner was originally accused of causing a false entry to be made in a marriage register at Bath, and in the course of the subsequent proceedings, extending over several weeks, evidence was given showing that between the years 1898 and 1914 he had married five different women, of whom two had died in their baths, one on the day following, and the other within a few weeks of the marriage ceremony. It was also a matter of public knowledge that a third woman had met with a similar fate.

Yesterday Mr Bodkin commenced a speech which occupied over four hours, with the dramatic announcement that the prisoner would now be charged with the wilful murder of three women:

Bessie Constance Annie Mundy, on July 13, 1912;

EDWARDS'

"HARLENE"

FOR THE HAIR.

The Great Hair Producer & Restorer.

THE FINEST DRESSING.
SPECIALLY PREPARED AND DELICATELY PERFUMED.
A LUXURY AND A NECESSITY TO EVERY MODERN TOILET.

UNDER THE ROYAL PATRONAGE OF
H.M. THE QUEEN OF GREECE.
H.I.H. THE GRAND DUCHESS GEORGE OF RUSSIA.
H.R.H. THE DUKE OF SPARTA.
H.R.H. THE DUCHESS OF SPARTA.
H.I.H. THE GRAND DUCHESS OF MECKLENBURG-SCHWERIN.
H.R.H. PRINCESS HOHENLOHE.
H.R.H. PRINCE GEORGE OF GREECE.
PRINCESS ANNA HOHENLOHE.
H.H. PRINCESS WINDISCHGRAETZ.
H.H. PRINCESS DI SIPINO.
H.H. PRINCESS RATIBOR,
&c., &c.

MR. HARRY DE WINDT,

THE GREAT EXPLORER,
WRITES:

"I think it right to tell you that on my return from my recent Land Expedition from Paris to New York I was practically bald, the few hairs I had left were rapidly coming out. I have only used your 'Harlene' for two months, and am perfectly astounded at its marvellous results. My hair has ceased dropping out, and is growing again quite thickly, and I can safely testify from personal experience to the marvellous effects of your 'Harlene.'"

45, Avenue Kleber, Paris.

1s., 2s. 6d., and (three times 2s. 6d. size) 4s. 6d. per bottle, from Chemists and Stores all over the World, or sent direct on receipt of Postal Order.

EDWARDS' "HARLENE" CO., 95 and 96, High Holborn, W.C.

Alice Burnham, on December 12, 1913, and

Margaret Elizabeth Lofty, on December 18, 1914.

Mr Bodkin described the case as one of exceptional gravity, remarkable for the skill with which sudden and silent death had been dealt out to these three women, and for the presence in each instance of the greed for wealth, which no doubt was the dominant motive. He indicated that the suggestion of the prosecution was that the unfortunate women had been drowned in consequence of their heads having been forced under the water in their baths.

Mr Bodkin continued: As a fact we shall show that from the deaths of two of these women something like £2,800 was obtained, and the prisoner was, when he was arrested, not far away from obtaining £700 more.*

These crimes were committed in the intervals of the prisoner's cohabitation with a woman with whom he went through the ceremony of marriage in 1908, a woman named Pegler, from whom every now and then, for weeks, and in some cases months at a time, he would suddenly absent himself.

After pointing out that in such cases as the present, where the attitude of the prisoner had been that each death was accidental, the law admitted a review of other cases in addition to the specific one charged, Mr Bodkin went on to state that the prisoner was the son of George Thomas Smith, an insurance agent, of Roman-road, Bow, East London, and was born on January 11, 1872. The next that was heard of him was on January 17, 1898, when, in the name of George Oliver Love, he married Miss Caroline Thornhill at Leicester. He did not live very long with her. She is still alive and is now on her way to this country from Canada.

In 1908 the prisoner met Edith Mabel Pegler, at Bristol; after a very short acquaintance, he married her at Bristol on July 30, 1908. He carried on business as a dealer in secondhand furniture, and the couple used to travel about, never being very long in one place. After 1908 they were at Luton, Bedford and Croydon, and in the summer of 1910 they were back again in Bristol. During the months of August and September he was absent from Miss Pegler for some three or four weeks, during which time he was in Weymouth.

Mention of Weymouth introduced the name of Beatrice Mundy. She was a single woman, aged about 33, and on August 26, 1910, at Weymouth, the prisoner, in the name of Henry Williams, married her. Miss Mundy had lived a rather solitary kind of life, staying at various boarding-houses and lodging-houses. She was a tall, well-made, and healthy woman, and was the daughter of a man who had been a bank manager in Wiltshire. Her mother was dead, but she had an uncle and brother living at Trowbridge. Her father had some property, and when he died he left the whole of it to his son and to this lady. Her share, which amounted to about £2,500, was invested in stocks and shares, and because she was not a very capable or businesslike person, she executed a voluntary settlement of the property, and the uncle and brother were trustees. The property was settled on conditions, one of which was that the trustees should pay to her during her life an income which could not

* The 1993 purchasing power of the 1914 £ is reckoned to be about £38.

be anticipated. Her income was about £100 a year, which was paid to her monthly by her uncle.

Shortly after the prisoner married her, he seems to have realised that the attitude of the solicitor he had consulted was not of a very friendly character towards him, and he instructed another solicitor to obtain a sum of about £130, which he had discovered had accumulated in the hands of the trustees. After some correspondence, a cheque for £135 2s 11d was forwarded on September 13, 1910.

That was a day crowded with events in this story. After the cheque had been cashed, the prisoner appears to have sent a telegram to himself. When it arrived Miss Mundy was out, and he opened it and said to the landlady, 'I have got to go to London on important business.' He left the house, and his wife did not see him again until eighteen months later. He took with him £130 in gold. When Miss Mundy returned, she was greatly distressed to hear that her husband had gone. A letter which he had left was handed to her.

For reasons which would be clear to the magistrate when he saw the letter, said counsel, he did not propose to read the first part of it. It contained a cruel and absolutely untrue statement in regard to this poor woman.* The latter part of the letter was, however, material: 'The best thing for you to tell the landlady and everyone else is that I have gone to France, but tell your uncle the truth, but even your uncle may not even know we are parted unless he happens to visit you. So you must keep him away, but if other relatives visit you, tell them I am gone to France on business, but to your uncle tell him the truth, also that you have promised to remain with the landlady here until I return. If he happens to ask you about the money, tell him you kept the money in a leather bag, and that two days after I had gone you happened to go on the beach and fell asleep, and when you woke the bag and the money was gone. If you do not carry out every word of my advice you will cause a lot of trouble, and bring disgrace on yourself and your relatives. Now, study this letter, and whatever you do stick to everything to say, and never alter it. When you have read this letter take it into the street and tear it up.'

Some instructions with regard to payments to be made to the landlady followed, and then the first portion of the letter was repeated, the conclusion being:

'If you do not I shall be angry when I return. Believe me, I shall be sure to return to you, even if it is years to come. Mark what I say.'

By what is believed to be the only genuine coincidence in the case, the footsteps of Smith took him in March, 1912, to Weston-super-Mare, where Miss Mundy had been stopping since February at the house of Mrs Tuckett. They met on the beach, and Miss Mundy was

* 'Dearest, I fear you have blighted all my bright hopes of a happy future. I have caught from you a disease which is called the bad disorder. For you to be in such a state proves you could not have kept yourself morally clean. It reminds me of what you told me in reference to the immorality of 'So and so'. Anyhow you have got the disease somehow. I don't wish to say you have had connections with another man and caught it from him. But it is either that or through not keeping yourself clean. Now for the sake of my health and honour and yours too I must go to London and act entirely under the doctor's advice to get properly cured of this disease. It will cost me a great deal of money, because it might take years before I am cured . . .'

willing to forgive and forget. After this, the re-united couple appear to have lived at Woolwich and Ramsgate, and eventually, on May 29, they took a small house at 80 High-street, Herne Bay, Kent.

As soon as they were settled there, there was correspondence between Miss Mundy and her uncle, and in consequence of her repeated requests, copies of the settlement and other documents connected with her father's will were sent to her. Smith then consulted a solicitor, who took counsel's opinion, which was to the effect that Miss Mundy had no power to set aside the settlement. When Smith heard that, he seems to have realised that the only way in which he could obtain this woman's property was that she should execute a will in his favour, and then die. Accordingly, the solicitor was instructed to prepare two wills, one for Miss Mundy, leaving everything to her husband, and one for Smith, leaving everything to her.

On July 8 Miss Mundy executed her will. Then came a feature which was present in all these cases, and which it was suggested by the prosecution was the prisoner's method of preparing for the deaths of these women. On July 10 Smith and his wife called on a Dr French, and Smith said the woman had had a fit on the previous day. The doctor prescribed a sedative, and they went away. On July 12 Miss Mundy sent a registered letter to her uncle, and at one o'clock in the morning Smith went round to the doctor and told him his wife had had another fit. The doctor called, but could not find any evidence of a fit. At eight o'clock Smith went to the doctor with a note:

'Do come at once. I am afraid my wife is dead.'

At the inquest, Smith and Dr French being the only witnesses, a verdict of death from misadventure was recorded.

THE SECOND CHAPTER

Alice Burnham was a young woman about 25 years of age, the daughter of Mr Charles Burnham, of Aston Clinton, Bucks. She married the prisoner in the name of George Joseph Smith on November 4, 1913, at the registry office at Portsmouth. She had been for some years a nurse at Southsea, and was possessed of a little property of her own. The circumstances in which Smith met her were not known, but by the end of September, 1913, they were undoubtedly acquainted. They became engaged, and spent a week with Mr and Mrs Burnham, who, it is quite clear, did not find the man a very acceptable prospective son-in-law. After the wedding, the couple went into lodgings in Regent-road, Blackpool, and Miss Burnham wrote a post-card to her mother in which she said:

'I am sorry to say I have again suffered from bad headaches, which necessitated going to a doctor and taking medicine. My husband does all he possibly can for me. In fact, dear, I have the best husband in the world.'

Smith and the woman had arrived in Blackpool on December 10, and the same evening they went to a Dr Billing, who was asked by Smith to prescribe for his wife for a headache. On the evening of the 12th, Miss Burnham said she would like to have a bath, and shortly after she had gone upstairs Smith came down with some eggs in his hand and said, 'We should like to have these for breakfast in the

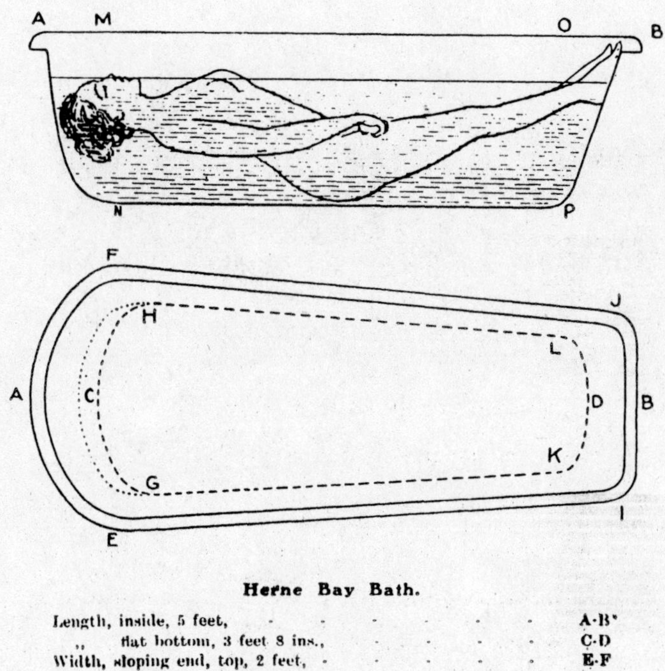

Herne Bay Bath.

Length, inside, 5 feet,	A-B*
,, flat bottom, 3 feet 8 ins.,	C-D
Width, sloping end, top, 2 feet,	E-F
,, ,, bottom, 1 foot 6 ins.,	G-H
,, tap end, top, 1 foot 7 ins.,	I-J
,, ,, bottom, 1 foot $1\frac{1}{2}$ ins.,	K-L
Depth, sloping end, 1 foot 4 ins.,	M-N
,, top end, 1 foot $4\frac{3}{4}$ ins.,	O-P

Height of woman, 5 feet 8 ins. or 5 feet 9 ins.

(Undertaker's measurement, 5 feet 11 ins.)

* B is the spot where the taps would have been fitted.

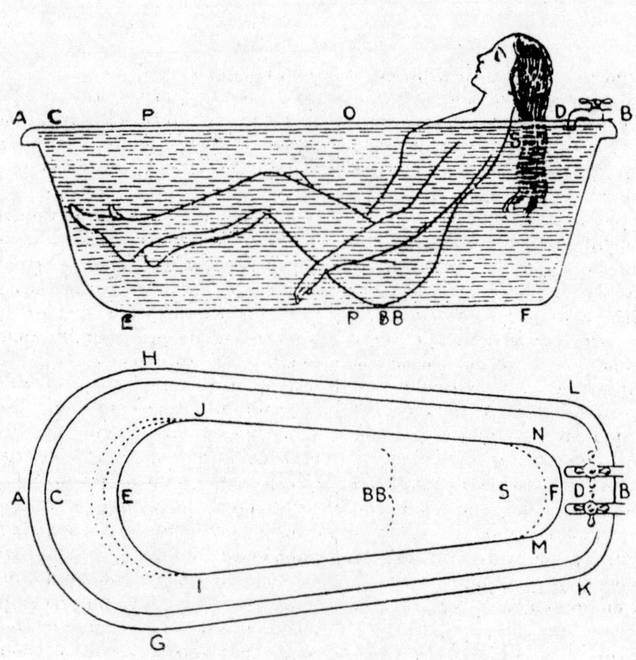

Blackpool Bath.

Length, over all, 5 feet 6 ins.,	A-B		
„ inside, 5 feet 3 ins.,	C-D		
„ flat bottom, 3 feet 9 ins.,	E-F	Position of buttocks.	BB
Width, sloping end, top, 2 feet 3 ins.,	G-H	Position of shoulder.	S
„ „ bottom, 1 foot 2 ins.,	I-J	Height of woman,	5 feet
„ tap end, top, 1 foot 3½ ins.,	K-L	(Undertaker's measurement, 5 feet 6 ins.)	
„ „ bottom, 1 foot,	M-N		
Depth, 1 foot 6 ins.	O-P		

morning.' He then called out 'Alice', and receiving no reply, he asked the landlady to go for Dr Billing.

Prisoner seems to have regarded the matter of his wife's death with extraordinary callousness. He went to an undertaker and stipulated that the woman should be buried as cheaply as possible and in a public grave. Previous to marrying Miss Burnham, he had introduced her to a Mr Pleasants at Southsea, and she had insured her life for £500, at the same time making a will leaving everything to her husband. On January 18, 1914, he received £506 from the insurance company, and with it he purchased an annuity.

ANOTHER 'MARRIAGE'

Going on to deal with the case of Miss Lofty, Mr Bodkin said she was 38 years of age, and was one of several daughters of a reverend gentleman who died some years ago in Bristol. She had been engaged to be married, but the arrangement had fallen through, and at the end of 1914 her family had no knowledge that she was contemplating marriage. As a fact, on December 17 she was married at the Bath Registry Office to Smith, who gave the name of John Lloyd, bachelor. She died on December 18 in a bath of a lodging-house, 14 Bismarck-road, Highgate, North London.

The couple had arrived at the house in the afternoon of December 17. That evening, Smith took Miss Lofty to see a Dr Bates, saying that she had got a headache. On the following day they both went to a post-office at Muswell-hill, and Miss Lofty withdrew all the money she had in the savings bank, about £19. She then appeared to be in her usual health.

In the evening she asked for a bath, which was prepared for her. She left the sitting-room about a quarter to eight. Shortly afterwards, Smith, who had just previously been heard in the house, knocked at the front door, and when it was answered he remarked, 'Oh, I forgot I had a key. I have been to get some tomatoes for Mrs Lloyd. Is she down yet?'

Smith then went upstairs and called his wife's name, immediately afterwards exclaiming, 'By God! there's no answer.' He struck a light and said, 'She is in the bath. Come and help me.' He went into the bath-room and asked if he should let the water out, although it would have been thought that from his previous experience he would have known what to do. The doctor was fetched, and he found the body lying on the floor, the woman being dead. Smith said, 'I hope this won't be brought in as suicide. I hope they won't find she was insane.'

An inquest was held, and a verdict of 'Accidental death; drowned in bath', was returned.

If, concluded Mr Bodkin, what I have opened is borne out by the evidence of the many witnesses who will have to be called, it is clearly, in my submission, a case in which the prisoner should be committed for trial on the three charges.

Evidence previously given by Detective-Inspector Neil and two other police officers having been read over, the prisoner was again remanded in custody.

At the trial, which began at the Old Bailey on Tuesday, June 22, the indictment referred only to the case of Bessie Mundy – who, so far as was known, was the first of Smith's 'brides' to die a watery death – but the judge, Mr Justice Scrutton, allowed the prosecution to introduce evidence relating to the deaths of Alice Burnham and Margaret Lofty, so as to prove a 'system' of murder.

Friday, July 2:

Yesterday was the ninth day of the trial,* and the attendance of the general public was larger than on any occasion since the case opened. Women, as usual in these trials, formed a very large proportion of the spectators.

Mr Justice Scrutton commenced his summing-up with a reference to a remark made by Mr Marshall Hall, leading counsel for the defence, as to what must be passing through all their minds at the present moment. 'It is one of the ironies of life,' said the Judge. 'Since last August, all over Europe, sometimes in Asia, sometimes on the seas, thousands of lives of combatants, and sometimes of non-combatants, have been taken daily with no warning, and, in many cases, with no justification. No inquiry has been made at all, as, for instance, in the case of the *Lusitania*, whether people should be sent to death. And yet, while this wholesale destruction of human life has been going on, for nine days all the apparatus of justice in England has been considering whether the prosecution are right in saying that one man should die. And it is quite right that it should be so. In England, in this national crisis, we have tried to carry on business as usual; we hope with confidence of victory as usual; and we are determined to maintain justice as usual. And so you and I approach, just as if this were a time of peace, instead of one of the greatest world disturbances ever known in history, the question of whether the prosecution have proved to your satisfaction that George Joseph Smith is guilty of murder.'

The jury had to consider whether the prisoner was guilty of the murder of Bessie Mundy. They would not be asked, 'Is he guilty or not of the murder of Alice Burnham?' or 'is he guilty or not of the murder of Margaret Lofty?'

'There is no direct evidence at all,' the Judge proceeded, 'that he murdered Bessie Mundy. There is no direct evidence that he was present in the bath-room when she died. If you convict him, you convict him on circumstantial evidence. But, gentlemen, like the character in Molière's play, who had been talking prose all his life without knowing it, you have been acting on circumstantial evidence all your life, and very likely without knowing it. It means that, having no direct evidence of the fact, you infer it from the evidence of the surrounding facts.'

* Making it the longest English murder trial since Palmer's.

The prisoner interrupted the Judge frequently. 'You may as well hang me, the way you are going on,' he exclaimed gruffly at one point. Mr Marshall Hall waved to him to be quiet, but he continued in a low, thick voice, 'Sentence me and done with it. You can go on for ever, but you can't make me into a murderer. I have done no murder.'

His lordship took no notice of the prisoner's outburst, and proceeded to refer to some houses which the prisoner had purchased.

'What about it?' said Smith. 'That doesn't prove I done the murder.'

'It's a disgrace to a Christian country, this is,' he went on, in a louder voice. 'I never murdered her. You are telling the jury I murdered the woman.'

The Judge asked the jury to consider whether thirteen facts were mere coincidences:

1. In each case there was a death in a bath in a house to which the prisoner had moved, or which he had fitted up, within a week before the tragedy.
2. In each case the bath-room door was unlocked, so that the prisoner might enter, although in two cases it was in a strange house, and in one place there was also a lavatory which might have led other lodgers to enter the room.
3. In each case the deceased

Increased Separation Allowances

for soldiers' wives and children.

FROM MARCH 1st the Separation Allowances paid by the Government to the wives and children of soldiers have been increased, so that the total weekly payment to the family, if the soldier makes the usual allotment from his pay, is now as follows:

		Corporal or Private.	Sergeant.
WIFE	per week	12/6	15/-
WIFE and 1 CHILD	per week	17/6	20/-
WIFE and 2 CHILDREN	per week	21/-	23/6
WIFE and 3 CHILDREN	per week	23/-	25/6

and so on with an addition of 2/- for each additional child.

Each Motherless Child 5/-

To wives living at the time of enlistment in the London area a further sum of 3/6 per week is paid as long as they continue to live there.

From February 1st, 1915, Separation Allowance is payable for all children up to the age of 16 years. This includes adopted children.

Allowances for other Dependants.

If an unmarried soldier has supported a dependant for a reasonable period, and wishes the support he gave to be continued, the Government will help, during the war, by making a grant of Separation Allowance, provided he will contribute part of his pay.

Full particulars can be obtained at any Post Office.

God Save the King.

woman made a will in favour of the prisoner a week before her death.

4. In two cases the deceased insured her life within ten days before death in favour of the prisoner, and in the third instance there was no insurance because there was property which would go to the prisoner.

5. In each case all the debts due to the deceased, and all the Savings Bank accounts, had been realised just before death.

6. In each case, two or three days before the tragedy, the deceased was taken to a strange doctor in a strange place, complaining of headache, and the same doctor was called in after the death.

7. In each case a letter was written to relatives the day before the death.

8. In each case the prisoner went to get food for future consumption just before the woman was found drowned – fish at Herne Bay, eggs at Blackpool, tomatoes at Highgate.

9. In each case the prisoner found the woman and left her in the water till someone had seen her, and did not get rid of the water without permission.

10. In each case it was a sham marriage – a bigamous marriage.

11. In each case the prisoner benefited more by the death than the life.

12. In each case the prisoner buried the woman as quickly, cheaply, and obscurely as possible.

13. In each case the prisoner immediately went back to Miss Pegler, in two cases changing his name and hiding his tracks.

Referring to the fact that the prisoner had not given evidence, the Judge said that it was for the jury to draw their inference from that fact.

An absence from court of less than half an hour was sufficient to enable the jury to arrive at the verdict that George Joseph Smith was guilty of the murder of Bessie Mundy. He gave no sign of having heard the foreman announce their verdict. He was asked if he had anything to say why sentence should not be passed upon him according to law, and there was an appreciable pause before he replied. Then, in a strained voice, he declared: 'All I can say is, I am not guilty.'

Mr Justice Scrutton assumed the black cap and addressed the prisoner. After saying that he entirely concurred with the verdict, he commented: 'Judges sometimes use this occasion to warn the public against a repetition of such crimes. They sometimes use the occasion to exhort the prisoner to repentance. I propose to take neither of these courses. I do not believe that there is another man in England who needs to be warned against the commission of such a crime, and I think that an exhortation to repentence would be wasted on you.'

Almost unnoticed, Miss Pegler, a pathetic figure in blue, sitting at the back of the court, showed great distress when sentence was passed. She hurried out with tears streaming down her face, and, sitting down in the central hall, gave way to a fit of weeping.

Outside in the street, a crowd of three or four hundred people waited patiently for the verdict. There was, however, a complete absence of

Leading article:

THE DROWNED BRIDES

Sentence of death has been pronounced upon GEORGE JOSEPH SMITH, and with his recommittal to prison, pending execution, there passes out of the life of this generation one of the most callous and inhuman wretches that ever felt the weight of English law.

The history of this criminal places him in a peculiar class of homicides, whose appearance in our courts is comparatively rare; those, that is to say, to whom the taking of life in cold blood is so much a matter of indifference that they can follow a systematic course of carefully-plotted murder for the mere motive of pecuniary gain. A single deliberate murder for the sake of money is a well-known type of crime, though in the greater number of cases in which cupidity has been the original motive, the actual shedding of blood has been done in a momentary access of ferocity or fear. Again, where a succession of murders have been the work of one person, it has commonly happened that strong evidence of insanity – or what would be treated as such at the present day – has been present.

But SMITH is a ruffian whose whole career and conduct, apart from his three consummate crimes, was simply that of an ordinary loafer and swindler, living by the comparatively common trick of entrapping women into supposed marriage, and then making off with as much of their property as he could lay hands on. His legitimate wife, who is still alive, was treated in this fashion; and Mr Justice SCRUTTON informed the jury, after the giving of the verdict, that the police had evidence of two bigamous marriages, followed by robbery and desertion, but by nothing worse, in addition to the three of which the hideous story was told in the course of the trial.

There was nothing whatever in SMITH's record upon which a plea of insanity could be founded. His loud outbursts in court were merely those of an imposter of a commonplace, uninteresting type, desperately brazening it out to the last. The touch of stupidity that mingled with his elaborate cunning was thoroughly normal. The only distinguishing feature of SMITH's story is the frozen cruelty with which he planned and carried out the killing, within eighteen months, of three innocent women who had given him their love and confidence.

Strange as it may appear, the securing of a conviction in this case was not at one time regarded as a foregone conclusion by any means. That the verdict of the jury was rendered with such promptness as it was may be ascribed, we have no doubt, to the admirable clearness with which the learned Judge marshalled the evidence in his summing-up, and especially to the series of thirteen articles in which he arranged the points of similarity between the cases of SMITH's three unhappy victims – a survey which even extended to the fact that in each case the murderer, by way of preparing for his feigned discovery of the dead body, had gone out of the house to buy food. In this, as in all the more essential details of his plan of crime, SMITH simply repeated himself without an attempt at variation, and that characteristic dullness was his undoing.

And yet his deeds might never have come to light – he might even have practised again and again the hideous scheme of assassination which he had systematised into a means of livelihood – but for one act of incaution, into which a far cleverer villain might have stumbled. In making Highgate the scene of his last crime, he unwittingly secured for the details of the death – which were published in the London papers – an enormously wider publication than they would have had in the columns of any local journal; and so the relatives of his previous victim, reading those details, were struck by the coincidence of the two cases. Scotland Yard was put upon the trail, and Inspector Arthur NEIL took up that tangled task of investigation, on the performance of which he was deservedly complimented from the Bench.

SMITH, then, vanishes from the world whose common instinct of humanity he has so fearfully outraged, leaving to the history of crime a case for which there can hardly be a near parallel. He leaves, too, to the student of psychology one more example of the recurrent problem of the fascination that can be exercised over intelligent and virtuous women by men so destitute of every visible attraction, physical or moral, as was this man, who showed himself, even at his best, an insolent and greedy adventurer. It is rarely indeed that a judge accompanies the sentence of death with such words as Mr Justice SCRUTTON addressed yesterday to SMITH; but who shall say they were not justified.

Saturday, August 14:

George Joseph Smith was executed at Maidstone Gaol at eight a.m. yesterday. For the first time for many years, no permits were issued to the Press.

During the ten days he had been incarcerated in Maidstone Gaol, Smith gave those in attendance upon him very little trouble. He was throughout the whole time very dejected. Soon after his arrival, he made known the fact that he was a Wesleyan, and as a result the local minister of his denomination visited him more than once, while the chaplain saw him several times daily. He made no confession. His statement to the chaplain was that he was innocent. The culprit had frequently been seen crying during the last few days.

1922

Leading article on Tuesday, December 12:

The trial of Mrs EDITH THOMPSON and her lover FREDERICK BYWATERS for the murder of her husband has excited, if we are to judge by the gathering of crowds, greater curiosity than any case which has been heard at the Central Criminal Court for some years.

It had, indeed, many elements which appeal to the imagination of the ordinary man and woman. The victim was killed by a sudden attack in the quiet dark of a suburban street, when he was trudging home, as hundreds of other middle-class husbands and wives are every night in the week, from a conjugal visit to the theatre.

From the moment that he fell, his wife made a mystery of it. The first queer stories of the murder set people asking whether the poor creature had lost her wits at the sight of her husband's blood, or whether she knew well enough that it was to be spilt that night. After BYWATERS was arrested, and to the horror and mystery of the murder itself was added the excitement of the crime of sex, the police-court revealed a history of long conspiracy in passion and hatred, a history which the woman herself had written in letters richly adorned with the colours of melodrama.

Human nature would have been changed out of knowledge if such a case had not drawn crowds to the Old Bailey. But to recognise this is not to pretend that there was anything in it strange in the annals of crime, or that the woman and her lover who stood in the dock showed any quality which dignifies or even palliates their guilt. The charge, as Mr Justice SHEARMAN carefully impressed on the jury, was nothing but 'an ordinary common charge of a wife and an adulterer murdering a husband'. The Judge could find in the facts before him no matter for sentiment, and his insistence that the jury and he were investigating a 'vulgar crime' according to the principles of human justice and common-sense well expresses the spirit in which English people would have all such cases tried.

A trial thus conducted could have but one issue. The facts, as Mr Justice SHEARMAN remarked in his summing up, 'were extremely short and simple'. The length of the proceedings was due to the length of the letters which the woman wrote to her lover, and to the efforts which advocates were in duty bound to make to prove, as the Judge put it, 'that this was a case of great love'. The appeal failed, and both woman and man were found guilty and sentenced to death. No sound judgment will doubt the justice of that verdict.

The facts were indeed simple.

In January, 1915, EDITH JESSIE GRAYDON married PERCY THOMPSON. There were no children of the marriage, and the wife as well as the husband did clerical work in the City. Last year BYWATERS, who is still only a lad of 20, stayed with Mr and Mrs THOMPSON. After he went away, he received many letters from the woman, which mixed protestations of passion and appeals for its return with assurance of hatred for her husband and melodramatic discussions of how he could be poisoned.

BYWATERS came back again; again he met Mrs THOMPSON. One day last October after he had had tea with her, she went to the theatre with her husband. On their way home, BYWATERS met them in an Ilford street after midnight, with a knife upon him. A little later, THOMPSON was found dead, stabbed in body and arm, and face and neck.

How were the accused to explain these facts? Their counsel protested that evidence of poisoning, save the voluble discussions of how to poison a husband in Mrs THOMPSON's letters, there was none. This is true. Whether she did in fact put poison in the food she gave him, the jury had not to decide, and those who have not the jury's responsibilities need not read more into the verdict than it says. But that these discussions of poison prove a murderous mind both in the woman and her lover we cannot doubt. The murder, however, was not thus done.

The onus of the case against the woman was that BYWATERS killed under her suasion. He was seeing her, as the Judge put it, whenever he could without her husband knowing. He left her only a few hours before he committed the murder. He knew exactly where and when to find husband and wife, and he took a knife in his pocket. It is not in human credulity to believe that the woman who had been writing to her lover of poisons was innocent of any guilty purpose. The explanation of BYWATERS was that he waited for the husband out there in the street after midnight, with his knife, in order to suggest a separation or divorce; that her husband then attacked him, and that he killed in self-defence. Such an invention has only to be set down to be rejected.

The case, indeed, was simple and overwhelming. There are, no doubt, questions of motive in it which may be debated. Some may ask why Mrs THOMPSON, who was not dependent on her husband, who was earning as much or more than he, and certainly enough to support herself, should have desired to murder the man. That he refused to divorce her seems an inadequate reason for adding the crime of murder to the sin of adultery. That BYWATERS and she, by an open liaison, would have been injured is again an insufficient cause for the desperate hazard of murder.

But with such problems, which are indeed not beyond solution, the jury were not concerned. It was within their provice to estimate the influence of one party to the crime upon the other. When a lad of twenty and a woman of twenty-eight are found concerned in the murder of the woman's husband, the antecedent probability that the woman is the leader in the deed is considerable. That probability is confirmed by the particular facts in the THOMPSON case.

January is a most important time to thousands who look to get

Great Bargains AT BURBERRYS

Outer clothing of good materials, well made, at a little above or below half their true value.

	SALE PRICE.
Lounge Suits Sizes 34in. to 46in. chest. Worsteds, Cheviots, Saxonys. Usual Price ... ... 10 gns.	$5\frac{1}{2}$ gns.
Sports Suits Cheviots, Lovats and Homespuns. Usual Price ... ... 9 gns.	$5\frac{1}{2}$ gns.
Sports Coats Models evolved during the past season. Usual Price ... ... 5 gns.	63/-
Grey and Lovat Flannel Suits Coats and Trousers. Usual Price ... ... 9 gns.	5 gns.
Fleece Weatheralls Comfortable walking weight. Usual Price ... ... 9 gns.	$5\frac{1}{2}$ gns.
Rusitors Fleece Coatings, lined to waist. Usual Price ... 11½ gns.	$6\frac{1}{2}$ gns.
Ladies' Ulsters Burberry Fleece. Warm, yet light weight. Usual Price ... 10 gns.	5 gns.
VELOUR-DE-LAINE Lined through Silk. Usual Price ... 12 gns.	5 gns.
Belted Burberrys (Ladies') Urbitor Coatings. Usual Price ... 8½ gns.	5 gns.
Costumes (Belted Designs) Shetlands and Homespuns. Usual Price - - 12 gns.	6 gns.
The Burberry Weatherproof Men's and Women's	73/6

Many Bargains for Boys and Girls.

Full List and Conditions of Sale post free on request.

LTD., HAYMARKET, LONDON, S.W.1.

What we find there is a crime suggested and compelled by sensuality. It is idle to attempt by sentimental appeals in the name of love – a word which has no place in this case – to throw some glamour over the man and woman who now lie condemned to death. The jury found, after long deliberation [of two hours and a quarter], no cause to ask for mercy upon either. To their silence there is nothing to add.

At 9 a.m. on Tuesday, January 9, 1923, Frederick Bywaters was hanged by Thomas Pierrepoint in Pentonville Prison, and Edith Thompson was hanged by John Ellis in Holloway Prison. The morning after the concurrent executions, it was reported that whereas 'Bywaters was calm to the end, partaking of a little breakfast and smoking a final cigarette before walking firmly from his cell', 'Mrs Thompson, after a night of semi-consciousness, with a doctor in constant attendance, was dazed, requiring assistance to walk to the scaffold'. Before very long, more imaginative reports, gratefully accepted by persons seeking the abolition of capital punishment, helped towards the creation of a legend that Edith Thompson was quite unconscious when Ellis hanged her. That legend, tacked on to the widely held and strongly based belief that she had been tried as much for adultery as for murder, caused her to become a sort of patron-saint of the abolitionist cause.

Ellis's resignation in March 1923, which may have been prompted by the offer of a lucrative contract to star in a mock-execution show at holiday resorts along the south coast, was taken by abolitionists to mean that he was 'afflicted by remorse' in regard to Edith Thompson; and so was his attempt, seventeen months later, to commit suicide by shooting himself in the neck (before discharging him from what was then the *crime* of attempted suicide, the presiding magistrate commented, 'If your aim had been as true as the drops you gave, it would have been a bad job for you.'); and so was his actual suicide, late in 1931, which he accomplished by slitting his throat with a razor that he had often used unblemishingly in his barber-shop.

1935

Letter published in the Daily Mirror, *June 9, 1967:*

> Every now and again I play an old gramophone record bought back in the Thirties. On one side is a song called 'Dark Haired Marie' and on the reverse side is 'You Brought My Heart the Sunshine'.
>
> The singer is the late Frank Titterton and his accompanist and the writer of the lyrics is named as 'Lozanne'.
>
> They are such melancholy songs that I wondered if you . . . could give any clue as to the composer's life.
>
> BALLAD-MONGER

'Lozanne' was the pen-name of Mrs Alma Victoria Rattenbury, an attractive Canadian woman whose talents as a pianist far outweighed her gifts as a lyric-writer. She and her husband Francis, a semi-retired architect, came to England in 1928, and settled down in a small house called Villa Madeira, in Manor Road, Bournemouth. She was then thirty-seven years of age, her husband about sixty.

In September 1934, the Rattenburys advertised in a local paper for a 'daily willing lad, 14–18, for housework; scout-trained preferred', and George Percy Stoner, who became eighteen in November, was engaged as chauffeur-handyman. Within weeks, he and Mrs Rattenbury were lovers.

On the night of Sunday, March 24, 1935, Francis Rattenbury was savagely beaten about the head as he sat sleeping in an armchair in the drawing-room. While under the influence of alcohol and morphia (the latter administered by a doctor), Mrs Rattenbury made several statements to the effect that she was solely responsible for the crime. Charged with doing grievous bodily harm with intent to murder, she was removed to Holloway Prison. Four days later, Stoner also was arrested; but this time the charge was murder, for Francis Rattenbury had died earlier in the day.

At the trial (before Mr Justice Humphreys at the Old Bailey), Mrs Rattenbury and Stoner refused to inculpate each other. The prosecution sought to prove that the crime was the result of a plot, but it soon became clear that Stoner, motivated by jealousy, had attacked Francis Rattenbury with a mallet that he had borrowed quite openly from his grandmother, and that Mrs Rattenbury had had no foreknowledge of the crime and had taken no part in it. After a retirement of forty-seven minutes, the jury acquitted Mrs Rattenbury, and brought in a verdict of guilty against Stoner, with a recommendation to mercy.

Leading article on Saturday, June 1:

Happily, the records of the English law courts offer no close parallel to the crime – the beating to death with a mallet of an elderly man, the husband of the woman prisoner – and so far as the evidence given in court was concerned, it was wanton and purposeless. The sordid story of the relations of the two prisoners, which has given a particularly unpleasant atmosphere to the whole trial, did not itself provide a motive, since what evidence there was on the point suggested that the situation was known to the murdered man and acquiesced in by him. The sole remaining inference was that the murder was the jealous act of an unbalanced boy.

Actually, there was no evidence before the Court as to who struck the blows, since STONER himself did not go into the witness-box. Nor was there evidence, as the judge was careful to point out, of such a condition of mind arising from the taking of drugs as would prevent STONER knowing what he was doing. The jury has come to the conclusion that STONER was solely responsible for the murder, and that he was not suffering from insanity at the time. With their verdict they couple a recommendation to mercy, which will no doubt be given its full weight by the responsible authorities, for there must be a sense of pity for this lad who, until he entered the RATTENBURY household, had apparently been of blameless life. Whatever the verdict, said Mr Justice HUMPHREYS, 'his position is due to the domination of that woman.' Disgust with the story of the association of Mrs RATTENBURY with this youth of half her age, as told by herself in – the witness-box, did not obscure the jury's view of the proved facts as regards the murder. It was not for them to decide or even to be influenced by the moral issue.

Thursday, June 6:

BOURNEMOUTH, Wednesday.

The body of Mrs Alma Rattenbury, recovered with six knife-wounds in it, from a River Avon backwater near here, was today identified by her maid, Miss Irene Riggs, a prominent witness at her trial. Miss Riggs was crying bitterly when she left the public assistance institution at Christchurch, where the body was taken.

Mrs Rattenbury went to a Bayswater nursing home last Friday, after her acquittal. She was immediately put to bed for a complete rest. Her nervous condition was said to be very bad, and she smoked cigarettes incessantly. After a time, she recovered somewhat, and began to live over again the experiences of her trial. According to one of her friends, a photograph of Stoner stood by the side of her bed, and she seemed 'never able to take her eyes off it'.

On Monday evening, according to

a statement issued by the nursing home, Mrs Rattenbury left with a woman friend who had been to visit her. From then until she was seen by the river, her movements have not been traced.

The pool where the body was found – where water lilies and wild irises grow – is an unfrequented spot. It is near a railway arch, about 300 yards across marshy meadows from a main road from Christchurch to Ringwood. Apparently nobody but William Mitchell, the local dairyman, saw her near the river.

Mitchell told me today that he went to the fields last night about 8.30 to see to some cows. Looking through a railway arch, he saw a woman walking towards the water.

'As I came over the top of the embankment,' said Mitchell, 'I saw the woman sitting down by the river bank. She took off her fur coat. Then I saw a knife in her hand, and she walked into the water, which is about 15ft deep just there. She walked straight in, it seemed to me. She got up and walked forward with her arms swinging from her shoulders in a determined sort of way.

'I had to go down the bank to get to the spot, and I tried to get hold of her. I cannot swim, so I got hold of her fur coat from the bank, held it out to her and asked her to try and catch hold of it. When I said that, her head went back away from me and I saw blood coming up through the water.' Mitchell went to fetch neighbours, and they recovered the body from the river.

Saturday, June 8:

Friday, May 31: 3.37 p.m., Mrs Rattenbury found not guilty of wilful murder.

Friday, June 6: 3.37 p.m., Mrs Rattenbury found to have committed suicide while of unsound mind.

This is the dramatic time-table of events in the last poignant chapters of the life of Mrs Alma Victoria Rattenbury, 37, of the Villa Madeira, Bournemouth.

At the inquest at Christchurch yesterday, P.C. Edward King stated that when he arrived at the scene on Tuesday night, he found Mrs Rattenbury lying on the north bank of the stream, fully clothed. About four yards away he found a handbag, in which were letters. Lying close to the handbag was a paper bag which contained a dagger-sheath.

The coroner, Mr R. B. Ingoldby, read extracts from some of the letters. The first extract was from a letter dated June 4:

'I want to make it perfectly clear that no one is responsible for what action I may take regarding my life. I quite made up my mind at Holloway to finish things should Stoner . . . and it would only be a matter of time and opportunity.

'Every night and minute is only prolonging the appalling agony of my mind.'

After reading this extract, Mr Ingoldby observed: 'Then this goes into quite a lot of neurotic statements.'

He added that there was another letter, dated June 3, written on the back of an envelope addressed to the 'Governor of his Majesty's Prison, Pentonville'. An extract from this read by Mr Ingoldby was as follows:

'If I only thought it would help Stoner I would stay on, but it has been pointed out to me all too vividly I cannot help him. That is my death sentence.'

The next extract was written on an envelope which had been addressed to Mrs Rattenbury. It ran:

'Eight o'clock. After so much walking I have got here. Oh, to see the swans and spring flowers and just smell them. And how singular I should have chosen the spot Stoner said he nearly jumped out of the train once at.

'It was not intentional my coming here. I tossed a coin like Stoner always did, and it came down Christchurch. It is beautiful here. What a lovely world we are in. It must be easier to be hanged than to have to do the job oneself, especially in these circumstances of being watched all the while.

'Pray God nothing stops me tonight. Am within five minutes of Christchurch now. God bless my children and look after them.'

The next extract, written on the night of June 4, was as follows:

'I tried this morning to throw myself under a train at Oxford-circus. Too many people about. One must be bold to do a thing like this. It is beautiful here and I am alone. Thank God for peace at last.'

Wednesday, June 26:

It was officially announced last night that Sir John Simon, the Home Secretary, had

> 'Recommended a reprieve in the case of George Percy Stoner, with a view to the commutation of the capital sentence to one of penal servitude for life.'

A petition for Stoner's reprieve was signed by 348,192 persons.

The appeal against his conviction was rejected by the Court of Criminal Appeal on Monday.

Stoner, a model prisoner, was released in 1942, when he was still only twenty-six. He joined the army, and took part in the Normandy Landings; after the war, he returned to Bournemouth, married, and settled down in his parents' house, which is still his home. He was again in the news in the autumn of 1990; but as the 'newsworthiness' had far more to do with who he was than with what he had recently done, it would not be fair to him to say what that was.

1952

Friday, October 31:

Mr Justice Hilbery at the Old Bailey yesterday sentenced Niven Scott Craig, 26, motor mechanic, and Cyril Burney, 27, both of no fixed address, each to 12 years' imprisonment for armed robbery.

To Craig, Mr Justice Hilbery said: 'You have by your record already shown that you are a young man determined to indulge in desperate crime.

'I have watched you carefully in the course of this trial and I can say that, with regard to both matters in respect of which you stand convicted, I do not remember in the course of some 17 years on the Bench, trying various crimes of violence, a young man of your age who struck me as being so determined as you have impressed me as being.

'You are not only cold-blooded, but from my observation of you I have not the least hesitation in saying I believe that you would shoot down, if you had the opportunity to do so, any police officer who was attempting to arrest you or indeed any lawful citizen who tried to prevent you from committing some felony which you had in hand.'

Mr Christmas Humphreys, prosecuting, said that on the night of 14–15th March five men wearing trilby hats and masks went to 55 Honey Lane, Waltham Abbey, Essex, where they threatened the occupiers with a gun. Mr and Mrs Whiten were tied up, and the intruders left after cutting the telephone wires, having taken £4 from Mr Whiten's trousers pocket and a petrol lighter.

It was stated that, when arrested in a bedroom, Craig reached for a loaded revolver under his pillow and that the officer arresting him jumped for the head of the bed, put his hand under the pillow and grabbed the gun.

Scotland Yard had been trailing Craig and Burney for several months and caught up with them in an apartment in Paddington. To avoid detection, Burney had dyed his hair black and Craig had bleached his.

Detective-Inspector Garrod said Craig had three findings of guilt as a juvenile and one previous conviction as an adult. At the age of 14 he was convicted of store-breaking. He absconded from an approved school and stole a tommy-gun.

In 1947, at a Field General Court-Martial, he received a five-years sentence for robbery while armed. He had escaped from an escort in Austria and made his way to Italy, where on four occasions he held up at pistol-point drivers of Army vehicles. He had 12 military convictions and his Army character was assessed as very bad.

Monday, November 3:

LONDON P.C. SHOT DEAD FROM ROOF

CROYDON, Sunday.

P.C. Sidney Miles, 42, was shot dead and Det-Con F. Fairfax, 37, was wounded after climbing on to the roof of a wholesale merchant's store and shop in Tamworth Road here to-night in pursuit of two suspects. Later two men were arrested. One of them is understood to be only a youth.

Sitting in the kitchen of her cottage opposite the scene tonight, little Edith Ware, who raised the alarm, said: 'I had been playing with my daddy's shaving soap, and then I went up to bed laughing and playing about.

'I got undressed and into my pyjamas and after I had said my prayers I looked out of the window for a little while. Then I saw two men coming down the road from West Croydon. They stood about and they looked very suspicious to me.

'One of them went over and tried to open the gate of Barlow and Parker's store. Then he got over the gate, and the other man, who was in a fawn raincoat, stood about waiting. Every time a car or a bus passed he pulled his hat down over his eyes.

'Then he climbed over the gate too, and that was the last I saw of them. I told mummy, and she called out to daddy, and he went and dialled 999.'

Within a few minutes a police wireless patrol car arrived. One policeman went into the premises, and then shots were heard. He called to his colleagues across the road to get reinforcements.

About 40 police, some of them armed and others with tear gas, answered the call for reinforcements. Fire brigades and ambulances stood by. It was quickly realised that a frontal attack on the long, glass-fronted modern building, with its flat roof, would be dangerous because of the position commanded by the two men who were on the roof.

Tamworth Road, which is about 600 yards long, is mainly residential, but contains a number of small shops and works premises. Barlow and Parker's store-place is about 200 yards from the main London road running through Croydon and about 30 yards from the John Ruskin Grammar School.

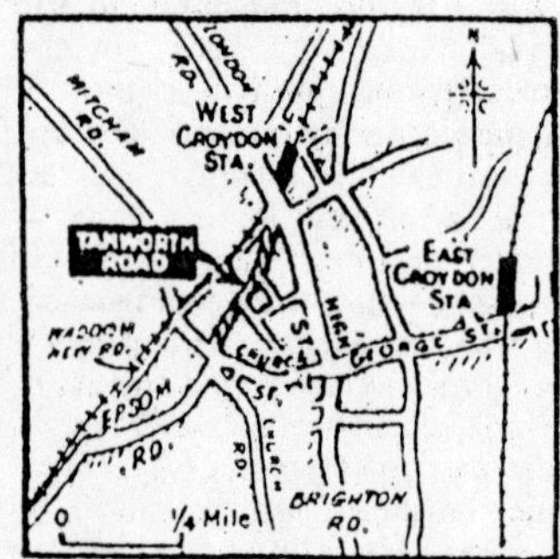

Police decided to carry out a flanking movement. They went through houses on either side of the premises and into back gardens. In one garden the occupants of the house heard heavy firing, and shortly afterwards a man's voice, inviting the police to 'shoot it out'.

People living at the back of the building said that they saw policemen armed with revolvers crawling on the roof, covering any retreat through the back way.

There was a short lull in the firing, and then a man jumped from the roof, crashing through a glass-house into a back yard. Police officers standing under cover immediately closed in.

SHOTS EXCHANGED
P.c. Was Hit in Head

Det Fairfax, who was armed, had climbed up a stackpipe to reach the roof and had fired before he was hit in the shoulder. He was taken to hospital and later allowed to go home. P.c. Miles got up through a door. He was shot as soon as he put his head above the roof.

The dead constable was married, with two children, and had 22 years' service. He was a driver of one of the police cars. He had taken detectives to the scene of the shooting, and led the way when the detectives decided to climb to the roof of the building.

AREA CLEARED
'Intermittent Shooting'

Mrs Tennant, the occupier of a house two doors from the store, said: 'We were watching the television when we first heard the sound of the firing.

'We thought at first that it was fireworks. Then a neighbour shouted that shooting was taking place, and everyone rushed to the front door. Within a matter of minutes dozens of police had arrived on the scene.

'Some police then came through our house and went into the back garden, which adjoins that of the store. From inside we could hear the sound of intermittent shooting, and a man shouting at the top of his voice. I heard him say: "Come on, I am enjoying myself."

'After this, the shooting stopped, and a man then jumped from the top of the building into the back-yard, crashing through a glass-house. The police officers who were waiting rushed forward and got a ladder and climbed over after him. He appeared to be injured.'

Mr E. Pillage, landlord of the Robert Peel public-house in Tamworth Road, said: 'I was serving in the bar when one of the regulars dashed in and said that some men had tried to get into Barlows, the wholesale confectioners, and were disturbed by police.

'I heard five single shots, three together, and then two more.'

Miss Helen Keable, who lives in Tamworth Road, said: 'First of all we heard shots, they were very loud and sounded like fireworks, which we thought they were. Then we heard a fire engine, ambulance, and police on loud-speakers, and went out to see what was happening.

'After about 10 minutes there were two more shots. The first two shots had been in rapid succession, and the next were slightly spaced.

'Then the police came in carloads, and by that time there were hundreds of people in the street. The police shouted to us to keep back and clear the road as there was shooting, so we did so with alacrity.'

LATE NEWS

MURDER CHARGE

It was stated early today that a man who had been detained at Croydon police station will appear before Croydon magistrates this morning, charged with murder.

20 AFRICANS ARRESTED

Bloemfontein, Sunday. – Twenty Africans, volunteers in non-European defiance campaign, were arrested here tonight for breaking curfew regulations under which they are obliged to be off streets before 11 p.m. unless they have special passes.

Tuesday, 4 November:

P.c.'s MURDER: YOUTH CHARGED

'CRAIG SHOT HIM' STATEMENT READ

DEREK WILLIAM BENTLEY, 19, electrician, Fairview Road, Norbury, was remanded in custody for a week by Croydon magistrates yesterday on a charge of being concerned with CHRISTOPHER CRAIG, 16, in murdering SIDNEY MILES, a police constable. The hearing lasted only three minutes.

All public benches in the court were filled and people were still trying to gain admittance when the hearing was over. Bentley was brought from the police station across the road through a tunnel connecting the two buildings.

Chief Det. Insp. JOHN SMITH said he saw Bentley at 5.30 a.m. yesterday at Croydon Police Station and charged him with being concerned in the murder at Tamworth Road, Croydon, at about 9.30 p.m. on Sunday.

'I HAVE NOT GOT GUN'

'I cautioned him and he said, "Craig shot him, I have not got a gun. He was with me on the roof and shot him between the eyes."'

The Chief Inspector asked for Bentley to be remanded in custody until Monday. When Mr B. STILL, the chairman, asked Bentley if he had any questions, he replied: 'No, sir.'

Mr STILL: Have you anything to say why you should not be remanded in custody? – No, sir.

Do you want legal aid? – I will see my father.

When the charge was read by the Clerk, BENTLEY said in a loud voice: 'Not me, sir.' Asked if he fully understood the charge, Bentley replied: 'Yes, I understand it.'

Throughout the hearing a police officer stood in the dock with Bentley, while another officer remained by the side. Later Mr William Bentley, his father, obtained permission to see his son. He also applied for legal aid, which was granted.

An hour and a half later, Bentley was taken by car to Brixton Prison. Detectives sat on either side of him.

While the court hearing was in progress, detectives waited by the bedside of CHRISTOPHER CRAIG, 16, of Norbury Court Road, Norbury, who is in Croydon General Hospital. He is believed to have broken ribs and a wrist. It was stated by the police that Craig will be the subject of a charge when he leaves the hospital.

Detectives are trying to establish where the weapon used in the shooting was obtained. It is likely that a new appeal will be made for all people possessing weapons as war souvenirs to hand them in to the police.

Sir Harold Scott, Commissioner of the Metropolitan Police, went to Croydon yesterday and met colleagues of the dead constable. It has not yet been decided whether there will be an official funeral.

Tuesday, November 18:

CRAIG SAID 'I WAS OUT TO KILL,' MAGISTRATES' COURT TOLD

Christopher Craig, 16, accused of the murder of P.c. Sidney George Miles, was said to have remarked to a police officer in hospital: 'That night I was out to kill because I had so much hate inside me for what they have done to my brother.'

Other remarks he was said to have made were: 'You are coppers. Ah! The other one is dead with a hole in his head. I am all right. All you b— should be dead . . .' 'If I hadn't cut a bit off the barrel of my gun, I would probably have killed a lot more policemen.'

Det-Constable Frederick Fairfax described how, with a bullet wound in his right shoulder, he engaged in a roof-top gun battle with Craig. On the roof P.c. Miles lay dead, shot through the head.

CRAIG, a fitter, of Norbury Court Road, Norbury, and DEREK WILLIAM BENTLEY, 19, electrician, Fairview Road, Norbury, are jointly charged with the murder of P.c. Miles and with attempting to murder Det-Constable Fairfax on Nov 2. They were sent for trial at the Old Bailey.

Craig listened to the evidence lying on a stretcher near the witness-box. His father, Mr Nevin Matthew Craig, a bank official, bent down and spoke to him before he was taken to Brixton Prison Hospital.

Det-Constable FAIRFAX, who showed no sign of his injury, said in evidence that on being called with other police officers to the confectionery warehouse, he climbed an expanded metal gate across the side entrance and up a drainpipe on the western wall.

'Having reached the flat roof, I saw Bentley and Craig standing about 15 yards in front of me and to my right between the roof lights and the lift shaft. As I approached them they backed behind the lift shaft.

CHALLENGE TO POLICE
'Come and Get Us'

'When I got to within six feet of them I said: 'I am a police officer. Come out from behind that stack.' One of them shouted: "If you want us — well, come and get us." I said: "All right."

'I dashed behind the stack, grabbed hold of Bentley and pulled him out in the open. Craig went to the opposite side of the stack. I then took Bentley round the stack, and as we got round the other side we came face to face with Craig.

'Bentley then broke away from me, and as he did so he shouted: "Let him have it, Chris." There was a loud report and a flash, and something hit my right shoulder which caused me to spin round and fall to the ground.

'As I was getting up, I saw one man moving away on my left and another on my right. I rushed at the man on my right, who was Bentley. I closed with him and struck him with my fist, causing him to fall to the ground.

'As he did so, there was a second report and flash and I dropped down, pulling Bentley in front of me behind a roof light. I ran my hands over his clothing to see if he was carrying a gun.

'I did not find a gun, but in his right-hand pocket I found a knuckle-duster. In his right-hand breast pocket I found a knife. Bentley then said to me: "That's all I have got, guv'nor. I have not got a gun."

'I then said to him: "I am going to work you round the roof to that doorway over there." I indicated the staircase head. Bentley said: "He'll shoot you." I did not reply but pushed him in front of me round the roof to the doorway. I pushed him against the wall and said: "If you stand still, you should be safe."

'I then heard P.c. MacDonald shout up to me: "I have tried to climb a drainpipe but can't make it. Can you help me up the last bit?" I said: "Yes, I think so." P.c. MacDonald then climbed the drainpipe and I pulled him up on to the flat roof.

'I shouted to Craig: "Drop your gun," and he shouted back: "Come and get it."

'As P.c. MacDonald and I were holding Bentley, P.c. MacDonald said to me: "What sort of gun has he got, Fairy?" Before I could reply, Bentley said: "He has got a .45 Colt and plenty of — ammunition for it."

'At this stage the door at the staircase head burst open and I heard officers call to me. I told them I was round to their right and the fellow with the gun was round to their left.

'I saw P.c. Miles jump from the doorway, and as he did so there was a loud report and he fell to the floor. I went out to him and as I did so there was another report.

'I dropped on to one knee, and caught hold of his shoulders. P.c. MacDonald came forward and caught hold of his legs, and we dragged him behind the staircase wall. I examined him, but he was beyond human aid.

'A second officer, P.c. Harrison, jumped from the doorway and rushed round to us. We decided to remove Bentley down the stairs. I went first through the doorway and the other officers pushed Bentley towards me. As I pulled Bentley into the doorway he shouted: "They are taking me down, Chris."

'DROP GUN' CALL
'Come on Then, Copper'

'I took Bentley down the staircase, and at the bottom I was handed a pistol. I returned to the roof and shouted to Craig: "Drop your gun. I also have a gun." He shouted back: "Come on then, copper. Let's have it out."

'I jumped from the doorway and there was another report, and I ran in a semi-circular direction towards Craig. I fired two shots as I went. Craig vanished over the roof. I went down into the street and into a back garden where Craig had fallen.'

Mr J. F. CLANTON, prosecuting, said Craig had a fractured left wrist, a fracture and dislocation of the breast bone, a fracture of part of the spine, and contusion of the chest. He was conscious when found, and said to the police officer who held him: 'I wish I was — dead. I hope I have killed the — lot.'

A statement Bentley was said to have made to the police read: 'I have known Chris since I went to school. We were stopped by our parents going out together but we still continued going out with each other – I mean we have not gone out together until tonight.

'I was watching television tonight and between 8 and 9 p.m. Craig called for me. My mother answered the door and said I was out.

'A little later two lads called. I did not answer the door or speak to them. My mother then said they had called. I ran out to join them and went to a paper shop and saw Craig standing there.

'Chris Craig and I got a bus to West Croydon. We walked down to

Tamworth Road, where you found me. There was a little iron gate which Chris climbed over, and he went up a drainpipe to the roof. I followed.

'I knew we were going to break into the place. I don't know what we were going to get – just anything that was going. I did not know Chris had a gun until he fired one.'

P.c. JAMES C. MACDONALD said that when he got on to the roof he heard someone shout, 'Come and get it', and a shot was fired. Det. Fairfax said: 'He has got me in the shoulder.' Bentley said, 'I told the silly b— not to use it.'

He saw a man with a gun fire twice in the direction of P.c. Harrison. He then saw him fire at P.c. Miles, who fell at their feet with a wound in his head.

P.c. ROBERT JAGGS, who also climbed on to the roof by a drainpipe, said he heard the man who was doing the shooting shout, 'Come on, you great coppers. Think of your wives.' Bentley said, 'You want to look out. He will blow your heads off.'

The constable added: 'Craig shouted, "Give my love to —", and he mentioned a girl's name. I missed the last part, then he dived head-first off the roof.'

P.c. NORMAN HARRISON said he was fired at when attempting to reach the roof and later went with other officers through the front entrance and up the stairs.

'P.c. Miles kicked the door open and I saw him fall as a shot was fired. I then saw Craig, who came from behind the lift shaft. He still had a revolver held in his two hands and fired another shot towards us. I thought I heard it hit the brickwork where I was standing.

'I leaned out of the doorway and threw my truncheon, a bottle of milk and a block of wood at him. He shouted, "I am Craig. You have just given my brother 12 years. Come on, you coppers. I am only 16."

'As I left the door, another shot was fired. I assisted to take Bentley down the staircase. He shouted, "Chris, they are taking me down," and another shot was fired. I then heard Craig call out, "Are they hurting you, Derek?"

'I saw Det-Constable Fairfax fire two shots towards Craig, who shouted, "You are going to make a shooting match of it. Come on, copper, let's have it out."

TWO COUNSEL REFUSED
'Mental State' Issue

Mr DAVID NELSON, for Craig, and Mr JOHN STEVENS, for Bentley, each applied for a legal aid certificate for two counsel. Mr Nelson, submitting that there were 'special difficulties', said: 'There may be a question of the mental state of my client. It is a most serious matter. It could not be any graver.'

The CHAIRMAN: Would not state of mind be a simplification rather than a complication?

Mr NELSON: That is something that counsel will have to consider.

The application was refused, the magistrates granting both a certificate of legal aid for one counsel.

(Subsequently, the application was granted.)

Wednesday, December 10:

FATHER SAYS CRAIG WENT TO BIBLE CLASS

Neither Christopher Craig nor Derek William Bentley can read or write. This was stated yesterday when their trial began at the Old Bailey.

Mr Christmas Humphreys, opening for the prosecution, said: 'The Crown's case is that Craig deliberately murdered Miles, and thereafter gloried in the murder and only regretted he did not shoot more.

'Bentley incited Craig to begin shooting, and although he (Bentley) was technically under arrest at the time of the murder, nevertheless he still mentally supported Craig in all he continued to do and was, in English law, and you may think in common sense, in every sense a party to that murder.'

The trial is being heard by the Lord Chief Justice, Lord GODDARD. It will continue to-day. Mr F. JOHN PARRIS, a Leeds barrister, is representing Craig. Bentley is represented by Mr F. H. CASSELS, son of Mr Justice Cassels.

Craig was able to walk up the steps from the cells into the dock. A stretcher had been prepared for him in the dock, but after he had made his plea of 'not guilty', he sat down in a wicker chair with a pillow at his back. He was dressed in a fawn suit.

Bentley wore a heavy belted tweed grey overcoat. They sat side by side, without speaking, throughout the hearing. Crowds had waited outside the Old Bailey, some of them from 6 a.m., but only a small number got into the public gallery.

Craig's father and mother sat behind the dock with one of their daughters, Miss Lucy Craig. Bentley's parents and his brother and sister were in court. Two benches in front of them sat Det-Sgt. Frederick William Fairfax, who last week was awarded the George Cross for his part in arresting the youths. The posthumous award of the King's Police Medal to P.c. Miles was announced at the same time.

A jury of 12 men was empanelled after Craig's counsel had challenged two women jurors as they were about to be sworn. Lord Goddard asked the two to stand down.

Exhibits produced included a .45 revolver, a piece of sawn-off revolver barrel, and a tin box containing 149 rounds of ammunition said to have been found under the floor boards in Craig's house.

WARNING TO JURY
'Gun Battle' Reports

Mr HUMPHREYS, who spoke for 45 minutes in presenting the case for the Crown, referred to reports of 'a gun battle, as a result of which one policeman was killed and another one wounded, of a spectacular jump or dive from the roof by Craig, and of an alleged confession by Bentley.' He warned the jury to disregard these reports as the case would be tried on evidence alone.

NIVEN MATTHEWS CRAIG, father of Craig, said he was chief cashier at a bank. He served as a captain in the First World War.

His son Christopher was the youngest of a family of eight. He went to a secondary modern school until he was 15, but in spite of that never managed to read or write. He suffered from word blindness.

Mr PARRIS: You tried night after night to teach him? – Yes.

The only reading matter he is familiar with is what are called comics? – Yes, just small works.

The only books he knows anything about are the books of Enid Blyton, which he gets other people to read to him? – Yes.

INTEREST IN SHOOTING
Taught Elder Boys

Asked whether he encouraged his family to take an interest in shooting because he was a good marksman himself, Mr Craig replied: 'I did teach my elder boys to shoot well with airguns and pistols, but not with revolvers. Christopher's ambition in life had been to become a gunsmith, but this was not taken seriously at home.'

Mr PARRIS: As a result of being unable to read, he started going to the films a lot? – Yes.

Was he ever to your knowledge a violent boy? – No, he was quite the opposite, gentle. Until about 18 months ago he went to a Church Bible class at Streatham. Unfortunately he did not wish to continue with that because he was afraid of being asked to read the lesson. All his life he has been very consious of the fact that he cannot read, and was mocked by other boys.

In reply to further questions, Mr Craig said he had been fined £5 for possessing a firearm without a licence in 1942. He did not know Christopher had sawn off the barrel of the revolver or that he had hidden in the house a large quantity of ammunition.

JUDGE SEES WEAPONS
Knuckleduster and Knife

Det. Sgt. FAIRFAX, after describing how he was shot in the shoulder and how he caught Bentley, produced the knuckleduster and dagger-type knife he found on Bentley. These were examined by Lord Goddard.

Mr CASSELS: I suggest that Bentley never said, 'Let him have it, Chris', or anything else. – Yes, he did, sir.

P.c. J. MACDONALD, who arrived at the scene of the shooting in the car with P.c. Miles, told how he followed Fairfax up the drainpipe to the roof.

He was unable to get up the last six feet and climbed down again, but he heard someone shout: 'Let him have it, Chris.' He did not know the voice. He heard two or three shots.

Mr CASSELS: I suggest Bentley never said, 'Let him have it, Chris', if anyone did. – I do not know.

Lord GODDARD: There were three people on the roof, Craig, Bentley and Fairfax, and you heard someone say, 'Let him have it, Chris'? – Yes, sir.

P.c. NORMAN HARRISON said he climbed to the sloping roof of the warehouse and watched Fairfax detain Bentley, who broke away and shouted: 'Let him have it, Chris.'

Police Sgt EDWARD ROBERTS said that, after being cautioned, Bentley said: 'I did not have a gun. Chris shot him.' On the way to the station in the police car, he said: 'I knew he had a gun, but I did not think he would use it. He has done one of your blokes in.'

Police Sgt. STUART LOWE described how he saw from below Craig sitting on the iron railings surrounding the flat roof. He was holding a revolver in both hands and pointing it towards the staircase where the police officers were and making disjointed remarks.

P.c. HENRY STEPHENS, driver of the police car which took Bentley to Croydon Police Station, said that

Bentley's remark about knowing that Craig had a gun was spontaneous.

JUDGE'S REGRET
JOURNEY BY DOCTOR 'UNNECESSARY'

Dr NICHOLAS JASMON, who was casualty officer at Croydon General Hospital when Fairfax was brought in for treatment for his shoulder, described the wound. Replying to Mr Parris, he said the bullet caused a skin wound and had gone up and over the shoulder.

Mr PARRIS: That would indicate that it was fired from a low position?

Lord GODDARD: It seems a self-evident proposition.

Mr PARRIS: Is it consistent with a ricochet off the floor, dropping down behind?

Lord GODDARD: The doctor is here to give medical evidence, not to speculate on the flight of bullets.

Mr PARRIS: If your Lordship will not allow me to put the question, then I will not put it.

Dr JASMON, who had come from Manchester to give evidence, said he did not think he could answer the question.

Lord GODDARD said he 'very much regretted' that the doctor had been brought there on a perfectly unnecessary journey. The purpose of binding over was to prevent doctors and other people from being brought to the court when their evidence was purely formal.

Dr GORDON HADFIELD, of Croydon General Hospital, produced records and gave evidence of the drugs administered to Craig in hospital. He said Craig had been given pethidine, codeine, pentothal and atropine to relieve pain and for operations.

Cross-examined by Mr Parris, he agreed that pentothal was sometimes called 'the truth drug' in America.

Mr PARRIS: It makes people talk; undermines the will, so to speak – it makes them talk freely? – Yes.

And say things, perhaps, that they would not normally say?

Lord GODDARD: Do you know if it is given for this purpose?

Dr HADFIELD: A small dose may be given over a long time to make a patient talk.

Mr PARRIS: If a large quantity is given suddenly, it will make a patient unconscious? – Yes.

Replying to a further question, Dr Hadfield said he would not agree that the effects of the drug would be felt long after the person had had it.

Mr PARRIS: People vary in their reaction, do they not? It might be that the effect would not have worn off long after? – That is unlikely.

But it is possible? – Yes.

Asked if the drug pethidine was sometimes administered because it made people 'feel on top of the world and boast of their achievements', Dr Hadfield agreed that it did induce a feeling of buoyancy.

Answering Mr Humphreys, Dr Hadfield said the purpose of giving the drug to Craig was to render him unconscious for the operation. When his wrist was being re-set, he was given a smaller dose, and these were the only occasions it was administered to him in the hospital. There was no evidence that anything he said was caused by confusion of mind as a result of the drug.

VISIT TO HOME
Ammunition Find

Det. Sgt. STANLEY SHEPHERD said he went to Craig's home and in his bed found a .45 bullet. Under the floor boards in an attic he found a piece of sawn-off revolver barrel and a considerable quantity of ammunition in tin boxes.

Cross-examined by Mr Cassels, Sgt. Shepherd said he did not know if Bentley was close to being a feeble-minded person. When signing the statement he made, he asked how to spell his name.

Mr CASSELS: Is it right that Bentley is illiterate and that he cannot read or write? – So he says.

P.c. BROWN said Craig said to him in hospital: 'If I had not cut a bit of the barrel off my gun, I would probably have killed a lot more policemen. That night I was out to kill because I had so much hate inside me for what they did to my brother. I shot the policeman in the head with my .45 – if it had been the .22, he might not have died.'

Thursday, December 11:

CRAIG COUNSEL ASKS FOR MANSLAUGHTER VERDICT

For nearly an hour yesterday, Christopher Craig alternately sat and stood in the witness-box at the Old Bailey and told the story of his 'mania' for guns which led to the shooting of P.c. Miles.

In reply to his counsel, Mr Parris, he said he was born on May 19, 1936. Until the events of the night of Nov. 2 he had always lived at home with his parents. The only time he had been in trouble before was in November, 1951, when he was fined for possessing a firearm without a certificate.

Mr PARRIS: When did you first take an interest in firearms? – When I was about 11, but I liked them when I was about seven.

Where did you get them from? – I swopped them with other boys at school.

Between the age of 11 and now, how many guns have you had? – Forty or fifty.

Keep your voice up, Christopher. Were there any other boys in the school who had weapons? – Five, maybe more.

How did your interest in weapons arise? – Through seeing my father.

What was your interest? – Finding out how they worked.

Were you interested in firing them? – I fired a couple of them.

Were you a very good shot? – No, sir.

Did you on one occasion go with your father to a shooting range? – Yes.

WHISPER TO JUDGE
Knew Firearms Killed

Lord GODDARD intervened at this point: 'Did you know that firearms kill?' he asked Craig. For a second or two Craig looked at the Judge, and then was heard to say almost in a whisper: 'Yes.'

In further reply to Mr Parris, he said his real interest in guns was in taking them to pieces, and re-making them, and his ambition was to be a gunsmith.

Did you ever take a gun to work? – Yes, nearly every day.

Why? – Because it made me feel big.

Did people ever say anything to you about not being able to read properly? – Yes, they used to take the Mickey out of me.

Do you go to the pictures? – Yes, three or four times a week.

What sort of films do you see? – Gangster films.

Coming to the Sunday night, you and Bentley were on the rooftop to get into the sweetshop. How long were you there before the police officers arrived? – About a couple of minutes.

Where did you first see Det. Fairfax? – At the main gate.

When he came on to the roof, where were you? – Behind the stack.

Tell us what happened. – He came from the drainpipe and came round and grabbed Bentley.

The officer said that Bentley said: 'Let him have it, Chris.' Did you hear any words like that? – No, sir.

When was the first shot fired? – He was level with the glass.

Where did you fire? – Down on the ground a few feet in front.

Did you fire another shot? – Not then, sir. The officer got up and rushed at Bentley and I fired another to frighten him off.

Did you fire at him? – Over the side.

Had you any intention of hitting that officer? – No, sir. I did it to frighten him away.

Lord GODDARD: How many rounds did you fire? – Nine, sir.

Then you re-loaded the revolver? – Yes.

Mr PARRIS: Did you see Miles come on to the roof? – I did not see him come on the roof. I saw someone come and I fired another shot to frighten them away. I fired it over the parapet.

Lord GODDARD: How did it come to hit P.c. Miles? – It might have ricocheted.

Mr PARRIS: Had you any intention at any time of killing that officer? – No, sir.

Had you any intention at any time of doing any officer harm? – No, sir. I wanted to frighten them away.

Why did you say the things you were alleged to have said on the roof-top? – It was all bluff.

You were standing there with a gun in your hands. What did you think you were like?

Craig hesitated for a moment, then ran his tongue around his lips and replied: 'Like the films.'

Lord GODDARD, intervening again, asked Craig: 'Have you ever expressed any regret or sorrow that you killed that officer?'

Craig replied: 'Yes.' But when the Judge asked him when, and to whom, his replies were inaudible.

When asked by Mr PARRIS why he dived from the roof, he said: 'I was upset and I wanted to kill myself.'

The next thing he could remember was being in hospital and 'someone hitting me on the mouth and calling me a murderous bastard'.

Craig nodded when Mr HUMPHREYS asked: 'On this night you shct P.c. Miles?'

And he died. You meant to shoot him, didn't you? – No, sir.

You meant to shoot any police officer who tried to prevent you from committing a felony? – No, sir.

You knew Bentley and had known him for some time? – No, sir. I have known him for about eight months.

You were with him frequently? – Not frequently, because I was often out with my girl. I was with him sometimes.

You sawed off the gun barrel so that you could carry it about more easily when you went house-breaking? – I did not go house-breaking.

Lord GODDARD: Shop-breaking, then? – But I used to take it to work with me.

Mr HUMPHREYS: You had ammunition at home. Where did you get it? – From an Army barracks.

You asked Bentley to go with you on this night? – No, sir.

He asked you? – No, sir, dared me to go with him and break into a butcher's shop.

WORE SHEATH KNIFE
Knuckle-duster Spike

You went home to get something to eat and to get that gun? – No, sir, it was already in my pocket.

Craig said he always carried a knife with him too. He turned to the jury and demonstrated how he wore a sheath knife on his left hip, under his jacket. He made the knuckle-duster at work.

Lord GODDARD, holding the knuckle-duster towards the jury, fitted it on his hand and asked Craig: 'What is this spike for?' Craig said he did not know.

Lord GODDARD: What is a knuckle-duster for? – To put on your hand.

To put on your hand to hit anyone. What is this dreadful spike for? You said you made this? Why did you put this dreadful spike in? – It was already there.

Bentley, he said, did not know he had a gun until they were on the roof-top and saw the policeman. Then he told Bentley that he had a loaded gun.

Lord GODDARD: Did you tell him you had a gun so as to make him feel safe up there with you? – No, sir.

'HATE INSIDE ME'
Statement Not Remembered

Mr Humphreys then referred to the statement Craig was said to have made in the hospital: 'That night I was out to kill because I had so much hate inside me for what they have done to my brother.'

CRAIG: Did I say that? I do not remember. I was injected with drugs every 12 hours.

Are you saying that on Nov 6 you did not know what you were saying? – I do not remember.

Lord GODDARD: The police had arrested your brother. He had been convicted and he had a gun? – Yes.

Asked by Mr HUMPHREYS about other statements he was said to have made, Craig replied: 'It is ridiculous.'

Mr HUMPHREYS: You intended to shoot any person who tried to prevent you from committing that crime? – No, to frighten them.

You shot Det Fairfax at six feet range? – No, 27 ft.

Lord GODDARD: Did you say, 'Come on, you brave coppers, think of your wives?' – I do not know.

What did you mean by that? – It was bluff.

'In other words, think of your wives who will be widows if you do come on?' asked the Judge. Craig did not reply.

Mr HUMPHREYS: You saw P.c. Miles fall and never move again? – He did move.

You saw the officers pull him in to cover. You knew he had been hit by you? – Yes.

Lord GODDARD: After P.c. Miles's body had been moved, did you fire again? – Twice.

After you had seen P.c. Miles lying there, and his body taken in, you fired again, twice? – More than twice, in the air.

Mr HUMPHREYS: You did not like fighting people when they had guns? – It was not that, but I realised I had hurt someone.

Lord GODDARD: Have you ever expressed any regret? – I have thought about it. Who was there to express it to?

You saw plenty of policemen, because they were watching you at your bedside. – I was hardly conscious.

Lord GODDARD: Nonsense.

BENTLEY: 'I DID NOT DARE CRAIG'

BENTLEY, a tall, well-built youth in a grey tweed suit, followed Craig in the witness-box and gave his evidence in a clear, firm voice.

Answering Mr CASSELS, his counsel, he said he first knew Craig at school, and after leaving school saw him on occasions. On the day of the shooting, he first saw Craig in the morning. No arrangements were made about later.

It was not true that he dared Craig to come with him to a butcher's shop. Later he met Craig at the end of the road. They stood together for a little time and then got a bus to Croydon.

Lord GODDARD: What were you going to do when you got to Croydon? – Walk around.

'On the bus Craig gave me a pair of knuckle-dusters. I had not seen them before. I put them in my pocket.' They then went down the road in Croydon where the warehouse was situated. Craig got over the fence and climbed up the drainpipe, and he followed.

At that time he did not know Craig had a loaded revolver. When they got on the roof, a light flashed in the garden and someone called out. Sgt. Fairfax then got on the roof, grabbed him and walked him across it.

'I made no attempt to struggle or to strike him. I did not say, "Let him have it, Chris." Until the shot was fired I did not know he had a gun.'

VIOLENCE DENIAL
No Incitement to Craig

Answering Mr CASSELS, he said: 'I never at any time told Craig to use the gun or use violence towards the police, and I did not use any violence myself.'

Mr HUMPHREYS: Why were you given the knuckle-duster? – I do not know. I just put it in my pocket.

When Bentley said he shouted, 'Look out, Chris. They are taking me down' because he thought he might have got hit by a shot, Lord GODDARD remarked: 'You were only thinking of your own skin.'

Mr HUMPHREYS: You were prepared to assist Craig in hitting with the knuckle-duster, stabbing with the knife, or shooting with the revolver in escaping from the crime you were committing? – No.

CLOSING SPEECH FOR CROWN
EFFECT OF DRUGS

Mr HUMPHREYS, in his closing speech for the Crown, said a lesser verdict than murder against Craig could only arise if the jury found there was an element of accident or excusable mistake in the shooting of the officer. They could only find a verdict of manslaughter against Craig if they were satisfied that the shooting was an accident in these terms.

What Craig was saying was that almost every one of the police officers was wrong – that three out of four witnesses for the Crown were wrong.

'He is only a boy, and in hospital he was receiving drugs from time to time. But because it might reasonably be said by the defence that he did not know what he was talking about when he made the statements, a doctor from the hospital was called to tell precisely what drugs he was given and what effect they would have had on him.'

Had the prosecution not been satisfied that he was capable of making the statements, the evidence would not have been given. The cumulative effect of the evidence was all one way.

Before he had had any drugs, his first statement was: 'I had six in the gun I fired at the policeman.' Mr Humphreys said this was clearly a precise statement of deliberate intent. 'It is difficult to choose words from the English language that would convey that intent more clearly.'

P.c. Miles was shot between the eyes by a young man who boasted that he was interested in firearms all his life, had shot from ten different firearms, and was in possession of an enormous quantity of ammunition.

On the roof, P.c. Harrison was a sitting target, utterly helpless, but Craig shot at him twice, and one bullet struck the chimney stack close to him. 'Out of nine bullets fired, he hit two human beings and had a not very wide miss of a third helpless target lying on the roof.'

BENTLEY'S CASE
'A Different Proposition'

Bentley was 'a different proposition' and different considerations applied. It was right that he never had a gun in his hand and was almost at the receiving end of Craig's fire when P.c. Miles was killed. To some extent he was under arrest.

The most important statement he made was the deliberate incitement to Craig to begin the shooting, the answer from Craig being the bullet which hit Sgt Fairfax.

Was it not amazing that in spite of Craig's boasting, Bentley did not know he was carrying a gun? Was it not also amazing that Bentley was carrying a murderous dagger and that he was given a knuckle-duster with a murderous spike at the end of it?

Referring to the incidents on the roof, Mr Humphreys said that at no time did Bentley say or shout anything to show that he was trying to stop Craig. 'Young though they be, they are both responsible for what they do, and I ask you to return a verdict of guilty of wilful murder against each.'

WAYWARD YOUTH SYMBOL
DEFENCE WARNING

Mr PARRIS, addressing the jury on behalf of Craig, said they would have to arrive at their verdict on the evidence and not on comments made by counsel or by what they might have read. They could not decide the case on prejudice, though vindictive things might have been said about Craig and pictures of him published portraying him as a young thug.

'The tragedy of this trial is that Craig has become the symbol of wayward youth. All the nation's anxiety and uneasiness about the state of youth has been fixed on him, and there is a danger that you may lose sight of him as he is and just regard him as a symbol of wayward youth.'

Pointing to Craig in the dock, Mr Parris said: 'He is not a thug. Look at his eyes, his mouth, the way he speaks. The picture that has been built up of him is a false one.'

BRAVE AND NOBLE
P.c. Died Doing Duty

Everyone must feel indignation and sorrow that a brave and noble police officer had died doing his duty, and Craig's mother must be the most tragic mother in England.

He did not ask the jury to acquit Craig entirely but to say that he was not guilty of murder but of manslaughter. The defence was that in the course of the events of the night of Nov 2, Craig accidentally caused the injury to the officer.

'The boy that night was a veritable walking armoury. The very extravagance of it showed that it was there for bravado and not for use. Look at him – the boy with a fascination for firearms since the age of 11. You may think that unfortunately he got that from his father's interest.

'He is a boy who likes to feel big and be admired by his schoolmates because he has got weapons. Think back to the days of your own childhood. Did you not on occasions carry the most sinister-looking knives? Recall the days when you played games of Cops and Robbers or Highwaymen or Cowboys and Indians or Bow Street Runners.'

This, said Mr Parris, was Craig's mental attitude on this night. 'There is a most deplorable alteration in the conditions in which young people are brought up these days, particularly through the influence of films, especially some American films. The gangster film is corrupting the youth of the nation and putting ideas into the heads of youth that would never be there but for this constant influence.'

The statements he was alleged to have made were only bravado. On the rooftop he saw himself behaving like one of the men in the films, melodramatic, play-acting, dramatising his position. 'But he was only a silly, misguided little fool.'

The jury might think it was a tragic, unfortunate, million-to-one shot that killed P.c. Miles and that the bullet was one which may have struck the parapet and ricocheted. They might think it was an unhappy, miserable and tragic accident.

Lord GODDARD intervened and said he would have to tell the jury that this was not the law, for reasons which he would explain later.

Mr CASSELS, in his speech for Bentley, said that before the jury could consider whether or not Bentley was guilty, they would have to be satisfied that Craig was.

Bentley never had the gun and never fired a shot. The jury would have to satisfy themselves on two points before giving their verdict on Bentley. The first was whether Bentley knew Craig carried a gun, and secondly, if he knew it, whether he incited, counselled, or inspired him to use violence to resist arrest.

Friday, December 12:

CRAIG TO BE HELD: DEATH SENTENCE ON BENTLEY

Jury's Mercy Rider: 'Terrible Case,' Says Judge: 3 Policemen Praised

Christopher Craig and Derek William Bentley were found guilty at the Old Bailey yesterday of murdering P.c. Sidney Miles. The jury took an hour and 17 minutes to reach their verdict.

The Lord Chief Justice, Lord Goddard, wearing the black cap, sentenced Bentley to death. He ordered Craig to be detained during Her Majesty's pleasure. He said the jury's recommendation of mercy in Bentley's case would be sent to the Home Secretary.

Neither Craig nor Bentley showed any emotion. Bentley was sentenced first, and Craig stood beside him as the black cap was placed on the Judge's head.

The Judge's summing-up took 45 minutes. Lord GODDARD said that in many respects the case was a 'very terrible' one. He and the jury must approach it as calmly as they could.

'Here are two lads, one 16 and one 19, admittedly out on a shopbreaking expedition at night, armed with a Service revolver, a dreadful weapon in the shape of a knuckle-duster, and two knives, which may or may not be described as daggers.

'The result is a young policeman is shot dead in the execution of his duty. You may think that it is almost a miracle that others were not shot too. One of them, you know, Det. Sgt. Fairfax, was wounded, fortunately not seriously.

'Let us put out of our minds in this case any question of films, or comics, or literature of that sort. These things are always prayed in aid nowadays, when young persons are in the dock, and they really have very little to do with the case.'

'HATE' MOTIVE
Brother's 12-Year Sentence

Both Bentley and Craig were of an age which made them responsible in law. As far as Craig was concerned, he had supplied the motive in his own words when he said he hated the police because they got his brother 12 years.

It seemed to show that his brother was convicted of a very serious offence to receive a sentence like that. It was not disputed that Craig fired the shot which killed the policeman.

The jury had been asked to say that the killing was accidental and that therefore the offence should be reduced to manslaughter. 'It may be, and indeed I think it is probable that you will say, when I have explained the law, that there is no room for a verdict of manslaughter in this case, though it is a matter for you.'

Explaining the law, Lord Goddard said: 'If in an ordinary case in which no police officer was concerned, you thought a prisoner only meant to fire wildly and to shoot off a revolver in a grossly negligent way, but was so negligent he deserved punishment and death resulted, that would only be manslaughter.

LAW'S PROTECTION
Policemen On Duty

'But you have to consider all the facts before you could come to that conclusion.' P.c. Miles was a police officer and the law had for centuries given special protection to police officers while in the execution of their duty.

'Perhaps it would be more accurate to say that in the case of a police officer who is killed, the law does not give the accused the same defence as in the case of other persons.

'I am going to direct you that this is the law: If a police officer has arrested or is endeavouring to arrest, and that includes coming on to the scene for the purpose of arresting a person and the arrest if effected would be lawful, and that person for the purpose of escape or preventing or hindering the arrest does a wilful, that is to say an intentional, act which causes the death of the officer, he is guilty of murder whether or not he intended to kill or do grievous bodily harm.'

A person who was doing such things as firing off a pistol at police officers could not say 'it was accidental because I never intended to kill him'.

'Now that I have explained the law to you, it may be you will have some difficulty, as I do not hesitate to say I have, in understanding what defence there can be for Craig.

'There he was on the roof with a loaded revolver, firing off shots until his revolver was empty.' He reloaded it and fired altogether nine shots and tried to fire eleven. 'If that is not a deliberate act, it is difficult to understand what would be.'

Referring to Craig's remarks made to police officers during the affray, Lord Goddard commented: 'You may wonder why he said "I am only 16." Possibly you may know that the law does not allow a capital sentence to be passed on a boy of 16.

'Was it a boast? "Ha, ha, I am only 16, I have got a gun. I cannot be hanged."' When they took all the facts together, was it possible that the shooting was accidental?

BENTLEY'S CRIME
Knowledge Of Gun

Dealing with Bentley, he said that where two or more persons were engaged together in an unlawful or criminal act, it was unnecessary to show that the 'hand' of both committed the act.

It was no answer for one to say: 'I did not think my companion would go as far as he did.' The first thing the jury would have to consider was: Did Bentley know Craig was armed?

'Can you suppose for a moment, especially when you have heard Craig say why he carried a revolver, that it was for the purpose of boasting and showing that he was a bigger man, that he would not have told his pal he had a revolver? Is it not inconceivable that Craig would not have shown him the revolver he had?

'I should think you would come to the conclusion that the first thing Craig would tell him if they were going on a shop-breaking expedition was: "It is all right. I have got a revolver."'

'HORRIBLE WEAPON'
Spiked Knuckle-duster

Referring to the weapons found on Bentley, he said: 'Where is that knuckle-duster?' The weapon was passed up to him and he fitted it on his hand and held it out towards the jury.

'Have you ever seen a more horrible sort of weapon? There you have got a dreadful heavy steel bar to strike anybody with on the face and even kill a person. Did you ever see a more shocking weapon?

'It has got this spike with which you can jab a person, as if the blow of the steel is not enough. It is a shocking thing. Here is Craig

THE REVOLVER used by Christopher Craig, 16, who with Derek Bentley was yesterday found guilty at the Old Bailey of the murder of P.c. Miles. The gun is a .45 with part of the barrel sawn off. RIGHT: The knuckle-duster, a spike welded on to it, which was found on Bentley.

armed with a revolver and that sheath knife, the big one. Hand it up.' The knife was passed up to him and he held it up for the jury to see.

'I do not know what parents can be thinking about these days, letting a boy of 16 – although they say they did not know – have a weapon like this to take about. It is not new, you can see. This is Craig's.

'Here is Bentley with a smaller knife which you can feel is sharp and pointed, and he carried it in his coat.' The most serious piece of evidence against Bentley was that he had called out, if the jury believed the evidence, 'Let him have it, Chris.'

DEADLY EVIDENCE
Statement by 3 Officers

These words were sworn to by three police officers. 'There is one thing I am sure I can say to all you 12 gentlemen, and that is that the police officers that night, and these three officers in particular, showed the highest gallantry and resolution.

'They were conspicuously brave. Are you going to say that they were conspicuous liars? If their evidence is untrue, these three officers are doing their best to swear away the life of that boy. If it is true, it is a most deadly piece of evidence against him.'

Referring to Bentley's other statement: 'They are taking me down, Chris,' he said this was nothing like so important. 'Whether it was an invitation to Craig to go on shooting, or an invitation to stop shooting lest he, the precious Bentley, should suffer, does not matter. By that time P.c. Miles was dead.'

Bentley had said he did not know Craig had a gun. Could they believe that he went on this expedition with 'this boastful young ruffian' without knowing that he had a gun?

The Judge concluded by saying that the jury had a duty to the prisoners, and they also had a duty to the community.

4 YEARS FOR ARMED ROBBERY

While the jury was out, NORMAN ERNEST PARSLEY, 16, schoolboy, Stratford Road, Thornton Heath, was sentenced to four years' imprisonment for armed robbery. He pleaded guilty.

Craig was with Parsley when the robbery took place. Both of them had revolvers.

It was stated that Parsley was of above average intellect, had won a scholarship to his grammar-school, and would have been going to a university next year. He had found Craig to be 'of magnetic personality'.

Mr J. S. BASS, prosecuting, said that on Oct 18, Mr and Mrs Christopher Howes were at their home in Brighton Road, Croydon, at about 7.30 p.m. when the doorbell rang. Mrs Howes, who answered it, was confronted by two men with masks over their faces.

They demanded money. Mr Howes came out and saw the two men, who pointed revolvers indiscriminately at him and his wife.

Lord GODDARD: The other one was Craig? – No doubt about that.

After Craig's arrest, the police saw Parsley, who at first denied the offence but later made an admission and statement. A .32 revolver and five rounds of ammunition were found at his home. The weapon was slightly defective but could sometimes be fired.

Lord GODDARD: 'Whether it was meant to be discharged or not, it was held at this unfortunate lady and her husband.'

Mr BASS then read a statement in which Parsley had said that Craig told him that he had something on that night and there was no risk. The statement ended: 'We agreed not to use the guns unless we had to.'

Lord GODDARD: 'Exactly.'

Mr JOHN HAZAN, defending, said that at the time of the robbery Parsley regarded it as a great adventure, but had since expressed regret. He was not an habitué of Craig's.

Lord GODDARD said: 'It is true you are only 16, and that you were in company that night with a young lad who is apparently a serious criminal. From your educational report, it is idle to pretend that you did not know the seriousness of what you were doing.'

For the sake of getting what money he could, he had terrified an old lady who might have died from a heart attack, and then terrified her husband. This type of crime was rife.

'I and other judges will do our best to let young men know what will happen to them if they do this sort of thing. There is not one word in your statement which shows you expressed contrition. You are under 21. If you had been older I should have sent you to prison for 12 years.'

JURY'S VERDICT
Two Youths Silent

When the jury delivered their verdict, neither Bentley nor Craig replied when asked if they had anything to say before sentence was passed.

Sentencing Bentley, the Judge said: 'You are 19 years of age. It is therefore my duty to pass on you the only sentence which the law can pass for the crime of wilful murder.'

To Craig he said: 'You are not 19, but in my judgment and evidently in the judgment of the jury, you are the more guilty of the two. Your heart was filled with hate and you murdered the policeman without thought of his wife, family or himself. Never once have you expressed a word of sorrow for what you have done.

'I shall tell the Secretary of State, in forwarding the recommendation in Bentley's case from the jury, that in my opinion you are one of the most dangerous young criminals that has ever stood in that dock.

HOLD-UP OF COUPLE
Led Another Boy

'While the jury were out considering the verdict in this case, I had to deal with another case in which you were concerned with another boy whom you led into it, holding up an elderly couple at the point of revolvers and stealing from them.

'It is quite obvious that the people of this country will not be safe while you are out of prison. I shall recommend the time I suggest to the Secretary of State that you shall be detained.

'The sentence is that you be kept in strict custody until the pleasure of Her Majesty is known.'

At the command 'Take him down' from the Judge, two warders with their hands behind his arms took Craig below.

Craig's parents and his sister Lucy had sat behind the dock throughout the trial. Bentley's parents with their son, Denis, 10, and daughter Iris, 21, had also been in the court.

When sentence was passed, only Mr Craig and Mr Bentley were in court. Their families left when the jury went out, and did not return. The result of the case was given to them outside and Mrs Bentley, sobbing bitterly, was driven away in a car.

Craig's father waved to his son as he left the dock. Crowds of people, some of whom had queued all night, waited outside to hear the result. Craig was taken to Wormwood Scrubs and Bentley to Wandsworth Prison.

THESE BRAVE OFFICERS
Judge's Commendation

When the case ended, Lord Goddard called for Det. Sgt. FREDERICK FAIRFAX, who was wounded in the shooting, P.c. JAMES MACDONALD and P.c. NORMAN HARRISON. Addressing Chief Det. Insp. John Smith, he said: 'The conduct of the men of Z Division on this night in the arrest of these two desperate young criminals is worthy of the highest commendation.

'The thanks of the community are due to the police for their gallant conduct. They are all deserving of commendation, but I have asked these three in particular to stand forward, as they showed such commendable courage on that night.

'It is no light thing to face a burglar or housebreaker in the dark while he is armed with a revolver and firing, in the way you did. I do not doubt that any of your comrades that night would have shown exactly the same courage.

'It so happened that you three officers were exposed to the worst of it, and therefore had more opportunity. The thanks of law-abiding citizens ought to be tendered to you.'

GANG'S GUNS WERE STOLEN OR BOUGHT ILLEGALLY

The ease with which Craig and his friends obtained firearms and ammunition has alarmed many parents. The 300 boys at Norbury Manor School, where Craig was a pupil, have been warned that anyone found with a gun will be severely punished.

Police inquiries have established that there is no centre at Croydon where arms are sold, but it is known that they can be bought in London. Some of Craig's weapons were given to him by friends of his brother, Niven.

The gun that killed P.c. Miles had been stolen from a Purley house. Its loss was not reported because the owner had no permit.

Craig's story in the witness-box that the ammunition found at his home had been picked up from shooting ranges was closely investigated by the police. They found nothing to support it.

Police believe some of it had been bought illegally and that the rest had been stolen and passed on to Craig. Other boys in the gang had guns originally obtained from people who had not handed in war souvenirs.

MANY DIFFERENT GUNS
Greatest Interest In Life

A 15-year-old pupil at Craig's old school said: 'I do not know how many different guns I saw him with. They seemed to be his greatest interest in life.

'He mostly had .22 calibre pistols,

but I have known him bring starting pistols and all sorts of guns. There was an old French revolver of which he was particularly proud.

'He seemed to change and become moody after leaving school and starting work. He often came round to my house in the evenings, and we all noticed that he seemed to be getting more and more miserable. When his brother Niven was sentenced, it seemed to finish him completely.'

The youngest of eight children, three boys and five girls, Craig lived at home with his parents in a seven-roomed terrace house in Norbury Court Road. At home he was not unduly troublesome but was naturally lazy.

He had a flair for engineering work and repairing wireless sets. Soon after leaving school he went to work as a petrol pump attendant in a Croydon garage. It was here that the 'ragging' referred to at the trial took place. He carried a gun to work because 'it made me feel big'.

REPORTED MISSING
Found Hiding On Beach

It was while employed at the garage that he clashed with the police. One day he left home for work but did not return, and in the evening was reported missing. Police found that he and another boy were trying to get out of the country.

A warning that the boys might be armed was sent to all police in the Southern Counties. Soon afterwards an officer found them hiding under an upturned rowing boat on the beach at Hove. Craig had a revolver with two bullets in it. He was fined for possessing a firearm.

He took to wearing slouch felt hats, smoked cigars, and went out with girls several nights a week. He was at a cinema with one of them on the afternoon of Nov 2, a few hours before the gun battle on the roof in Croydon.

BENTLEY'S WEAKNESS
Injured In Bombing Raids

It was during this period that he renewed his association with Bentley, whom he had met some years before. Bentley, lonely because he thought everybody knew of his year at an approved school for stealing tools, encouraged the friendship.

Bentley was always physically and mentally weak. When only a few hours old, he had an operation which left a permanent chest weakness. Twice during the war he was buried under the debris of his home in Southwark during bombing raids. He received head injuries.

He was convicted of shopbreaking, and in 1948 was again in trouble with the police and was sent to an approved school at Bristol. He returned home in 1950 and was so ill that he was unable to keep a job. His father, an electrician, took him on as an assistant.

Mrs Craig, referred to by counsel at the trial as 'England's most tragic mother', has been interested in the work of approved schools and once gave a broadcast talk. Her subject was 'War and the Young Offender'.

REPORT ON CRAIG BY SCHOOL HEAD

'MENTAL LAZINESS'

Croydon Education Committee were told last night that one of the reasons for Christopher Craig's low educational standard mentioned during his trial was lack of co-operation on the part of his parents.

Mr F. H. Glogg, headmaster of Norbury Manor, Craig's former school, in a report to the committee said: 'I formed the opinion that his trouble was not so much inherent inability as mental laziness, and matters were not made any easier for us by the fact that his elder sisters consistently read to him during the evenings.

'There was no co-operation whatever on the part of the parents and certainly no evidence of any interest in the boy's education. They made no effort to be present when the youth employment officer had the boy's future employment in hand.

'In conclusion, I would add that Craig was perfectly amenable to school discipline, and on no occasion did he show resentment to corporal punishment, nor did he evince any anti-social tendencies.

'He presented no special problem other than his low standard of attainments, and had I not known of his background I would have entertained no misgivings about his future.'

Mr Glogg explained that Craig could not be sent to a special school because at the time of his transfer to the senior school his intelligence quotient test, based mainly on verbal questions, showed that his intelligence was not low enough to warrant such a course.

'The suggestion that he was completely illiterate when he left school is not true. He could make out simple words and read easy passages, but I doubt whether he could comprehend, for example, the leading article in a newspaper.'

Monday, December 15:

DEREK BENTLEY TO APPEAL

The Registrar of the Court of Criminal Appeal will today receive the appeal form which Bentley signed on Saturday.

Mr John S. Stevens, Bentley's solicitor at the trial, visited the condemned man on Saturday afternoon. Though Mr Stevens's duties under the legal aid certificate ended when the trial finished, he said that 'out of ordinary humanity', he felt he should help him to fill up the appeal form. Bentley cannot write.

Tuesday, January 13, 1953:

BENTLEY APPEAL NOT REACHED

Derek William Bentley, 19, waited for two hours in a cell beneath the Court of Criminal Appeal yesterday, only to learn that his appeal against conviction on a murder charge had not been reached and would be heard today.

Wednesday, January 14:

BENTLEY PLEA REJECTED

An hour before the appeal was due to be heard, people began to form a queue outside the Law Courts. Women outnumbered men in the public gallery, which was crowded. Bentley's father sat with his daughter, Iris, but Mrs Bentley waited in the corridor with her younger son, Denis, 10.

Bentley, who was brought from Wandsworth Prison, remained seated while his counsel, Mr F. H. Cassels, addressed the three judges – Mr Justice Croom-Johnson, Mr Justice Ormerod and Mr Justice Pearson.

Mr CASSELS said that the grounds of the appeal were that Lord Goddard, the Lord Chief Justice, who tried the case, had failed to put Bentley's defence adequately before the jury. This, he submitted, amounted to misdirection.

The only references to Bentley's defence in the summing up were a denial that he had said 'Let him have it, Chris', the statement that Bentley did not know Craig was going to shoot, and that he did not know Craig had a gun. The defence went further than that.

The question of Bentley's knowledge of the fact that Craig had a gun was a major issue in the case, but the Lord Chief Justice had made no reference to this.

Mr Justice CROOM-JOHNSON: The Lord Chief Justice is summing up the case for the defence when he says 'Bentley's defence is "I did not know he had a gun and I deny that I said I knew he had one."'

NEGATIVE DEFENCE

Mr CHRISTMAS HUMPHREYS, for the Crown, said the defence was of a negative type. It was that the case had not been proved and that the police were not telling the truth. It could be put to the jury in summing up in a few words.

Mr Justice CROOM-JOHNSON, giving judgment, said there was overwhelming evidence that Bentley knew what Craig was ready to do. It had been suggested that the Lord Chief Justice, in summing up, had not given sufficient attention to denials made by Bentley, and had not indicated that statements made by the police had not been accepted by the defence.

'Speaking personally, after almost a lifetime of experience of jury actions in criminal cases, I am bound to say that these arguments come to me, I will not say with a sense of unreality, but as something far divorced from what one usually finds at criminal trials.'

He could see nothing wrong with the way the Lord Chief Justice had dealt with the matters raised. That was the opinion of all the members of the court.

MOTHER BREAKS DOWN
Friends' Petition

Mrs Bentley broke down in the corridor on hearing the decision and had to be assisted to a seat. She cried repeatedly: 'The fellow who did it is getting away but my boy has to die. It isn't fair.' It was half an hour before she had recovered sufficiently to leave the building.

Outside the Court, Bentley's father declared: 'It is up to public opinion now to save to my boy.' He told me there was nothing more he could do about the verdict, but he hoped that a reprieve would be granted.

He also spoke of petitions which friends were organising at New Addington, Surrey, and at Norbury, London, where the Bentleys live.

Saturday, January 17:

EXECUTION OF BENTLEY ON JAN 28

The execution of Derek William Bentley, 19, sentenced to death at the Old Bailey for murdering a police constable at Croydon, was yesterday arranged for 9 a.m. on Wednesday week at Wandsworth Prison.

Tuesday, January 27:

MESSAGE SENT TO PREMIER

'NO COMMENT' REPLY

Mr William Bentley, the father of Derek Bentley, yesterday received a letter from the Home Office stating that Sir David Maxwell Fyfe, the Home Secretary, had 'failed to discover any sufficient ground to justify him in advising Her Majesty to interfere with the due course of the law'.

Immediately the Home Office letter was received, Mr Bentley sent a cable to Mr Churchill, on board the Queen Mary, on his way to Britain, asking him to intervene. A reply was received last night saying, 'I have forwarded your message without comment to the Home Secretary.'

A telegram was also sent to Queen Mary, saying, 'We plead with you to save our son's life.'

Earlier Mr and Mrs Bentley, with their daughter Iris, 21, visited Derek Bentley at Wandsworth Prison. Ten minutes before they arrived, Mrs Craig, mother of Christopher Craig, entered the prison.

Mrs Craig also visited Mr Frederick Harris, Conservative MP for Croydon North, to tell him that her son had never been called 'Chris' by Bentley, who, she said, always used a nickname. This information was passed on to the Home Secretary.

As it became known during the day that a reprieve had been refused, many messages were received at the Bentleys' home. People telephoned to ask if they could help. Letters, some containing money, and telegrams arrived in hundreds.

In the morning Mr Bentley drove with his daughter to the Home Office, where he handed in another 4,000 petition signatures.

About 200 telegrams urging a reconsideration of Bentley's case reached the House of Commons last night for MPs. A large number were also addressed to the Home Secretary. The Commons post office reported that there had not been so many telegrams delivered to MPs in a single evening for many years.

Among the people who visited Mr Bentley at his home last night was a man who said: 'I am an ex-convict. In the name of Edward Patrick Heggarty I was tried at Stafford Assizes on Feb 27, 1925, with a man named Crossley for the shooting of a policeman.

'We were both sentenced to death, but I was under age and could not hang. The Home Secretary reprieved us both.'

Edward Patrick Heggarty, 17, waiter, and William Crossley, 19, labourer, were found guilty of the murder of P.c. A. Willitts. The policeman was found shot through the head in Vicarage Road, Wolverhampton, on Jan 18, 1925.

Both were refused leave to appeal on March 23. Their executions were fixed for April 7. They were reprieved on April 2.

SPEAKER REJECTS MOTION ON DEREK BENTLEY

The Speaker, Mr W. S. Morrison, announced to a crowded House of Commons to-day that it had no authority to intervene in the case of Derek Bentley.

Sir David Maxwell Fyfe, Home Secretary, sat silent through nearly an hour of argument which arose out of his refusal to recommend a reprieve. Raising the issue, Mr S. Silverman (Soc., Nelson and Colne) challenged the action of the Speaker in removing from the Order paper a motion dissenting from Sir David's decision.

The Speaker explained that he had removed the motion because it was 'wholly out of order'. He refused to allow the matter to be debated on a motion for the adjournment of the House.

Wednesday, January 28:

BENTLEY: PLEA BY 200 MPS REJECTED

The Home Secretary, Sir David Maxwell Fyfe, late last night rejected an eleventh-hour appeal by a deputation of Socialist MPs, headed by Mr Bevan, which had urged him to reprieve Derek Bentley, who is due to hang at 9 a.m. to-day in Wandsworth Prison.

The deputation presented a petition signed by about 200 Socialist MPs, including a number of former Ministers and members of the National Executive of the Labour party. It was received by Sir David at the Home Office.

For 45 minutes the Home Secretary listened to the MPs' arguments. They urged that a new factor, strong public reaction against the execution of Bentley, had made itself apparent since his decision not to recommend a reprieve.

Later, he sent a message to the deputation in the House of Commons. In this, received just before the House rose at 10.30 p.m., he said he had given careful consideration to their point of view and had not listened with a closed mind.

He was well aware that they had added further points of emphasis, but all the same he felt there was not sufficient reason to change his mind. The balance was still the other way.

PROTEST MARCH BY CROWD IN WHITEHALL

A crowd of 200 demonstrators calling for the reprieve of Derek Bentley marched last night from the Home Office to Great Peter Street, Westminster. They thought that the Home Secretary, Sir David Maxwell Fyfe, lived there, but he moved about nine months ago.

Efforts to save the life of Bentley, due to hang this morning, continued all day. His father went to the Home Office. Mr Craig, whose son was convicted with Bentley, sent a telegram to the Duke of Edinburgh. It asked the Queen's 'gracious intervention' to save Bentley.

The Bentley family were at the House while the Home Secretary considered the MPs' petition. They left for home after Mr Bentley had been told of its rejection.

Earlier in the day, the Bentley family had visited their son in prison. When they left, Mrs Bentley and her daughter were weeping. Mr Bentley said: 'Derek was cheerful, even under the shadow of the gallows.'

Thursday, January 29:

GAOL CLASH AS BENTLEY DIES

Police and demonstrators clashed and two men were arrested when Derek Bentley, 19½, was executed at Wandsworth Prison yesterday.

At 8.40 a.m., 20 minutes before Bentley was due to die, Mrs Van Der Elst, the campaigner against capital punishment, arrived at the prison by car. People who recognised her began cheering.

'AN INNOCENT MAN'

Mrs Van Der Elst hammered on the gate with the massive iron knocker. A police inspector and sergeant forced their way through the crowd and stood in front of her. 'I must see the governor,' she shouted. There were cries of 'Freedom', 'They are hanging an innocent man', and 'Let her talk'.

At 9 a.m. by the prison clock, the crowd, which had grown to more than 500, stood silently. Men removed their hats. Mrs Van Der Elst led the singing of 'Abide with me' and the 23rd Psalm, 'The Lord is my Shepherd'.

There were angry scenes when the execution notices were hung outside the prison gates. A crowd of more than 500 people shouted and booed. Coins, apple cores and other missiles were flung at the prison officer who posted the notices and at the police. Repeated efforts were made to tear down the notices. The glass of the black-framed board was smashed. Extra police were brought up.

At an inquest at the prison, a verdict of death by judicial hanging was returned. The deputy coroner for Battersea, Mr C. W. Robertson, said to the jury: 'You are in no way involved in the controversy which rages in this case.'

Mr W. J. Lawton, the prison governor, said he or his deputy had seen Bentley twice daily since Dec 11. Bentley had made no complaint. The execution was carried out expeditiously and humanely.

Dr David Haler, pathologist, said there was a trivial scratch mark on the right shin. Apart from that there was no mark of violence except where the noose had encircled the neck.

Excerpts from Letters to the Editor:

Sir – It is to be deplored that certain newspapers should have endeavoured to foment the feelings of gullible members of the public by irresponsible and unnecessary publicity in what will now inevitably become known as 'the Bentley Case'.

Bentley was found guilty (after a regular and proper trial) of murder, and his appeal and various later approaches were carefully and regularly considered and dismissed. Far from holding him out as the dangerous and irresponsible criminal he was, the sections of the Press I mention above were assisting him to be raised to a pedestal where he started to become a popular figure – a martyr and one worthy of pity or even praise.

The ones to be pitied are surely the victim and his dependants, who appear to have been overlooked in the recent Press campaign.

I am extremely sorry for the parents and family of the wrongdoers, but not to the extent that their son's crime should be made to appear almost justifiable, judging from the noise and outcry made by certain sections of the Press.

The Home Secretary has had a most unpleasant duty to discharge and the public should be glad indeed that he has shown himself equal to the occasion in insisting that the law be upheld, however unhappy his personal feelings at his undoubtedly distasteful task.

Sir – To pursue the public controversy upon the merits of the Bentley case would seem indecorous and without purpose. The happenings in Parliament, however, charged as they were with strong emotion among those hoping for a reprieve (most, if not all, of whom knew that the House of Commons could not deal with the matter) occasion reflection upon the constitutional quality in modern times of the royal prerogative of mercy.

Former days knew the personal intervention of the Sovereign. In the 18th century the famous Commentaries of Blackstone cite with approval the statement that

> 'Laws cannot be framed on principles of compassion to guilt, yet justice by the Constitution of England is bound to be administered in mercy: this is promised by the King in his Coronation Oath and it is that act of his Government which is the most personal and most entirely his own. The King condemns no man; that rugged talk he leaves to his Courts of Justice. The great operation of his sceptre is mercy.'

In the previous century the great Sir Matthew Hale had written that the King might by command or precept under his Great or Privy Seal, Privy signet or Sign Manual, 'Yea, by signification under the hand of the Secretary of State,' command the reprieve of one condemned of treason or felony.

Now in constitutional theory that royal prerogative, dating indeed from Saxon times, has remained untouched by the centuries, but in reality the Sovereign now remains aloof. The decision whether the death sentence shall be carried out in every case, be there a petition or not, is in the hands of the Home Secretary.

In recent years there have generally been about 30 murder convictions annually without a finding of insanity. Last year, for example, there were 27 cases and the death sentence was carried out in 19. There were three cases of supervening insanity, which constitutes a statutory respite. Reprieve was accorded in the remaining five cases.

Such figures as these show that the Home Secretary is faced with the consideration of life or death almost continuously, and if his decision was subject to debate, resolution or vote in Parliament, it is difficult to see how an examination of the case of any convicted murderer could be kept within bounds.

When the passions aroused by particular cases subside, it can be seen clearly enough that the exercise of the prerogative of mercy is best left where it at present lies, and that Parliament has been wise in maintaining the immunity which, by the Speaker's ruling this week, was accorded to the fateful decision.

Sir – It would be of greater value to us all if the public indignation aroused by Bentley's hanging were directed against the hanging rather than against the Home Secretary.

No one has any doubt as to Bentley's guilt, but many people are shocked by the penalty. Abolish capital punishment, and the clamour would disappear too.

Sir – In regard to the Bentley affair, English people who have pride in their country, and doubtless also many observers abroad, will be wondering which is the more shameful spectacle – that of some politicians always alert for the opportunity to attract publicity to themselves, showing themselves not unwilling to use it to stir up illwill towards the Government, or certain organs of the Press exploiting the private grief of Bentley's relatives for its sheer sensationalism and circulation-boosting properties.

From none of these unscrupulous people does one hear one word of pity for a brave policeman, shot down in cold blood, or his unfortunate wife and children. Nor do they display the slightest consciousness of the fact that, unless they receive the full support of both the law and public opinion, the country will soon cease to have the type of police who will face these armed blackguards with bare hands.

The great redeeming factor in this unsavoury spectacle is the sight of a Home Secretary, well known for his humanity, together with members of the British Judiciary, doing their painful and unpleasant duty with calm integrity, despite the moronic clamour that these agitators have evoked.

FOG AND MORTALITY

Sir – The mortality figures during the recent fog period, produced in the House of Commons, must give all students of public health ample food for thought.

Wednesday, December 21, 1960:

5 YEARS' GAOL FOR BROTHER OF MURDERER

Niven Scott Craig, 34, elder brother of Christopher Craig, was sent to prison yesterday for five years.

Craig, a motor fitter, of Du Cane Road, Shepherd's Bush, was found guilty, with two other men and a woman, of safe-blowing and stealing £26 16s 11d from a shop in Church Street, Marylebone.

Det-Sgt. Leonard Read said Craig had two previous convictions.

Sunday, June 5, 1961:

Ten men, several of them dangerous criminals, broke out of Wandsworth Prison yesterday after overpowering and tying up three warders in a workshop. They scaled the prison walls with ropes and escaped in two cars taken from a bowling club.

One of the men is George Peter Madsen, 47, known in the underworld as 'Cigs', which stands for Chief of the Illegal Gelignite Squad. It is his second escape from Wandsworth and the third in his criminal career.

Another of the men is Niven Scott Craig, 34, brother of Christopher Craig.

Friday, February 8, 1963:

CRAIG TO BE FREED AFTER 10½ YEARS

Christopher Craig, 26, is to be released from prison on licence in May. The decision to release him was announced in the Commons yesterday by Mr Brooke, the Home Secretary, replying to Mr Lipton, Labour MP for Brixton. Mr Brooke said that Craig's case, in common with others similarly sentenced, had been kept constantly under review.

He had to take into account the circumstances of the offence, the offender's age and character, his development in detention, and the need to protect the public from any person who might be dangerous if he were released.

Mr Lipton asked why Craig and Frederick Emmett-Dunne, a convicted murderer, were to be released while Joseph Doyle, serving life imprisonment for an Irish Republican Army raid on a British Army unit, was still detained. Mr Brooke replied that Doyle's offence took place two years after that of Craig. His case was under review.

Sgt. Emmett-Dunne was sentenced by a Dusseldorf court martial in 1955 to be hanged for the murder of Sgt Reginald Watters. The sentence was confirmed, then commuted to life imprisonment.

Sunday, June 27, 1965:

CRAIG MARRIES TYPIST

Christopher Craig has married.

Craig, 28, who is working as an engineer in Buckinghamshire, was married at Bletchley register office on April 3. His bride was a 25-year-old shorthand-typist.

Craig, who is still on licence, was a model prisoner and has made good since his release. His marriage is regarded by Home Office officials as a further step in his rehabilitation.

The Earl of Longford, Lord Privy Seal, has taken a close interest in the case of Christopher Craig and that of his brother, Niven Scott Craig, 38. In his memoirs, Lord Longford says that Niven played a leading part in Christopher's rehabilitation.

Niven, who is serving sentences totalling 12 years for safe-breaking, assault with intent to rob, and other offences, was recently placed on the hostels scheme at Wormwood Scrubs five years before he was due for release. He goes out to work every day and stays with relatives at week-ends. He wanted to attend his brother's wedding. He could not under the conditions of his limited freedom.

Parliamentary Report, Friday, May 26, 1972:

MR KERR (Feltham, Lab.) asked whether the Home Secretary had yet had an opportunity of seeing the BBC2 film *To Encourage the Others*, produced by David Yallop; and whether, in view of the documented evidence it contains, he was prepared to recommend a public inquiry into the circumstances surrounding the trial and execution of 19-year-old Derek Bentley.

MR MAUDLING, in a written reply, said:

I have fully reviewed the facts of this case in the light of Mr Yallop's book and television production, and the Commissioner of Police of the Metropolis has at my request made some further inquiries into those matters on which it is suggested that new or different evidence is now available.

In the light of these inquiries and of my study of all the facts I have found nothing to justify any action on my part in regard to the conviction, or to warrant more extensive inquiries.

Mr Yallop's book and play propound the theory that Police Constable Miles was accidentally killed by a bullet from a police weapon. My inquiries show this to be quite contrary to the available evidence.

Statements taken in the course of the original investigation make it clear that at the time that PC Miles was shot, no police officer at the scene was armed and that police weapons were sent for only after he had been shot.

Five .32 calibre automatic pistols, each with eight rounds of ammunition, were then issued to police officers, and with the exception of that used by Detective Constable Fairfax, all were returned unfired. The only ammunition not returned intact was the two rounds fired from that pistol after PC Miles had been wounded.

Nor can I find any basis for the doubts that have been raised as to the calibre of the fatal bullet. These appear to have been derived from an opinion attributed to Dr Haler, the pathologist who performed the post-mortem on PC Miles. He is said to have told the author that the wound could have been caused by a bullet of calibre between .32 and .38 (whereas the weapon that Craig was firing was known to be a .445 revolver).

Dr Haler has been seen and has made a statement in which he denies having expressed any such opinion. He adheres to the evidence which he gave at the trial that the wound was caused by a bullet of large calibre, and says that by this he meant a calibre of more than .38.

Former Detective Constable Fairfax has also been seen and made a statement in which he adheres entirely to the evidence which he gave at the trial and to which there is nothing that he is able to add.

Apart from considering the material in Mr Yallop's book, I have also had inquiries made into statements made independently by a Mr Philip Lee, who claims to have been an eye-witness of an alleged gun battle on the roof of the warehouse in Croydon on the night in question.

Mr Lee has now made a long statement to the police describing fully what he claims to have seen, and other consequential inquiries have been made to verify the details given in this statement. My inquiries show that this account of events is so inconsistent with other available evidence that I should not be justified in taking any action upon it.

Although there are some understandable discrepancies of detail in the accounts of witnesses of the confused events on the warehouse roof, the essential facts of the shooting are clear.

There is no information before me to cause me to think that the verdict of the jury was wrong.

Saturday, July 1, 1972:

Jail for man with 'arsenal'

A man who had been banned for life from possessing firearms was sentenced at the Central Criminal Court yesterday to two years' imprisonment for having at his flat what was described by Mr Justice Swanwick as a veritable arsenal.

Niven Scott Craig, aged 45, a fitter and welder, of Stroud Green Road, Finsbury Park, north London, pleaded guilty to possessing firearms without a certificate, and similarly possessing ammunition. The court accepted pleas of not guilty to conspiracy to contravene the provisions of the Firearms Act and shortening a shotgun.

Thursday, July 26, 1990:

LETTER TO THE EDITOR

Sir – Efforts to establish that there was an appalling miscarriage of justice when Derek Bentley was hanged for the murder of a policeman in 1952 fail to take into account the highly charged concern at the time. This could be compared to public anxiety over rape and child abuse today.

I covered the full drama of the trial as the Press Association's star shorthand writer. The background, largely ignored in the current campaign, was one of general public concern about growing signs of youthful lawlessness. The only important issue now is whether Bentley should have been found guilty of murder, because his companion actually fired the gun.

A young policeman had been shot dead, and ordinary decent citizens felt that something had to be done quickly to make it clear that the use of firearms by criminals would not be tolerated.

Far from being two misguided young men out doing a bit of 'scrumping', the impression I had throughout the trial was that of two young thugs out for kicks. They had a revolver and a knuckle-duster.

Lord Goddard, the presiding judge, shared the public view that such crimes must be seen to be checked. I remember him breaking off during his summing-up to peer down at the table loaded with exhibits. 'Where's that knuckle-duster?' he demanded. 'Let's have another look at it.' Trying in vain to force it down over his well-fleshed fingers, he jabbed it towards the jury: 'A dreadful weapon. A terrible weapon.'

Every householder in the courtroom felt just what it would be like to have it smashed into their faces.

Criminal law in those days was more effective than it is now. The shoot-out and arrests occurred on Nov 2, 1952; the trial was all over by Dec 11.

None of us in court really doubted that Bentley, in the custody of a policeman and sheltering with him behind a chimney, actually did call out 'Let him have it, Chris' before the gun was fired.

That was recognisable as the language of the day, and one could only admire the Rumpole-like defence which argued that it meant 'Hand the gun over to the policeman, Chris'.

The jury took the view that Bentley was as guilty of murder as if he had pulled the trigger himself. We had seen what sort of boy Craig was during Christmas Humphreys's devastating cross-examination, which reduced him to a mumbling idiot, shaking and nodding his head, muttering 'Yes' or 'No'.

Nearly 40 years afterwards, efforts are being made to establish that *perhaps* Bentley never uttered those fatal words; that *perhaps* the dead policeman was actually shot by the bad marksmanship of one of his fellow officers.

We thought at the time that the Home Secretary should have commuted Bentley's death sentence because Craig himself was too young to be hanged. The fact that he did not was merely a potent argument for the subsequent abolition of the death penalty.

REGINALD TURNILL
Sandgate, Kent

Saturday, August 17, 1991:

The case of Derek Bentley, the teenager hanged 38 years ago for the murder of a policeman, was reopened yesterday by the Home Secretary.

Mr Kenneth Baker has asked the Metropolitan Police to investigate evidence given to him in the past year. The decision follows new evidence from books and television documentaries that throws doubt on some key aspects of the case.

Miss Iris Bentley, 59, said the development could be the first step towards a pardon for her brother. 'I am amazed and very pleased,' she said. Miss Bentley, of Colliers Wood, south London, said her brother had made her promise on his last morning in the condemned cell to carry on the fight to clear his name.

Saturday, September 7, 1991:

Clophill, Bedfordshire, is a better place than most in which to disappear. Christopher Craig could not have known that when he went there in the mid-1960s, but he knows it now: Clophill swallowed him up. This is how it is supposed to be in the Badlands and the Essex Marshes – a man who is accepted here finds that the gate swings shut behind him.

The anonymity a place like this can confer was what Craig needed most. Having served ten years of a prison sentence, he was released in 1963. Then he seemed to disappear. When he resurfaced last week to give a television interview to Thames Reports, some people were astonished. Some thought he was dead.

The interview was fascinating as much for its appearance – the breaking of a silence of decades – as for its content. Craig, a stocky man of about 5ft 10in with a van Dyke beard, took a lie-detector test in which he swore that Bentley never said the fatal phrase – the sombre, rhythmic phrase whose ambiguities have been irresistible to authors, song-writers and film-makers: Let him have it, Chris.

Two years ago, a news agency heard that Craig was living in Clophill and found his address in the phone directory. Craig has since gone ex-directory, but the appearance in 1989 of a song by the pop singer Elvis Costello – called 'Let Him Dangle', and protesting at Bentley's hanging – made enough of an excuse for a story in *The People* about him. The attention which followed included two weeks of knocks on his front door, at the same time each evening. Still he said nothing.

Craig contacted Roger Cork, the director of the television programme, in July. Cork found him talkative, engaging, the kind of man who knew a lot of jokes and remembered all the punch-lines. He came across as a regular guy – married, two kids, living in a semi-detached. He does not drink or smoke and his hobby is scuba diving.

There must be hundreds like Craig: men who have put the knife or gun-wielding exploits of youth behind them, and found themselves subsumed in normality. Craig's case happened to be different. 'Of course there is a mystique about him,' says Cork. 'But it springs from his refusal ever to talk, and his refusal to admit that Derek Bentley ever said those words. He told me he could have knocked it all on the head years ago, if he had simply agreed with the prosecution. But that would have been the easy way out.'

But at the same time, Craig never took part in the Bentley family's campaign to have Bentley's conviction reassessed. 'I have never seen Chris Craig since the day he was taken down from the dock,' says Bentley's sister Iris, who has fought for a posthumous pardon since her brother was hanged. 'My father tried to see him in 1956 in Wormwood Scrubs. The governor said it was all right as long as Craig agreed, but he refused.' Nevertheless, she feels no resentment towards Craig. 'I knew where he lived, but I never wanted to get in touch with him. It was something he had to do himself.'

Comment: Quality of Mercy

If Derek Bentley was as innocent as he now seems to have been, then we may take comfort that these cases of judicial over-enthusiasm are not a recent development, as people might have feared.

But if Bentley's ghost is to be given a free pardon, as I have always felt it should be, I hope the authorities will take the opportunity to review the free pardon given to the ghost of Timothy Evans in October 1966 by Roy Jenkins, the then Home Secretary, for the murder of his daughter.

If we accept the evidence produced by Ludovic Kennedy in his book '10 Rillington Place', it is apparent that Evans must have been an accomplice to the murder after the event, and it seems much more likely than not that he was an accomplice before the event as well.

I have always been of the opinion that Evans was guilty. On the other hand, one cannot expect the Lord Chief Justice to pass the death sentence on him a second time, since the death penalty has mercifully been abolished; even the present mandatory life sentence seems inappropriate when one reflects that Evans is no longer, as it were, alive.

Perhaps we should concentrate on present-day excesses. It seems to me that the sentence of nine months imprisonment passed by Judge David Miller at Isleworth on a 36-year-old housewife who massaged two male French teenagers in her bedroom was altogether excessive. Must we wait another 38 years before justice is done?

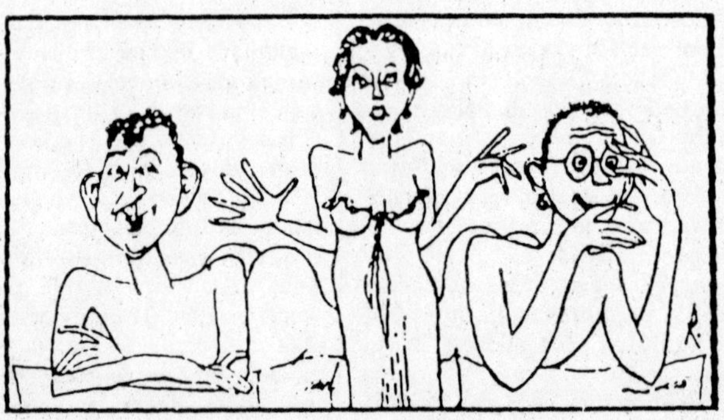

Friday, October 2, 1992:

Clarke rejects a free pardon for hanged Bentley

DEREK BENTLEY was yesterday refused a posthumous pardon.

Campaigners and relatives who have fought to overturn Bentley's conviction reacted with anger and disappointment to the announcement at a press conference that despite 'exhaustive consideration', Mr Clarke, the Home Secretary [since April], had found no grounds for recommending a pardon or ordering a public inquiry.

Mr John Parris, now 77, one of the defence lawyers, said: 'It is terrible news. I am outraged.'

Mr Clarke, a QC, recalled that he keenly followed press coverage of the case 'as a reasonably political schoolboy of 12'.

But he said: 'However much many of us may now disagree with the decision to allow the execution to proceed, the sentence passed was the only one available for the offence of which Derek Bentley was convicted.

'Having examined the relevant Home Office papers, I am satisfied that the issues were properly and fairly considered by the Home Secretary of the day and his officials.'

The jury heard police evidence that Bentley admitted knowing Craig was armed with a gun, and was entitled to disbelieve later denials.

'There was no evidence that Bentley took any action to bring the joint criminal enterprise to an end before the killing of the police officer,' Mr Clarke said. 'He was consequently equally guilty in law of the killing as Craig, who fired the gun and killed the officer. This was the law then and it is the law today.'

It was suggested that Bentley should be pardoned not because he was innocent, but because it was wrong that he was not reprieved. But he had been properly sentenced in accordance with the law then applying to murder.

A decision whether to grant a reprieve rested with the Home Secretary alone. Mr Clarke said: 'I do not believe I would have reached the same decision. But none of this provides sufficient reason to set up a public inquiry or recommend a posthumous free pardon.'

Mr Clarke has ordered the release of papers held at the Public Records Office even though, under the 30-year rule, they should have remained undisclosed until 1996 because the last item was filed in 1966. They show that Sir David Maxwell Fyfe, who as Home Secretary refused to reprieve Derek Bentley in 1953, over-ruled his senior advisers when he decided that the execution should go ahead.

In a hand-written note at the end of submissions from Sir Frank Newsam and Mr Philip (now Lord) Allen, respectively permanent secretary and assistant under-secretary at the Home Office, Sir David stated: 'Let the law take its course.'

Sir David had balanced the advice of his civil servants against the views of the then Lord Chief Justice, Lord Goddard, who had sentenced Bentley to death.

In his letter to the Home Secretary, the day after the trial ended at the Old Bailey, Lord Goddard added: 'So far as merits were concerned, I regret to say I could find no mitigating circumstances in Bentley's case. He was armed with a knuckle-duster of the most formidable type I have ever seen and also with a sharp pointed knife, and he called out to Craig when arrested to start the shooting.'

The Home Office memorandum prepared by Mr Allen concludes: 'Shocking though this murder was, it is suggested that it would on the whole be right to give effect to the jury's recomendation to mercy, principally on the ground, which has been held to be valid in previous cases, that it would not seem right when the principal offender is escaping with his life.'

On Jan 22, 1953, in a memorandum explaining his decision, Sir David, who died as the Earl of Kilmuir in 1967, referred to mitigating factors. But he said it would be dangerous to give the impression that 'an older adolescent could escape the full penalty by using an accomplice of less than 18 years of age'. He also spoke of the need to protect unarmed police.

The case file also contains anonymous murder threats against the Home Secretary and Prince Philip and a letter to Sir David from a juror, Mr N. E. Finburgh, regretting his refusal of a reprieve.

Mr Clarke's decision was a crushing blow for Miss Iris Bentley, who has fought for 39 years for a pardon for her brother.

She was given a brown envelope by a Home Office official at her solictor's offices in Borough High Street, London, at 1.02 p.m. yesterday.

In Whitehall, meanwhile, Mr Clarke was making public his findings at a press conference. Miss Bentley, 61, said: 'I just read the first bit. I couldn't read any more. It said "no".'

Miss Bentley, who is divorced, promised her brother in his cell on the eve of his execution that she would clear his name.

Each year, on the anniversary of his death, she lays a wreath at Wandsworth prison. His grave at Croydon Cemetery remains unmarked, and she will not erect a headstone until he is pardoned. Despite having cancer for 20 years and undergoing 14 major operations, she continued the campaign. 'I'm going to write to the Queen,' she said.

'I won't give up. No way. Not until the day I die.' The champagne she has saved for 20 years at her home in Colliers Wood, south London, in the event of a pardon, will be put away again.

Leading article:

Of sentences past

With hindsight, and a quarter of a century after we abolished capital punishment in this country, it is open to anyone to see the hanging of Derek Bentley in 1953 as a blunder, and to impute the worst motives to everyone involved in the decision to send him to the gallows. Kenneth Clarke, the Home Secretary, has made a different assessment. Reviewing the evidence, after a long campaign to secure Bentley a posthumous pardon, he has concluded in effect that a verdict of almost 40 years ago ought not to be upset simply because such an outcome today would be unthinkable. It is, he says, easy in 1992 to make a judgement on what Sir David Maxwell Fyfe, the then Home Secretary, decided in a different climate of opinion. On all the evidence available, he stresses, the jury's decision and the death sentence were correct at the time. Mr Clarke's decision will be condemned as outrageous in some quarters, but in our view it is the right one.

Under the doctrine of constructive malice which applied at the time, an intention to kill or cause grievous bodily harm was inferred if, in resisting arrest, a police officer was killed. Though the doctrine was repealed by the Homicide Act of 1957, it bore directly on Craig's liability to murder in 1952. Because this was a joint criminal enterprise, Bentley was likewise incriminated. Craig has subsequently declared that Bentley did not utter the words: 'Let him have it, Chris!'* But what equally concerned the jury, as Mr Clarke points out, was whether or not Bentley knew that Craig was carrying a gun, and they concluded that he did.

The case roused high feelings at the time, and these will now be revived. Mr Clarke's critics will accuse him of taking a decision designed to mollify the police. In reality, he has done something more fundamental. He has refused to judge the past through the eyes of the present.

Thursday, July 8, 1993:

JUDGES BACK BENTLEY CAMPAIGN FOR PARDON

The sister of Derek Bentley, hanged for murder in 1953, yesterday won a historic victory in the High Court which recommended a posthumous conditional pardon and accepted that 'an injustice was done'.

After a series of appeals had been rejected over the years, the three judges delivered a 21-page ruling which concluded that there were grounds for a pardon. It should be possible, they said, to devise some formula that amounted to a clear acknowledgement that 'an injustice was done'.

Lord Justice Watkins, sitting with Lord Justice Neill and Mr Justice Tuckey, said they were 'far from satisfied' that Mr Kenneth Clarke, when he was Home Secretary, gave sufficient consideration to his power to grant a conditional posthumous pardon.

Lord Justice Watkins called on Mr Michael Howard, who succeeded Mr Clarke as Home Secretary, to consider a conditional pardon 'to give full recognition to the now generally accepted view that this young man should have been reprieved'.

* EDITOR: Craig's retrospective negative 'evidence' has received far more publicity than it deserves. The fact (if it *is* a fact) that he cannot remember hearing The Words does not mean that they were not spoken.

The court had no power to direct the Home Secretary on how the Royal prerogative of mercy should be exercised and it would not be right to make any formal order, Lord Justice Watkins said, 'Nevetheless, we would invite the Home Secretary to look at the matter again,' he added.

Despite a submission by the Home Secretary that even to grant a limited pardon might lead to a flood of other applications to review past convictions, the court was satisfied the Bentley case was exceptional.

Mr Clarke, now Chancellor of the Exchequer and in Tokyo for the economic summit, said: 'As far as I am aware, my judgments in the case have not been challenged. My judgment was that the verdict of the jury was safe, and that Mr Bentley was in fact guilty of murder.

'My opinion was that he should not have been hanged because of his mental handicap, and because, though more culpable, the other man was not hanged.

'I followed the precedent that a royal pardon was only given where innocence was established. The court has decided that a pardon should be given where the penalty should be lifted, even if guilt is established.'

Leading article:

JUDGMENT – NOT SENTIMENT

Yesterday's High Court ruling on the 1953 case of Derek Bentley reflects a remarkable lack of intellectual rigour. At a time when justice is under sharp scrutiny, three judges may suppose that their judgment will earn praise from libertarians for its humanity, and decent sympathy for the dead man's sister who brought the case. Yet it is not the business of judges to adopt positions which may win them momentary acclaim from tabloid readers, but to deal in cold reason.

It is most unlikely that, in the climate of 1993, Derek Bentley would have been convicted.

It was to the deep discredit of Sir David Maxwell Fyfe that he did not reprieve Bentley. But, as Mr Kenneth Clarke robustly and sensibly declared last October, it is a hopeless task to seek to impose the values of 1993 upon a judgment made 40 years earlier. The fact that today, for instance, we are far more sceptical of police evidence than were our fathers may enable us to take a different view of testimony that was found acceptable in 1953, but it does not give us the right to impose a retrospective judgment upon it. It is the job of pundits and historians to reassess history, but an abuse of our system of justice and of government resources to do so at public expense. If we advance down this route, there is no limit to the scope for altering the verdicts of our ancestors. Such fatuous acts as that of the then Transport Secretary, who reopened inquiries in 1989 on some circumstances of the 1912 loss of the Titanic to appease uneasy descendants, is an abuse of public responsibility.

Plainly, the High Court has now placed the new Home Secretary, Mr Michael Howard, in an unenviable position. If he declines to grant some form of posthumous pardon to Bentley, he will be accused of insensitivity to the feelings of Iris Bentley, who has campaigned long and hard for her dead brother. But Mr Howard's first responsibility must be to take a sensible view of the public interest, and to avoid opening the floodgates to a torrent of such cases at the expense of the taxpayer. Even if three judges have suddenly suffered an outbreak of ill-judged sentiment, there is no reason for the Home Secretary to do likewise.

Saturday, July 10:

LETTER TO THE EDITOR

Sir – Following the three High Court judges' decision on posthumous pardons, I hope the way is now clear for a pardon for poor old Guy Fawkes.

This unfortunate young fellow was arrested on scanty circumstantial evidence, his right to remain silent not explained to him, and a confession extracted from him under duress. He was refused a trial by jury (despite the Magna Carta) and he and his alleged fellow conspirators were tried collectively by an ad hoc court of six earls and three judges.

He was not allowed any representation and the prosecution was conducted by the most formidable advocate in England. His so-called confession was the only real evidence against him, but the verdict was a foregone conclusion.

Of all the possible miscarriages of justice by today's standards, Guy Fawkes deserves the first consideration for a posthumous pardon.

JOHN BARNETT
Farnham, Surrey

Saturday, July 31:

BENTLEY GIVEN PART PARDON 40 YEARS AFTER BEING HANGED

Derek Bentley was granted a limited pardon by Mr Howard, Home Secretary, yesterday.

The unprecedented decision came three weeks after the High Court urged the Home Secretary to recognise that an injustice had been done.

The posthumous pardon is 'limited to sentence', meaning that Bentley was properly convicted at the Old Bailey but that he should not have been executed for the murder of Pc Sidney Miles.

Mr Howard's decision is also a vindication for Lord Allen of Abbeydale, then a senior Home Office civil servant, who urged Sir David Maxwell Fyfe, Home Secretary, to reprieve Bentley. Mr Howard said he would have followed that advice.

Only one executed man, Timothy Evans, has been granted a full posthumous pardon.

Yesterday's decision by Mr Howard has created a new category of pardon – as he was invited to do by the High Court in a 21-page ruling this month.

Mr Howard, a barrister like Mr Clarke and since 1991 an opponent of capital punishment, said a free pardon remained 'inappropriate' because Bentley was neither morally nor technically innocent.

He added: 'The issue before the court was my predecessor's decision not to recommend a posthumous free pardon. Successive Home Secretaries have reserved free pardons for cases where moral and technical innocence is established.

'The court recognised the strength of this position and made no criticism of the decision not to recommend a free pardon in this case.'

Christopher Craig is now 56 and living at Clophill, Beds. His wife said yesterday: 'He does not want to say anything.'

Speaking at a champagne celebration, a tearful Miss Iris Bentley, who has cancer, said: 'The battle goes on. What I want now is a pardon to clear his name completely.' But she said she would treasure the document granting the pardon.

'I will keep it in a safe place because I have not long had burglars. I want it to be buried with me.'

1964

Wednesday, July 8 (entire report, near foot of page 22):

DEATH SENTENCE ON 2 DAIRYMEN

Two Preston dairymen, Peter Anthony Allen, 21, and Gwynne Owen Evans, 24, were sentenced to death at Manchester Crown Court yesterday for the capital* murder of John Alan West, 53, a laundry vanman, at his home in King's Avenue, Seaton, near Workington. Their trial, before Mr Justice Ashworth, had lasted seven days.

Mr J. Cantley, QC, prosecuting, said they hit Mr West with a cosh and stabbed him in the heart. They stole a gold watch and two bank books. Each accused the other of the attack.

Friday, August 14 (entire report, near foot of page 17):

TWO EXECUTED

Two Preston men sentenced to death for the capital murder of a Cumberland man were hanged yesterday. About a dozen people were outside Strangeways Prison, Manchester, when Gwynne Owen Evans, 24, was executed. The other man, Peter Anthony Allen, 21, was executed at Walton Prison, Liverpool.

These executions turned out to be the last.

* In March 1957, Parliament had passed the Homicide Act – often referred to in legal circles as the 'Reggie-cide Act' since Sir Reginald Manningham-Buller, the Attorney-General, was primarily responsible for the compromise legislation – which retained the death penalty for five categories of murder: 'in the course or furtherance of theft; by shooting or by causing an explosion; in the course or for the purpose of resisting or preventing a lawful arrest, or of effecting or assisting an escape or rescue from legal custody; any murder of a police officer acting in the execution of his duty or of a person assisting a police officer so acting; in the case of a person who was a prisoner at the time when he did or was a party to the murder; any murder of a prison officer.' The death penalty also applied to persons convicted of murder on a previous occasion, and to persons convicted on the same indictment of two or more murders done on different occasions.

1992

Monday, July 13:

ALBERT PIERREPOINT, who has died aged 87, was Britain's leading executioner for 25 years, but later campaigned for the abolition of the death penalty.

Short and dapper, with mild blue eyes, a pleasant singing voice and a fondness for cigars and beautiful women, Pierrepoint was fascinated by bar tricks with coins and matchboxes – which were in plentiful supply at the oddly-named Help the Poor Struggler, a pub he kept in Lancashire.

While employed as a hangman, he never spoke of 't'other job', and he hated the thought of any impropriety, unseemliness or vulgarity connected with his craft, which he viewed as sacred.

Pierrepoint was undoubtedly a first-rate hangman: 'I hanged John Reginald Christie, the Monster of Rillington Place,' he wrote, 'in less time than it took the ash to fall off a cigar I had left half-smoked in my room at Pentonville.'

During his career he hanged more than 400 people – his record was 17 in a day ('Was my arm stiff!). In 1946 he went to Vienna where he ran 'a school for executioners'; the British authorities had sentenced eight Polish youths, but refused to hand them over to Austrian hangmen, whose methods were brutally unscientific. Pierrepoint hanged the youths at the rate of two a day, and stayed on for a fortnight to give further instruction.

He recalled only one awkward moment in his career. 'It was unfortunate. He was not an Englishman. He was a spy and kicked up rough.'

In 1956 Pierrepoint resigned, incensed at the meanness of the Home Office, which had granted him only £1 in expenses, and began his campaign against capital punishment.

'If death were a deterrent,' he wrote, 'I might be expected to know. It is I who have faced them at the last, young lads and girls, working men, grandmothers. I have been amazed to see the courage with which they take that walk into the unknown.

'It did not deter them then, and it had not deterred them when they committed what they were convicted for. All the men and women whom I have faced at that final moment convince me that in what I have done I have not prevented a single murder.'

Albert Pierrepoint was born on 30 March 1905 at Clayton, a district of Bradford in the West Riding of Yorkshire, and brought up in Huddersfield and Manchester. His father, Harry, had been an executioner for 10 years, and his uncle for 42. Young Albert was nine when he first conceived the ambition to become an executioner.

When he moved with his mother to Manchester, he spent half a day at school and the other half working in the local mills, a practice which the law then allowed boys over the age of 12½.

HELP THE POOR

STRUGGLER

Six months later, he left school and started work as a piecer at the mills. In 1926 he found another job as a horse-drayman at a wholesale grocers, and by 1930 had become a motor-drayman. It was then that he wrote his first application to the Home Office to be included in the list of official executioners, but there were no vacancies.

A year later Pierrepoint was invited to an interview at Strangeways Prison, where he was disappointed to learn that he was the tenth applicant to be interviewed, his chagrin only slightly lessened when he noticed that the previous applicant was clearly drunk. None the less, he was accepted.

After a week of intense training by the prison engineer, Pierrepoint was placed on the list of approved assistant executioners – subject to his attendance at an execution to test his nerve.

The first execution he attended was not, however, authorised by the Home Office, but by the Irish government. Tom Pierrepoint (Albert's uncle and then the chief hangman) was contracted privately, and was allowed to select his own assistant. He chose his nephew.

Pierrepoint's first British execution was at Winson Green Prison in Birmingham, where the executioner, once again, was his uncle. The role of assistant involved pinioning the condemned man's legs and getting off the trap as fast as possible, but it was the gravity of the occasion that was the real test.

It was 1940 that marked the turning point in Pierrepoint's career. After acting as assistant to an executioner who had been less than competent, he was asked if he would be prepared to be head executioner.

His first execution as principal hangman was that of a gangland murderer at Pentonville in London, and further engagements soon followed.

In 1943 he was sent to Gibraltar to execute two saboteurs. During the Second World War there were 16 spies convicted in Britain, and Pierrepoint hanged 15 of them (the 16th was reprieved).

He always maintained that there was no glamour in taking the lives of others, and he abhorred all publicity, so he was displeased when General Sir Bernard Montgomery announced from his headquarters in Germany that Pierrepoint was to hang the convicted staff of Belsen. Appointed an honorary lieutenant-colonel for the purpose, he duly travelled to Hameln in Germany, where, on Friday, December 13, 1945, he hanged 13 people before lunch. There was a strange sequel to these executions: every Christmas thereafter, for a number of years, Pierrepoint received a £5 note in an envelope, with a slip of paper reading simply 'Belsen'.

At the end of the war Pierrepoint became a publican. His pub attracted ghoulish sightseers by the coach-load, but he denied press reports that he ever discussed 't'other job' with his customers. He did admit, though, to having hanged one of them, a man convicted of the murder of his mistress.

He hotly denied, too, the existence of a sign reading 'No Hanging Round the Bar', though several people claimed to have seen such a sign – among them the late Diana Dors, the actress, who also claimed that Pierrepoint had sung amorous songs to her over the telephone.

In 1954 Pierrepoint himself was 'sentenced to death' by the IRA for his execution of a terrorist in Dublin in 1944.

After his resignation, he settled down as landlord of another pub, the Rose and Crown at Hoole, near Preston, which he had taken in 1952, but the ghouls put him off pub-keeping, so he concentrated his energies instead on his small farm.

Among the mourners at Albert Pierrepoint's funeral was an elderly but still dapper man named Harry Allen. He caught a cold during the ceremony, and soon after his return to his home at Fleetwood, Lancashire, was admitted to hospital.

Monday, August 17:

Harry Allen, who has died aged 80, succeeded the late Albert Pierrepoint as chief executioner in 1956. On August 13, 1964, he executed Gwynne Evans at Strangeways Prison, Manchester. Evans's partner, Peter Allen, was hanged at the same time in Liverpool by the assistant executioner. They were the last death sentences carried out in Britain.

The following year, Parliament abolished the death penalty for murder; but Harry Allen always maintained that he was never officially stood down. As recently as 1976, the Home Office put him on stand-by to await a telegram from the Irish Republic, where three men had been sentenced to death for the murder of a police officer.

Before becoming the chief executioner, Allen had served as an assistant, at first to Thomas Pierrepoint, and then to the latter's nephew, Albert. Altogether, he was involved in more than 100 executions. As well as performing the task in Britain, he carried out executions of EOKA terrorists in Cyprus, and official hangings in Spain and the West Indies.

Like Albert Pierrepoint, Allen was a publican by trade, and for many years was the landlord of the Junction Hotel at Besses o' the Barns, near Manchester. He found that 'the regular customers protect me against the vultures – that's what I call the sightseers. When they see me, they're often surprised. I look so normal.'

Indeed, Harry Allen reminded many observers of a civil servant. He had a tendency to careful circumlocution, a mild air of self-importance, and a taste for formal suits with waistcoats and a bowler hat.

On arriving at prisons for an execution, he would also affect one of 'a wide range of multi-coloured bow-ties, so anybody demonstrating outside the jail would assume I was a doctor or lawyer'.

'It's just another job,' he used to say. 'I'm the man to do it. I took it on out of a sense of duty.'

Allen was a stickler for detail. The night before an execution, he would have 'a dummy run', using a sack filled with sand and a mannequin's head. 'The rehearsal takes all the stretch out of the rope and makes sure the drop is exact,' he explained.

'The noose, about a thumb's width thick, was placed around the prisoner's neck, with the knot underneath one of his ears. This will break the neck at the fourth vertebra and sever the adjacent nerve.'

While Allen placed a white hood, 'like a pillow case', over the prisoner's head, his assistant would strap his legs together around the knees and ankles. 'This,' he said, 'is to stop any *post-mortem* nervous twitching. I'd then step to one side, 3ft from the condemned man, and pull the lever. The trapdoor, 4ft wide and 3ft across, opens. Death is instantaneous. We'd leave the prisoner hanging there until the doctor went below to certify death.

'We'd haul the body back with a pulley and gently lower it down. There's never any mark on the corpse. Then my assistant undressed the body and we'd put it in a coffin and our job was over.

'After breakfast I always used to return home, have a bath, and go to bed. I slept like a baby for the next eight hours. I've never been bothered with dreams or nightmares.'

Harry Allen was born in 1911 and brought up in the Roman Catholic faith. His father apparently refused to speak to him for five years when he discovered, from a newspaper article, that he was a hangman.

In 1939 Allen applied to the Home Office for a position. 'They offered me a job as assistant executioner,' he recalled. 'Unfortunately, I accepted. My wife was completely against it, but at that time I had no choice but to take it on.'

Although Albert Pierrepoint eventually took the view that capital punishment did not act as a deterrent, Allen remained a lifelong supporter of the death penalty. 'Since the rope was scrapped,' he said in 1983, 'discipline has gone right out of the window.' He blamed 'the well-meaning do-gooders for the mess society is in today'.

Allen married first (dissolved 1962), Marjorie; they had a son and a daughter. He married secondly, in 1963, Doris Dyke. After his second honeymoon, he went straight to Bristol to carry out an execution. He was the same jolly Harry on his return, his new wife said. Allen's son, Brian, assisted his father at five executions, but resigned as assistant hangman in 1961 after qualifying as a state-registered mental nurse.

Index

Illustrations are shown by a page number in italics

TIM TATE
and RAY WYRE

Murder Squad

- This year alone there will be 550 homicides
- At least as many other, unsuccessful, murder attempts will be made
- The most common causes of death will be wounding and strangulation
- The most common motives will be sex and jealousy
- More than half the victims will know their killers: most will be members of the same family
- In 92 per cent of all cases Murder Squad detectives will bring the killers to justice

Granted unique access to a London Murder Squad, and drawing on research from the Thames Television series, Tim Tate and Ray Wyre go behind the headlines to examine the business of murder – its investigation, detection and punishment.

CHRIS RYDER

The RUC

According to Interpol, Northern Ireland is the most dangerous place in the world for a policeman. The RUC costs £1 million a day to operate, and in the last twenty years has seen nearly 300 of its members killed and more than 9,000 injured. Amazingly, there are almost twenty times more applicants than vacancies in the force, whose techniques and expertise are emulated worldwide.

Journalist and Ulsterman Chris Ryder tells the inside story of the men and women whose courage and disregard for danger are almost routine. Authoritatively impartial, he traces the turbulent and increasingly complex history of the force.

The RUC covers the controversial use of plastic bullets, the innovative management style of Kenneth Newman, the ill-starred Stalker affair and the continuing ramifications of the Anglo-Irish Agreement. For all those interested in the more notorious terrorist and paramilitary groups of the sectarian divide, *The RUC* is required reading.

'Chris Ryder's book will help all those concerned to move along the road to a peaceful Northern Ireland'
Merlyn Rees

'I know of no other journalist who has Chris Ryder's knowledge of the Ulster troubles . . . At last we have an account which gives full credit to the extraordinary courage, dedication and professionalism of the men and women of the RUC'
Sir Kenneth Newman

CHRIS RYDER

The UDR

An Instrument of Peace?

In July 1992, the UDR and the Royal Irish Rangers amalgamated to form the Royal Irish Regiment, whose dual role as part of the British Army is to continue the fight against terrorism in Northern Ireland and to provide an infantry battalion for frontline service throughout the world.

This book traces the turbulent history of the UDR and examines the background to the merger with the Royal Irish Rangers. It show how Catholic confidence in the UDR was undermined by repeated instances of its soldiers taking the law into their own hands and becoming involved in terrorism and crime. At the same time, it explains that many Protestants, ever fearful that the British government will give in to the IRA and agree on a united Ireland, regard the UDR as their last line of defence.

'Ryder's fine book has the efficiency and detachment of the working journalist'

Daily Telegraph

'Chris Ryder's book is an objective survey – shirking neither the awful tragedy of 200 UDR men killed by the IRA nor the involvement of some UDR soldiers in dreadful wrongdoing'

Times Educational Supplement

'A valuable study of an aspect of 'the Troubles' that few on the mainland understand'

Publishing News

BILL BUFORD

Among the Thugs

A book about the experience, and the attractions, of crowd violence.

'[Buford] gatecrashes a social world that most of us have spent some portion of our lives avoiding and brings it to life on the page with a ferocious relish that only someone who was a foreigner to soccer could manage, or stomach'

Jonathan Raban

'Compelling, intelligent and fully engaged'

Martin Amis, *Independent on Sunday*

'Buford's reportage is vivid and pacey, dropping you in the thick of the madness with a Wolfe-like immediacy'

Daily Telegraph

'The excellence of [Buford's] descriptive writing takes the reader to the centre of the mob . . . His words have the fragmented accuracy of a hand-held television camera in a war zone'

John Stalker, *Sunday Times*

'Possesses something of the quality of *A Clockwork Orange*'

The Times